NEW ENGLAND'S FAVORITE

Seafood Shacks

NEW ENGLAND'S FAVORITE

Seafood Shacks

Eating Up the Coast from Connecticut to Maine

Elizabeth Bougerol

The Countryman Press
Woodstock, Vermont

Library of Congress Cataloging-in-Publication Data has been applied for.

ISBN-13: 978-0-88150-708-9
ISBN-10: 0-88150-708-3

Book design and composition by Melanie Jolicoeur/Jolicoeur Design
Cover photographs by David Brownell and Elizabeth Bougerol
Illustrations by Lynn Gimby-Bougerol
Interior photographs by Tanya Braganti, Stephen Lenz, Ian MacKenzie, Pierre Bougerol, and Elizabeth Bougerol, except as noted: Ron Howard, Leslie Look, Robert Schellhammer, Peter Simon, Betsy Corsiglia, Nicole Friedler, and Debbie Grant for the Martha's Vineyard Chamber of Commerce (pp. 84, 87, 98, 99, 107); the National Oceanic and Atmospheric Administration (p. 5); Jeremy Keith (p. 22); the Maine Lobster Festival (pp. 31, 227); Newport Harbor Corporation (p. 49); Tom Gilbert (p. 83); the Historic American Buildings Survey/Historic American Engineering Record (pp. 97, 112, 118); Roger Sherman (p. 101); John Bigenwald (p. 106); Massachusetts Office of Travel and Tourism (p. 128); Brian Talbot (p. 169); Mick Robinson (p. 190); and David Brownell (p. 217).

Additional photographs and ephemera graciously provided by the restaurants herein, with the author's thanks

Published by The Countryman Press, P.O. Box 748, Woodstock, Vermont 05091
Distributed by W. W. Norton & Company, Inc., 500 Fifth Avenue, New York, NY 10110

Printed in the United States of America

10 9 8 7 6 5 4 3 2 1

For my parents, who met by the sea

contents

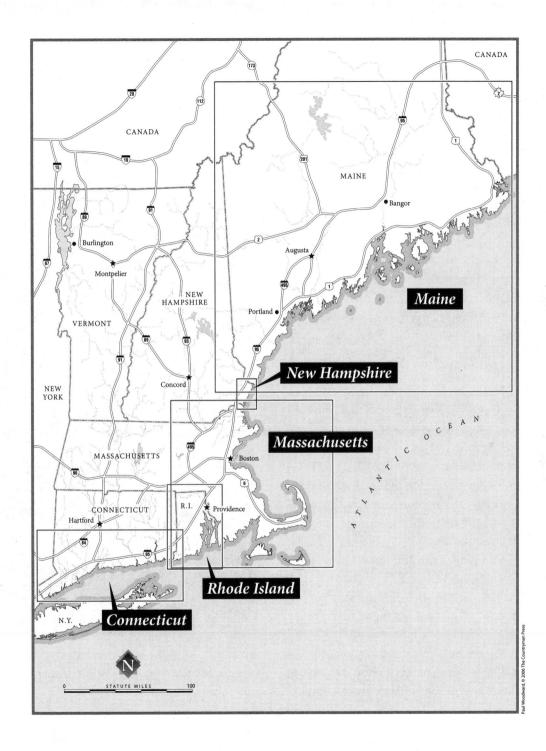

thanks

To everyone who embraced and buoyed this project in a thousand ways, by taking pictures, sending clippings, being wonderfully opinionated about whose fried clams are tops, and opening their minds, hearts, and homes to me and my little seafood book. Special thanks to Stephen Lenz; Richard Berlin; Jane and John MacKenzie; Kim, Jen, and Oonagh Last; Christine and Lou Olmsted; Fausto Braganti; Mona Lichman; Jeff Glasse; Gillian MacKenzie and Andrew Miller; Pat and John Shea; Adrien Glover; Ann Volkwein; and Ames Friedman.

To John Michel, for explaining everything to me in plain English;

To Kermit Hummel, Jennifer Thompson, David Corey, and the rest of Countryman Press, for being gung-ho;

To Tanya Braganti, for her uncommon eye and support, and unabashed love of the Clam Box;

To my family, for taking life lightly and eating seriously; especially my parents (for raising me in the kitchen) and my grandmother Madeleine (for teaching me about butter);

To Moxie, for being a steadfast travel companion and tirelessly dedicated taster;

To Ian MacKenzie, for his New Englander's heart, his French palate, and his New York driver's license;

And to all the shack owners, lobstermen, fry cooks, clam diggers, crab pickers, chowder makers, oyster shuckers, and busboys I was lucky enough to meet along the way, for showing me why they love what they do and couldn't imagine doing it anywhere else.

introduction

*I*f you're holding this book on a summer morning, say around 11 or so, things are starting to happen in restaurant kitchens in Norwalk, Connecticut and Calais, Maine, at the tip of Cape Cod, on tiny Block Island, and everywhere in between.

Up and down the Eastern seaboard, as you read this paragraph, Fry-o-lators are starting to sizzle and pop with fat the color of molasses. Prep cooks are giving full-belly Ipswich clams a silky coat of cornmeal or crumbs. In a few minutes, these'll be dumped—fried to a perfect caramel crunch—into a cardboard box, spotting it with hot, salty grease. Kitchen hands are slicing pickles for tartar sauce, lemons for littlenecks, bacon for chowder. Snowy slabs of haddock are being set on ice for later, lined up alongside plump pillows of freshly picked crab that'll be stuffed into a butter-griddled bun by noon. Secret ingredients are being slipped into fifth-generation recipes for bisque or pie. Cabbage grown two towns over is being slivered for slaw. And on a wharf somewhere, as you set this book on your coffee table or dashboard, a man in waxy overalls who's been up since four o'clock this morning plops an inky-colored, shimmering-wet lobster onto a stainless steel scale. Across the cove, his son pulls another lobster (tomato red, this one, and puffing with steam) out of a huge vat of roiling seawater perched over a wood fire.

A thousand other things are taking place right now—traps are being hauled, corn is being husked, onions are being ringed, oysters are being shucked,

butter is being drawn, lines are starting to form at takeout windows, and traditions are being carried on in a thousand ways, proudly and deliciously, the same way they have for nearly a century.

I'm getting hungry just writing this, so I'll keep it short:

Welcome to New England. Grab a plastic fork.

how to use this book

What's a New England seafood shack?

You say "seafood shack," it conjures up an image. I'd start by saying it's a dining establishment in the clam shack/chowder house/lobster pound family, or some combination thereof (or aspiration thereto), found along the coast of Connecticut, Rhode Island, Massachusetts (and her islands), New Hampshire, and Maine, that serves classic New England seafood dishes. But ask a hundred

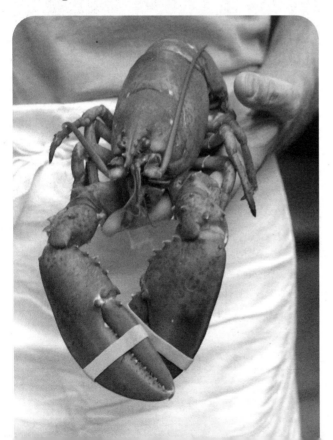

different people to define it, and you'll get a hundred different answers. For one, it's "someplace where you can eat lobster in the rough–on a picnic table outside, with paper plates. Sometimes they have sinks nearby for washing up." For another, it's "any place where they barely do anything to the seafood. It's fresh, they do it right, and that's that." Still another says that "any restaurant where you can toss a french fry into the air and a seagull will catch it" qualifies. For writer Nathaniel Reade, it "should look like it can be towed away . . . If a few guys in yellow slickers are loading buckets of herring onto their lobster boats right next door, then this particular shack is probably 'a real corkah,' which is Yankee for 'good.'" To you, it may be something else entirely. The most anyone can agree on is that it captures and distills something elemental about seaside New England–in other words, a seafood shack is a state of mind.

best vs. favorite

Now, ask a hundred people to tell you their favorite seafood shack, and the disparity is greater still. But one thing's for sure: Theirs is tops, hands down. They've tried a million others, they'll tell you, but only their place gets it right. It fries the crispiest clams, it has the freshest lobsters and the creamiest chowder, and they've been going for years, if not since childhood, when happiness was fried fish on a paper plate after a day at the beach.

Okay, so the food's good at this place, maybe even great. But is it unparalleled? Objectively, does it serve the very best seafood in New England? It doesn't matter: It's their favorite. The meals we recall most fondly are sometimes, but not always, about the food alone. Something about them seduces, and not necessarily with stratospheric eats. Could be the location: a bait shop perched on stilts rotting in the tide (Round Pond Lobstermen's Co-op, Round Pond, Maine), or the gleaming white yachts bobbing in a tony marina (The Black Pearl, Newport, Rhode Island). Could be the floorshow: lobstermen unloading their catch (Shaw's Wharf, New Harbor, Maine), or barefooted kids tracking in sand from the beach nearby (Aunt Carrie's, Narragansett, Rhode Island). Could be the soundtrack: Patsy Cline on tinny speakers (Johnny Ad's, Old Saybrook, Connecticut), a blasting fog horn (The Lobster Shack, Cape Elizabeth, Maine), the wonderful accents of the regulars (Tall Barney's, Jonesport, Maine), or the cawing of gulls (everywhere). Could be the history of the place, apparent in the old menus lining the walls (The Village Restaurant, Essex, Massachusetts), or that the owner caught the bluefish you ate himself (Chopmist Charlie's, Jamestown, Rhode Island). Could be that the place has been doing what it does longer than anybody else, with a great respect for seafood and tradition (The Union Oyster House, Boston, Massachusetts). And sometimes it is the food itself: a bowl of exalted haddock chowder that makes the view–grease dumpsters in a shopping plaza parking lot–disappear with each perfect, buttery slurp (Westfair Fish and Chips, Westport, Connecticut).

beyond this book

This book should in no way be taken as a definitive list: Think of it as equal parts treasure map and scavenger hunt invite, but above all, think of it as a starting place. I'm guessing some of the greatest meals you've had happened because you set out looking for one thing, and got lost and hungry—and New England is one of the best places on earth to succumb to serendipity. An open mind, eager palate, and full tank of gas are all that's required.

seasons

Regrettably for chowhounds, most seafood shacks are seasonal operations, open in the summer (often bookended by Memorial Day and Labor Day weekends) and closed during the winter months. Some have started extending their season to Columbus Day and even beyond to cater to leaf-peepers; still others stay open year-round. I've included seasonal openings in each restaurant profile, but consider these a general guideline only: As a rule of thumb, always call before you go, to avoid disappointment

hours

Some places observe regular hours, some have different hours depending on the day of the week or the tides, and some simply close up shop when they run out of clams to fry. Weather is also a factor: Beachside concession stands are at the mercy of fog and rain. Call before you go to make sure your destination is open and serving.

addresses and directions

Many restaurants are in small towns with one main street, or they're the only business on some remote dock. Usually, you can't miss them (and they have official addresses like "At the flagpole"). Whenever necessary, I've tried to include additional information to help you get there.

reservations

Assume they're not accepted, with some exceptions–certain places listed herein are more "restaurant" than "lean-to with a Fry-o-lator," so if reservations are de rigueur (or you're bringing an entourage), call ahead and suss it out.

pricing

The market price of seafood can fluctuate wildly from one day (or one red tide) to the next, and businesses often adjust their prices accordingly (so you'll find very few prices in this book).

Also, a surprising number of people arrive at the seashore thinking they'll hand over $5 for a lobster dinner, and are stunned to find prices on a par with what they'd pay at a restaurant with candles on the tables in Dubuque. You're not paying less because you're eating at the source; you're paying as much because this kind of freshness is simply unavailable anywhere else. Sure, fried clams overlooking yachts on Nantucket will cost you more than fried clams in a scruffy diner in far Down East Maine. But the main ingredient–seafood–is itself expensive, notoriously fragile-flavored, highly sensitive to temperature, and easy to ruin in any number of ways (which is why it's easy to find a seafood meal in New England, but not so easy to find a good one). Shellfish, in particular, is the only ingredient to arrive in kitchens while it's still alive, because this freshness is so crucial to the flavor. Simply put, it's the least shipping-friendly food on earth: Quality of flavor starts to deteriorate almost immediately after it leaves the water. A lobster on your plate in Bar Harbor was submerged in saltwater as little as five minutes ago. A lobster in Dubuque, despite Fed Ex's very best efforts, has been out of the water for at least a day, usually more. Also, commercial fishing is still a wringing, dangerous, uncertain way to earn a living. All told, the $20 you just paid for that lobster is a bargain. (Besides, there's something a little, well, fishy about bottom-dollar seafood.)

liquor

You'll find that a lot of the restaurants in this book don't have a liquor license, especially among lobster pounds and co-ops, and places that really are just roadside (or wharfside) shacks. Also, I've flagged up dry towns here and there, where there is no alcohol for sale, period. The good news is that all booze-free establishments are more than happy to have you BYO.

best bites

You'll find my completely subjective picks of each place's menu at the top of its profile, for easy scanning—but this shouldn't discourage you from being adventurous. Add your own best bites to these suggestions.

additional listings

An extra bunch of places rounds out each state's restaurant profiles, just in case you can't get enough seafood. Some of these are very good, whereas some are noted as being more about view or atmosphere than food.

a short word on butter, batter, and cream

S hack fare can be a dietary conundrum in these heart-health-aware times: Seafood, one of the healthiest things you can eat, is routinely drenched in butter, enrobed in crunchy batter, and thickened with half and half or heavy cream–if you do it right.

My grandmother, Madeleine Bougerol, had a few dietary quirks–seeing someone add salt to a dish gave her hives, and I still don't know what she did with all those lemons, purchased by the bagful–but she was also a food lover with the utmost respect for good ingredients, especially where fat was concerned.

She made the best crêpes in the world (with whole milk, of course), fruit tarts with a meltingly buttery crumb crust, and a flaky potato pie with tarragon and shallots, in the top layer of which she punched a hole to pour in a pint of heavy cream 10 minutes before the cooking time was up. She maintained that these ingredients made everything taste (and turn out) better–without them, what was the point of eating at all? (Very French.) She kept her slender figure, complete with gams to make a Rockette green with envy, until she died just shy of 90.

Yes, some of this is genetics, but most of it is moderation, and knowing when to live a little. Eating mounds of fat for breakfast, lunch and dinner isn't a good idea, but a bowl of buttery chowder and a pint of fried clams won't kill you. And it if does, well, something has to. I can think of worse ways to go.

connecticut

1

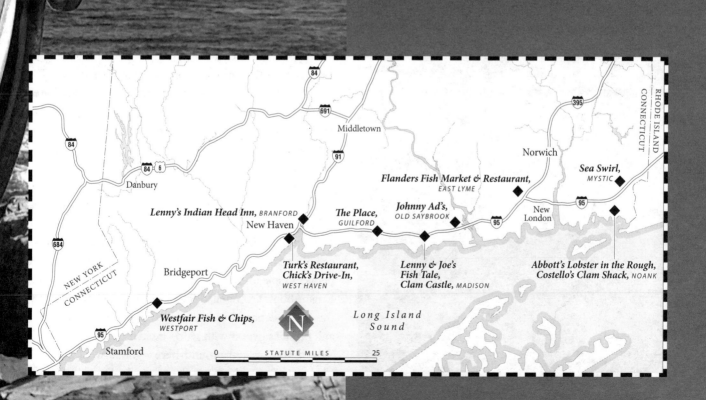

Flanders Fish Market & Restaurant, EAST LYME

Sea Swirl, MYSTIC

Norwich

Middletown

New London

Lenny's Indian Head Inn, BRANFORD

The Place, GUILFORD

Johnny Ad's, OLD SAYBROOK

New Haven

Danbury

Turk's Restaurant, Chick's Drive-In, WEST HAVEN

Lenny & Joe's Fish Tale, Clam Castle, MADISON

Abbott's Lobster in the Rough, Costello's Clam Shack, NOANK

Bridgeport

NEW YORK
CONNECTICUT

RHODE ISLAND
CONNECTICUT

Westfair Fish & Chips, WESTPORT

Long Island Sound

Stamford

0   STATUTE MILES   25

Abbott's Lobster in the Rough

117 Pearl Street, Noank 860-536-7719 • www.abbotts-lobster.com • Open May to mid-October

Costello's Clam Shack

145 Pearl Street, Noank 860-572-2779 • www.costellosclamshack.com • Open Memorial Day through Labor Day • BEST BITES: Hot lobster roll, Noank chowder, steamed whole lobster (Abbott's); fried belly clams, clam fritters, onion rings (Costello's)

Yes, Virginia, there is a Santa Claus—he's alive and well, he's got a bushy white beard and twinkling eyes, and he wears red. He has a pet bass. His name's Jerry Mears, and he runs a lobster shack in Noank, Connecticut.

And it may be the quintessential lobster shack. It's all here, in glorious Technicolor: the perfect, tucked-away spot that appears at the end of a seemingly endless winding country road that opens, all of a sudden, onto the sea. The striped awnings, the red and white paint on weathered wood and tin, the hand-painted signs, the picnic tables dotting the patches of lawn sloping down to the water. The various takeout windows (including one for ice cream alone), the apple-cheeked teens earning tuition at the pickup counter, the boats going by and, on occasion, heading in to dock and dine. And everywhere you look, families tucking into big, beautiful lobsters, rolls, chowder (even the odd roasted chicken). Blur out the clothing and a couple of cell phones, and it's easy to imagine that you're enjoying a perfectly splendid seaside afternoon in the 1940s, when Ernie Abbott first opened the place. And then there's Jerry, the aforementioned St. Nick, who bought Abbott's in 1981 and presides over it with giddy excitement.

"If you walked around here right now," he beams, "and asked people how they heard about the place,

almost all of them would say, 'My parents brought me here, or my grandparents.' That's the best compliment I can think of."

Owning a lobster restaurant may seem an unlikely trajectory for a man who spent most of his life working a double career as a commercial airline pilot and an industrial biochemist, and who himself didn't even like lobster until he was in his 40s. That's because it was the only white meat at the Mears household throughout his childhood, as the son of a fisherman who plied his trade in Rockland, Maine, a region hit hard by the Depression. "He went out and caught lobster in a rowboat. In the winter. Try it sometime!" he cackles. "It was the only way for him to make a living, and whatever he couldn't sell, we'd eat." (Nowadays, it's his daughter, Dierdre, who doesn't touch the stuff: She manages Abbott's, but can't stand lobster.)

The double career took its toll, and Jerry would frequently meet his wife Ruthie at Abbott's at the end of the day for a bite, to unwind. The restaurant was good, he says, but not great. "We'd sit at one of the tables by the water and say, 'Boy, what we could do if we got our hands on this place.'" They started talking about it seriously, made their intentions known and, after a proverbial

middle-of-the-night phone call informing them that the place was up for sale–and that they had mere hours to make a decision–scrounged every last penny, becoming restaurateurs overnight. "The first day we ran out of butter and my wife said, 'I'm gonna buy a case!' 'You reckless thing, you,' I said. 'A whole case!'" he chuckles. "We had no idea what we'd gotten ourselves into."

But they got up to speed, fast. Abbott's serves about 2,000 diners a day. A summer Saturday might see the kitchen turning out a thousand of their signature hot lobster rolls–a quarter-pound of hand-torn lobster tossed in creamery butter on a toasted, buttered bun, served with a fork and extra drawn butter on the side, a bold butter trifecta that you just have to applaud. (I was skeptical of the sesame-seed hamburger bun at first, but the flavor, preparation and, yes, butter, won me over.) There's a lobster salad roll, too, where the lobster is served cool, the meat tossed with a little mayo. Abbott's also sells gallons of "Noank-style chowder," a briny, broth-based, creamless mixture that Jerry describes as "basically clams, clam juice, and potatoes. It's Ernie Abbott's original recipe, and we'd be run out of Noank if we changed it."

And then there are the lobsters themselves. Jerry

swears by a steam-cooking method: "Once they're caught, they never touch water again. Out of the ocean, right into our steamers," which he says prevents the critters from getting waterlogged and accounts for the intense, lobstery flavor. "Some people run them through a broiler," he says, shrugging. "My father would roll over in his grave." For a sampling of nearly everything that Abbott's does best, order the New England lobster feast, which packs in a lobster, clam chowder, shrimp cocktail, steamers, and mussels.

Just down the road, in Noank Shipyard, sits Abbott's sister restaurant, Costello's (get it?). Customers had been asking for fried goods for years–especially clams–but Jerry and Ruthie didn't want to mess with a good thing by introducing a Fry-o-lator at Abbott's. Costello's embodies a similar cheery spirit and equally plum right-on-the-water spot, with a menu built on all things golden and crispy, from delicious full-belly Canadian clams and center-cut cod to clam fritters to deep-fried ice cream.

Maybe it's the surroundings, maybe it's the food, maybe it's Jerry himself, but people love Abbott's with an uncommon intensity. Take the first arrivals: Next to the register is a wall of photos of beaming folks who've made the trek–from all over the country–to be the first customers of the season, camping out to be at the head of the line when that takeout window opens on the first Saturday in May. And then, of course, there's Jersey Joe, Abbott's most dedicated customer, who won't eat lobster anywhere else (see sidebar).

So go to Abbott's. If it's not too busy, Jerry might purloin some chowder crackers from the counter and toss them to his eager, leaping pet bass, one of a few fish who've made Abbott's stretch of dock their home.

the legend of Jersey Joe

The phone call comes early, every Saturday, like clockwork. Before picking up, the staff at Abbott's already knows who it is.

The voice is gruff. There's no hello. "What's the biggest today?"

"We got a nine-pounder today, Joe."

"Okay. Have him ready. I'll be there at noon."

Jersey Joe is Abbott's most loyal customer. Every week of the shack's summer season, on Saturdays, when he has the day off from his job as a sanitation worker, he drives nearly four hours from New Jersey to Noank to eat lobster. Not just any lobster: The biggest lobster off the boat. "Biggest I did was 17.6 lbs.," he says. "That took a while." And not just any place: He only eats lobster at Abbott's. "Nobody does like this place. When they close for the season, that's it. No more lobster 'til May."

Chick's Drive-In

183 Beach Street, West Haven 203-934-4510 • Open year-round • BEST BITES: Foot-long lobster roll, split hot dog, soft-shell crab sandwich (in season), crabcakes, fried oysters

Vincent "Chick" Celentano is the kind of guy you want to sit next to on an airplane. The man has stories. So many stories. Like how he bought Jackie Mason's house in Fort Lauderdale–after he sold Susan Hayward's. Or how he financed the '80s movie *Cage* with Lou Ferrigno, of *Incredible Hulk* fame. But the best story of all is how Chick's Drive-In, a 55-year-old institution on the Connecticut coast, got its start because of a traffic jam.

Chick's family bought their little house across from the water in West Haven well before a stretch of beach down the road became a major tourist destination. It was

quiet, he says–his dad used to fish right off the breakwater across the street. But Savin Rock Amusement Park changed all that, along with the landscape of coastal Connecticut, drawing the kinds of crowds it wasn't quite equipped to handle. "There was one road in, and the same road out," he says, recalling the beginning of the summer season at Savin Rock. "Cars would be at a complete standstill, backed up for hours at a time. And, you know, people would get hungry."

In 1950, teenaged Chick convinced his dad to let him sell a few lunch items out of the Celentanos' garage. The makeshift roadside stand was a godsend to weary travelers. Soon he'd installed some basic equipment in there, next to his dad's car–a fryer, a grill. Hot dogs happened (still one of Chick's most popular items), and so did french fries (these days, the menu refers to them as "freedom fries"). The Celentanos added on to the garage. The menu kept growing. Soon, there was shrimp. Chick and his father realized that parking was a problem, and they turned the other side of the house into a small lot. Chick came up with the restaurant's slogan– "Through these doors pass the world's finest customers"– painted it on a sign and hung it. Eventually, the house was razed to build a bona-fide restaurant, more or less as it is today: A long takeout counter faces the water, behind

which sit a few indoor booths, and there's a broad patio stretching out to the side, peppered with bright blue picnic tables and some very eager-looking gulls. "All in all, we took down 18 houses here over the years," Chick says of the last half-century.

Savin Rock is long gone, but the Drive-In continues to thrive as a favorite spot for bunnies headed to the beach across the street. The place is a well-oiled machine: Some 50 people work in the huge kitchen and takeout counter in the summer, including Chick himself, who does a little bit of everything (he's refilling the ketchup pump when I arrive). And yet some things haven't changed, including most of the menu, which comprises drive-in basics plus a selection of fried seafood platters and rolls. "No frozen food, ever," says Chick. "Everything is prepared to order–all the seafood is breaded right before we fry it, which is right before you eat it. It takes a little longer, but it makes a difference."

Speaking of worth it, some may blanch at the higher-than-most price of the lobster roll, but consider this: Just like the famous hot dogs, Chick's lobster rolls are served on foot-long buns.

Chick himself doesn't appear to be slowing down anytime soon. He's gearing up to spend six

shack classic: Fried Oysters

They're more often associated with cuisine of the South (mmm, fried oyster po'boy), but they'll pop up occasionally alongside the more common clams, scallops, and shrimp on New England menus like Chick's. They're popular with the raw bar-squeamish, though naysayers claim frying overwhelms their delicate texture and taste—while ultra-purists couldn't imagine cooking an oyster at all. Try one for yourself.

months in Florida (at the ex-Mason estate, natch), he's excited about the latest award from *Connecticut Magazine,* and then there's his son: a months-old bouncing baby boy named Luke. Over the register hangs a photo of Chick from the '60s taken at the very same register. The man himself, aside from white hair and glasses, doesn't even look all that different from his younger self. At this rate, Chick's Drive-In could be around for another half-century.

Clam Castle

1324 Boston Post Road (Route 1), Madison 203-245-4911 • Open Memorial Day to Labor Day
BEST BITES: Fried clam bellies, soft-shell crabs (in season), fish chowder, broiled seafood platter

Pull in to the "World Famous" Clam Castle, order your dinner, and while you're waiting count the cartoon clams. There are three on the big yellow sign, grinning away with polka dots for eyes. There's the impossibly cute pair on the roof's wooden "Fresh Seafood" sign, set against an American flag. Two more on the trash cans outside. Cartoon clams are smiling, smirking–one even looks like it's yodeling–all over this squat, one-room restaurant from the '60s, a mildly down-at-the-heels place done up in reds and yellows that, honestly, doesn't really look like it's going to serve you good food.

Looks can be deceiving–while the Castle won't give you the best meal of your life, for the most part, the menu is solid. Days after my visit, the *New York Post*'s Page Six reported that food A-listers Jean-Georges Vongerichten and Jacques Pépin (who lives near Madison) had been spotted grabbing a bite at the Castle. I'm willing to bet they ordered the big, crunchy, briny full-bellied clams (the Castle uses Maryland bivalves, an unusual choice around these parts) or the in-season fried soft-shell crabs, both served up with fries or rings and slaw, or available in a little cardboard boat sans extras. Maybe they went for something lighter, such as the broiled seafood sampler, which features cod, shrimp, and sea scallops (done up with lemon, butter, and garlic–ask them to hold the Parmesan cheese), or something heavier, but in a good way: The decadent fish chowder, packed with bacon, cream, cod, and potatoes, is a real steal at about $3 a bowl

and the winner among their soups, which also include New England– and Rhode Island–style clam chowders, and a thin lobster bisque. No word on whether Jean-Georges and Jacques skipped the "raw bar," platters of pre-shucked clams and oysters on the half shell, sitting on ice under plastic wrap with cocktail sauce in a glass case by the till (my advice: stick with the hot food). There's also a duo of yummy lobster rolls, one hot with butter, one cold with mayo.

If you're not feeling seafoody, the Clam Castle offers a small array of basic diner fare like BLTs and chicken tenders. And there's a separate window serving Razzles and all sorts of other ice cream concoctions. Eat in at one of the shiny red booths, or take your tray out to the Picnic Grove, a roofed patio of tables set behind the restaurant that's lovely on days when it's raining (but not hard enough to drive you inside).

Flanders Fish Market & Restaurant

22 Chesterfield Road (Route 161), East Lyme 860-739-8866 • www.flandersfish.com • Open year-round • BEST BITES: Onion rings, fish and chips, clear chowder, lobster bisque, charbroiled scallops

Popular wisdom (and common sense) holds that if a restaurant is also a fish market, it's usually a good sign. First, because in cutting out the middleman, the fish doesn't have far to go (and fish less traveled is fresher fish) and second, because if they're willing to show it to you raw, it usually means they have nothing to hide. And fish with secrets is almost always bad news.

Flanders Fish Market, located inland on a nondescript stretch of commercial businesses where you might not think to look for a fantastic seafood dinner, takes this unspoken rule to a whole new level: the market comes first. Just inside the front door (which offers your first glimpse of Cappy, Flanders' chipper walrus mascot, lounging on an anchor in a cap'n's hat and jacket), you're greeted by a set of refrigerator cases displaying every locally (and some less locally) caught item imaginable, with a live lobster tank on the side. Move farther into the converted Colonial, and you'll come upon the dining rooms or find your way onto the deck or canopied patio. Spanking-fresh fare is all over the menu here, prepared with a light touch that lets the goods speak for themselves.

In true fish-market style, the menu is staggering in its variety, from the plain (the standards, fried or broiled—including farm-raised catfish or salmon) to the fancy (Dijon swordfish tips, anyone?). But first, kick off your meal with a bowl of something: The chowder comes

"clear" or "creamy." Go for the former: Owner-chef Paul Formica's clear-broth clam chowder—a specialty around these parts that's closer to Rhode Island clam chowder than the New England version—has been a bestseller since

the place opened in 1983. It's brimming with slices of sweet, tender clams and potato and topped with a sprinkling of parsley. Or try Cappy's Luscious Lobster Bisque, a creamy pink concoction shot with impressively large chunks of sweet lobster meat, but be advised that you won't need more food after a bowl of this stuff. (Get it to go. It reheats nicely and is a perfect meal on its own with some oyster crackers and an icy beer.) It's hard to choose a follow-up, but here are some winners: The sea scallops, fished in nearby Stonington, are almost sugary sweet–get them fried or charbroiled with a hint of lemon and ginger, but skip 'em stuffed (overkill).

The fish and chips is another dish that the FFM, as the place calls itself, is known for (the recipe's been featured on the Food Network's *Fingerlickin' Favorites*): Flavorful cod falls away when your fork breaks into the crunchy crust, and the fries are heavenly things the color of brown sugar. Sweet potato fries are also available, but what you really want is a side of onion rings, sliver-thin curls of virtually greaseless, oniony goodness. A bucket of steamers served with butter and broth is almost as good as the bucket of Chesapeake Bay shrimp, boiled with Old Bay and served hot, also with butter (or order them cold with the house cocktail sauce, dubbed "Tears of Joy" sauce). Finally, some swear by the flounder sandwich, others by the buttery lobster potpie. It's almost hard to go wrong on the menu (though dishes like gorgonzola shrimp with bacon on garlic toast make the seafood itself an afterthought), and the family-friendly Flanders also offers a good, cheap menu for kids. If you can't pick just one or three dishes, show up on Sunday: Flanders' famous, massive seafood buffet opens at 11 AM, ends around 3, and may just make you want to relocate to the neighborhood.

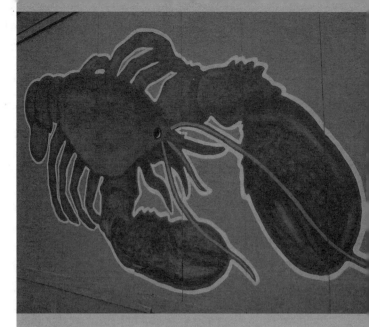

some lobster lingo

- *Chicken:* Lobsters on the small side, usually 1 to 1 1/4 pounds, so-named because they're young and their meat is so tender.

- *Cull:* A lobster that's lost one of its claws. This doesn't affect the flavor, so these tend to be used for dishes where looks aren't a factor, such as lobster rolls.

- *Pistol:* A lobster that's lost both claws, usually in self-defense, and hasn't grown them back yet.

- *Sleeper:* A live lobster that's been out of the water so long, it's too lethargic to hold up its claws. If you come across a sleeper, eat elsewhere.

Johnny Ad's

910 Boston Post Road (Route 1), Old Saybrook 860-388-4032 • Open year-round
BEST BITES: Fried clams, fried scallops, hot lobster roll, chili-and-cheese hot dog

If this little place, on a patch of asphalt set back from busy Route 1, has a name that sounds like a 1950s heartthrob–the kind of squeaky-clean crooner, with unsuggestive moves and a crisp suit, who your parents might have approved of–it's for good reason. Johnny Ad's opened in 1957 and has barely changed since, from the hand-painted diner-style sign that lights up at night to the '50s jukebox favorites cranked out to the patio through tinny speakers that double as a PA system when your order's ready. And while there's no ocean view, it has the feel of a beach cottage in every sense, a sweet little three-room structure painted all in light blues and whites with spring-hinged doors. Collages of photos taken at the restaurant share space

with brass anchors, retro-kitschy tin signs, and yellowed newspaper reviews, all slightly askew on the paneled walls. Everything about Johnny Ad's–named after its original owner, John Adinolfo–is modest, right down to the motto: "The little seafood restaurant with the big ocean taste."

Order from the no-frills, marquee-style menu, white plastic lettering arranged in three tidy glass cases between the window where you place your order and the one where you pick it up. With some exceptions (such as the broiled swordfish steak platter) nearly every dish here is fried or sandwiched, and in some cases, like the fried chicken sandwich or the scallop or oyster rolls, both. But before you order, know that Johnny Ad's has three offerings that–while owner Bob Hansen may not call them signature dishes–are the ones that have the most rabid following.

First, the clams. Oh, the clams. All the fried seafood here is wonderful–especially the juicy scallops, the shrimp and, when they have them, the soft-shell crabs–but the clams win. Available as bellies or strips, crumb-breaded with a light hand and fried 'til they sing, these clams' reason for being is to make Massachusetts jealous. Get them as a side order, get them as part of a platter, get them on a roll–just get them. I can't figure out why these clams are so sweet, and I doubt it has to do with the fact that Johnny Ad's is one of the few shoreline shacks in Connecticut to use Maryland clams. Do they put something in the coating? The woman who calls my number and slides the tray through the pick-up window isn't talking. "Just the way we do 'em, I guess."

Next, the hot dog. I love how a foot-long Hummel, split and grilled, is unapologetically stuffed into a New England–style top-loading bun about half its size, leaving inches of wiener overhang at either end. Have the dog with a simple coating of mustard and relish, or go for it the way the locals do, oozing with chili and cheese. You might even try it topping-free, so you can give the smoky meat and the bun–which is butter-griddled to a perfect exterior crisp–your full attention.

Finally, the lobster sandwiches. The lobster salad roll is done up with a little mayo binding the chilled meat together, and served in the same crispy bun they use for the hot dogs. If this were the only roll on the menu, it would be an excellent pick: flavorful, tangy, just right. But this being Connecticut, it shares the spotlight with a hot lobster roll available for the same price, an item Adinolfo added in 1976. Comparing the two is almost unfair: The cold version is the plain-sister-with-braces to the hot roll's prom queen. It's like having a miniature lobster dinner, with the warm chunks of perfect pink lobster tossed with butter and heaped into that already buttery bun. Maybe I was hallucinating, but I think they drizzle more of the melted stuff over the top as a finishing touch. There's so much butter going on here that the structural integrity of the bun is soon called into question, leaving you with handfuls of glistening lobster, chewy toast, and butter, butter everywhere, dripping down your arms. It's an experience that goes nicely with a root beer.

shack classic:
Lobster Roll

"Those of you who spend little time in the northeastern United States may have some difficulty appreciating the spiritual qualities of the lobster roll."

–Jeffrey Steingarten, *It Must Have Been Something I Ate*

Most everybody agrees on the bun: It should be a soft, chewy top-loader, toasted and buttered. Beyond that, anything goes. In Maine, New Hampshire, or Massachusetts, ask for a lobster roll and you're most likely to get a mound of chilled lobster, usually with just a luster of mayonnaise or other creamy dressing on the meat (or served on the side for dipping, like they do at Red's Eats in Wiscasset, Maine), and sometimes with a little something extra mixed in (diced celery, or a dash of paprika or Old Bay seasoning). It's this cold, mayo'd version of the sandwich that's become the gold standard of rolls, the Platonic roll ideal that chefs in San Francisco and New York try to replicate when they put the dish on their menu. In Rhode Island, they tend to go heavier on the dressing and the extras and call it a lobster salad roll. Finally, Connecticut is home to the lobster roll of my dreams: The meat is warm and naked, save for a glow of melted butter—like a lobster dinner on a bun.

Lenny & Joe's Fish Tale

1301 Boston Post Road (Route 1), Madison 203-245-7289 • www.ljfishtale.com • Open year-round
BEST BITES: Fried scallops, hot buttered lobster roll, scrod and chips, Rhode Island–style clam chowder

*I*first discovered Lenny & Joe's en route to Cape Cod from New York. The heart of clam shack country was still a ways away, but it was lunchtime, I was hungry, I wanted seafood, and I wanted it now–not in four hours, when I would arrive. Hunger pangs are hell along this stretch of I-95–each highway rest stop's food court is identical to the last, always leaving me frustrated and disoriented, my clothes smelling like McNuggets. But this time around, I'd been tipped off to a restaurant that was "just a couple minutes off the highway." And sure enough, there it was:

a low-slung building, in the proverbial middle of nowhere, with some cute cartoon fish painted on the sign. But no one had told me about the carousel.

From the road, it looks like any other: a slowly spinning cylinder of old-fashioned, glazed animals carrying kids clutching poles who are waving to parents with cameras. But look closer, and don't expect horsies–instead, you'll find lobsters, whales, and seals. The whimsical designs are original, built by the Dentzel Carousel Company in Port Townsend, Washington. The only thing better than the carousel's pieces is the price for a ride–one

dollar, and it goes to charity.

Okay, even better than the dollar is the killer combination of carousel music and fried seafood smell. And saltwater taffy, if that's your thing, and ice cream, which is pretty much everybody's. Lenny & Joe's may be right on Route 1, where the view comes down to which parking lot you want to overlook, but they've successfully recreated a small-scale fairground atmosphere, a sort of mini-theme park on an otherwise bland strip of road.

At the center of all this summery hubbub is Lenny & Joe's kitchen, which turns out New England seafood classics, some good, some great. The fried clam bellies are hugely popular, but I beeline for the scallops: stunningly sweet with just the right flesh-to-crunch ratio. Another winner is the fish and chips, made with scrod. The clams are done better justice in the chowder: It's Rhode Island–style (brothy, not creamy), and it tastes like a marina in the very best sense. In season, the kitchen also deep-fries soft-shell crabs to great effect. Finally, as far as the fried menu goes, it's worth noting that unlike at most restaurants, the tartar sauce here is not an afterthought, but made fresh, and with heaps of chopped dill pickles. The tang perfectly complements the crunch. Their hot buttered lobster roll has won awards, which isn't surprising; my only complaint is that it's on the small side, an anomaly here where nearly every portion is gigantic enough to share. And kids will want dessert–there's a separate structure for this outside by the carousel. Lenny & Joe sell almost as many flavors of ice cream and frozen yogurt as they do colors of logo-emblazoned T-shirts and caps.

Check Lenny & Joe's other restaurant, in Westbrook, farther up the Connecticut coast. But don't expect carousels.

shack staple: Oyster Crackers

The concept of the cracker goes back to Roman times, and ship cooks paired hardtack—dense bricks of unleavened, baked flour that were sliced into "crackers"—with chowders long before English bakers Adam and John Exton came to New Jersey in the 19th century. But come they did, and the oyster cracker as we know it is a direct descendant of their "Exton Oyster and Butter Cracker and Wine Scroll Biscuit," cooked up in Trenton in the 1840s and so popular, it spawned dozens of imitations. The Extons used wheat flour, vegetable shortening, yeast, and salt to create their puffy little discs—no oysters. So why call them oyster crackers? It's unclear, but most attribute the name either to the original crackers' roundish, lumpy shape, or to how popular it was to pair them with shellfish chowders, which sometimes included oysters.

Lenny's Indian Head Inn

205 South Montowese Street, Branford 203-488-1500 • www.lennysnow.com • Open year-round
BEST BITES: Shoreline chowder, zuppa d'clams, soft-shell crab sandwich, strawberry shortcake

Lenny's looks like nothing more than what it is, an old log cabin on a salt marsh, but it smells like heaven, if you assume that heaven smells like fried clams and sea, which I do. The restaurant has been here, with its Indian head on the sign (a nod to Indian Neck, the strip of land where it's located) for decades. It's a summer standby, but I love it come October when the boating crowd deserts Branford's marinas, resuming their city lives and turning this scruffy hole in the wall back over to the locals.

These locals are a big part of Lenny's appeal, along with the wooden booths, the fragrant marsh, and the unfussy seafood dishes that have hardly changed since the place opened in 1968. The lobster dinners are as straightforward and scrumptious as you'd expect, and there are some fantastic entrées like baked scrod that was swimming when you got in your car to drive here, but the truth is, you could make an entire meal out of the appetizers alone.

First, you'd want an order of Maine oysters on the half shell, and you'd want to suck them down on the marshside patio so that their metallic liquor could mingle with the heavy, seaweedy air. Next up, clam chowders: rich and creamy New England–style, or the "shoreline" version, a brothy, sippable nod to Connecticut's neighbors to the east.

And then you'd get the zuppa d'clams, for which some have been known to drive all the way from Providence or Manhattan: a half-dozen musky cherrystones steamed in a silky, lemony, herby, red peppery broth, with enough garlic to make you vampire-proof for months. It's served with plenty of Italian bread on the side, guaranteeing that none of this ambrosial liquid will go to waste.

Though this is Connecticut, home of the hot lobster roll, Lenny's serves a salad variety only, with mayo-laced meat served cool. It's good, but a better pick from the sandwich line-up is the soft-shell crab, when it's available. It's possibly the best of the menu's fried fare, which includes all the usual suspects, with a preference for batter breading over crumbs. It's the kind of sandwich that makes you wish Lenny's were closer to the Interstate, because just the sight of Branford on an exit sign is enough to make one's mouth water for it.

As a chaser, get the strawberry shortcake–sugary berries stuffed into a split, baked biscuit, crowned with frothy folds of cream–which disappears from the menu when fresh berry season ends. St. Patrick's at Lenny's is especially fun–swing by on March 17 for the sloppy, salty, satisfying corned beef special.

trick: The Box Degreaser

Walking by open-door kitchens, you may see fry cooks shaking cardboard boxes around. What gives? It's a shack trick: Foods are pulled out of the bubbling oil and immediately dumped into cardboard flats—the kind soda cans come packed in—and jostled around for a bit. The cardboard absorbs the oil better than anything else, resulting in light bites where you taste the seafood, not the grease.

Ten Festivals for Seafood Fans

Summer isn't just shack season—it's festival season along the coast, and local seafood specialties are the guests of honor. Bring your appetite and sunscreen to these 10 tasty events.

1. *Hampton Beach Seafood Festival,* Hampton Beach, NH, September
Local restaurants serve every kind of seafood imaginable to more than 300,000 hungry attendees, nearly all of whom have trouble parking.

2. *Wellfleet OysterFest,* Wellfleet, MA, October
About 30,000 bivalves are slurped, rain or shine, in this Cape Cod hamlet that's home to the famed Wellfleet oyster.

3. *Schweppes Great Chowder Cook-Off,* Newport, RI, June
Chefs come from as far as Australia to test the mettle of their kettle, serving up 3,000 gallons of chowder for big money.

4. *Maine Lobster Festival,* Rockland, ME, August
The big daddy of lobster fests, with lobster crate races, the Maine Sea Goddess pageant, and 20,000 pounds of bug.

5. *Chowderfest,* Boston, July
The Boston Harborfest counts nearly 200 events, but it's the Chowderfest you won't want to miss: More than 11,000 taste the entries.

6. *Norwalk Oyster Festival,* Norwalk, CT, September
Tall ships, live entertainment, oysters, and more than 100,000 attendees.

7. *Yarmouth Clam Fest,* Yarmouth, ME, August
The population of 8,500 swells to 125,000, as an old-fashioned fairground takes over the 19th-century town.

8. *Charlestown Chamber Annual Seafood Festival,* Charlestown, RI, August
Every Rhode Island gastronomical quirk under one tent: Stuffies, clear chowder, clamcakes, and more.

9. *Scallop Festival,* Bourne, MA, September
Nearly 40,000 convene to worship the scallop.

10. *Essex ClamFest (and ChowderFest Competition),* Essex, MA, September
Come hail the mighty Ipswich clam in the town that fried the first, and help crown Cape Ann's best chowder.

HONORARY LOBSTER FISHERMAN

COURTESY
MAINE DEPT. OF SEA & SHORE FISHERIES

CLAM FESTIVAL—BUS STOP

The Place

891 Boston Post Road (Route 1), Guilford 203-453-9276 • Open Memorial Day to Labor Day
BEST BITES: Roast clam special, grilled bluefish, grilled chicken, grilled whole lobster

Guilford, Connecticut's most famous restaurant is a bit of a magical thing, part clambake, part floorshow, entirely al fresco, and never better than right before sunset.

First, you have to find it: It's not hard, as the restaurant's a mere minute off I-95 at a traffic light on Route 1, but from the front, it looks like any other house, albeit one with a red-and-white "The Place" sign dangling off a pole out front, and one right below it that reads, enigmatically, "An Unusual Restaurant." Even if you miss the signs, it's hard not to see or smell the smoke billowing up through the tall oaks. Follow it around the little house until you

hear the crunch of clam shells under your feet and come upon a wide clearing in the trees, scattered with bright red "tables" (cable spools) and "chairs" (tree stumps) and in the middle of it all, a massive wood fire, where a handful of cheery men in short sleeves and long fireproof gloves are moving some of life's greatest pleasures–lobsters, clams, and corn on the cob–on and off the biggest, most ramshackle grill you've seen this side of a Texas county fair. This, as the poem goes, must be The Place.

Co-owner Vaughn Knowles can recite the poem in question by heart: "There's no other place just like this place any where near this place, so this must be the place." He came across these words years ago, when he and his brother Gary just worked here – back then, it was a roadside clambake known as Whitey's Roast. Whitey had the poem on a little plaque tacked up at the restaurant. "The idea was mostly the same," Vaughn says. No Fry-o-lator, no kitchen: just fire burning under a bunch of rails and racks suspended over cinderblocks, food that tasted good grilled, roasted, or steamed, and weather permitting. Whitey, gloves and all, would pull a dozen roasted clams off the flames, delivering the white-hot wire rack right onto your table with a warning not to touch the metal. The Knowleses do the honors today–same wire rack, same warning–and the staff's gone from 6 to 22, but not much else has changed since the brothers bought Whitey's restaurant in 1971.

A giant tent strung up to a pulley-and-rope system sits gathered at one end of the "dining room," ready to be hoisted across the clearing in case of rain. It's red and white, as are the signs inviting patrons to "Put your rump on a stump," and then there's the bill of fare, a 15-or-so foot tall series of planks nailed to a post, looking more like a road sign between Montana ghost towns than a clam shack menu. "Everything we serve is up there," says Vaughan. "We have some specials that change, but that's all. If we don't have it, bring it."

The short menu makes ordering easy. You'll want to start with a dozen clams, set live on the grill until the heat pops open their shells, revealing a pearly pink crescent inside. Purists can go for the plain roast kind, but if you do this, Vaughan may come over and quietly suggest you try the roast clam special. He takes the juicy littlenecks and dabs them with a mixture of cocktail sauce and butter before placing them back over the flames just long enough to make everything melt and sizzle. Sounds straightforward enough, but the sauce, the fat, and the bivalve's natural liquor all come together in the kind of harmony that makes you want to take a snapshot with your taste buds. This is a definite food moment. Some have been unable to order anything else at The Place, putting away as many as a dozen orders of these little suckers in one sitting (that's 144 clams, people), and truth be told, it is hard to move on from this dish. But if you do, try the lusty grilled bluefish, or plump pink shrimp by the dozen or half-dozen, or go whole hog and get a lobster—they're all caught off Branford, on Long Island Sound—served up with little cups of melted butter and cocktail sauce. As a side, get some corn on the cob, roasted to summery bliss in the husk, or try the veggiebob, a simple skewer of grilled vegetables. Frankly, even the chicken rules at The Place: Everything here gets imbued with smoky notes of hickory and oak, which is all the Knowleses use to fire their grill.

"Newcomers, fancy folks, and amateurs eat the clams with forks. Pros prefer to slurp from the shell. My personal best . . . 12 dozen."

—MICHAEL N. MARCUS, FOUNDER, UNITED CLAM LOVERS OF AMERICA, ON THE PLACE'S ROAST CLAM SPECIAL

Since 1971

THIS MUST BE THE PLACE

ROAST CLAM SPECIAL	DOZ.	$9.45
PLAIN ROAST CLAMS	DOZ.	$9.35
STEAMERS	LB	$10.45
WINE AND GARLIC MUSSELS	LB.	$9.45
SHRIMP ½ DOZ. $4.50	DOZ.	$8.95
BLUEFISH OR CATFISH		$8.95
SALMON		$11.95
LOBSTER 1¼ $18.95 1⅛ LB. $16.95	1 LB.	$14.95
RIB-EYE STEAK		$13.95
CHICKEN PLAIN OR BBQ		$6.95
VEGGIEBOB		$5.95
ROASTED CORN		$1.85
SODA · APPLE JUICE COFFEE · TEA · MILK $1.35 Poland Spring · Snapple ·		$1.75
CHEESECAKE MS MUD CAKE CARROT CAKE PECAN PIE KEY/LIME PIE SPL		$3.95
ICE CREAM $2.40 HOT FUDGE SUNDAE		$3.95
BYOB		

Throw your clam shells on the ground (how do you think all those shards got there in the first place?) and have a slice of Mississippi Mud or Key lime pie for dessert. Wait for the sun to set and the strings of fairground lights to flicker on overhead, and watch the flames light up the faces of the staff flipping lobsters on the grill or carrying big nets of littlenecks from the cooler. Pull out a deck of cards, finish the wine you brought. Maybe even stay long enough that you get hungry again and order another roast clam special. You've come to the right Place.

etiquette at The Place

Vaughn and Gary Knowles's restaurant has its own etiquette, or lack thereof: As long as you order something, you can wear anything, you can bring anything, you can do pretty much anything at The Place, and the result is a kind of local ritual. On a sunny Friday evening, carful after carful of diners pulls up, and what happens next goes something like this: They send someone ahead to score an empty table. Once that's done, they proceed to disgorge the contents of their VW Bugs and Mini Coopers, marching armfuls of baskets, boxes, and bags over to the spot. Then, the unpacking begins: For some, it's just BYOB—a nice Shiraz or a six-pack of something foreign, and maybe an ice bucket so they can stay awhile. Others BYO enough trimmings to put a picnic at Martha Stewart's house to shame, from linen tablecloths and napkin rings to martini shakers and silver place settings. Here, a bunch of dahlias is rescued from a Ziploc bag and slipped into a blown-glass bud vase; there, a Greek chopped salad or maybe some sushi is transferred from Tupperware to Terence Conran.

And once the table's set, they—like all of the Place's diners—turn their attention to the main event: the food.

Sea Swirl

30 Williams Avenue (Route 1), Mystic 860-536-3452 • www.seaswirlofmystic.com • Open "during baseball season" • BEST BITES: Fried clams, fried cod, onion rings, Buck's ice cream

Is the Sea Swirl an ice cream stand moonlighting as a clam shack, or the other way around? There's been heated debate between the ice cream crowd and the clamheads for the two decades the Swirl's been in business. Historically speaking, the ice cream came first, and the slanted glass-walled hut looks like a greaser-era soda shop for a reason: It housed a Carvel for nearly 30 years before current owner David Blaney arrived and began frying what many defend as the best belly clams in the Nutmeg State. He knew he didn't want to lose Carvel's sweet-tooth fan base, so ice cream stayed on the menu and the Sea Swirl became known for both. The restaurant's name and even the logo—a seemingly content fish, fin-clutching a cone—suggest ocean treats with a sugary, creamy chaser.

While there's no indoor seating in the Swirl itself (there's barely room for a kitchen and a takeout window), a couple of picnic tables flank the building, and there's a tented dining area over to the side where you can carry your meal and settle in for a spell. But the happy hubbub of families surrounding the takeout window makes it a pleasure to chow down even perched on your car hood. Sunsets are an unofficial specialty at the Swirl, and if you time it right and the weather's nice, you'll catch a beauty right there in the parking lot. There's also the definite smell of sea in the air—thank the Mystic River flood tide, which creeps up to a marshy cove right next to the restaurant. This is where your dog can get all slimed with seaweed and make your car smell like a marina for the entire drive home.

How hungry are you? The first time I happened upon the Swirl, I cursed the bad highway lunch I'd choked down mere minutes before and discovered that a roll of fried clams (I got the bellies, but strips are available) was small

enough for a nice-sized snack. (I gave my bun to a gull, not because it wasn't good, but because a girl has to know her limits. That said, please don't feed the gulls. They're ornery enough as it is.) For hungrier moments, clams, scallops, cod nuggets, and big Gulf shrimp are available as side orders, with tartar sauce (or cocktail, but get the tartar), and as dinners, with all the trimmings. Without exception, these bites are fresh and succulent within a perfectly done amber crust full of crunch, and virtually greaseless (the Swirl uses soybean oil). If you're in a hot dog mood, upgrade to the smoky grilled kielbasa on a toasted bun. There's also a juicy burger that the Swirl staff can top with everything

> "It's like I get in line, and my circuits jam. Do I want clams? Do I want scallops? What about the shrimp? I love the shrimp. Damn them for not having a combo plate!"
>
> —SUSAN PHEE, BOSTON, ON ORDERING ANXIETY AT THE SEA SWIRL

from cheese and bacon to sauerkraut and homemade chili, and if a quarter-pound of meat isn't enough for you, order the double. Or get the sweet, brittle onion rings on the side.

A yummy chilled lobster roll rounds out a long list of sandwiches that includes grilled chicken and BLTs, though I can't say I've managed to get past the seafood and burger to sample any.

A note on dessert: If we're going by volume alone, the ice cream camp wins. There's soft serve, hard packed (Buck's, made in nearby Milford), and yogurt; shakes, floats, and sodas; flurries, sundaes, and banana splits the size of a small hubcap–few ice cream parlors can touch the Swirl for sheer variety.

SEA SWIRL
FRESH SEAFOOD
FAMOUS FOR CLAMS
ICE CREAM

crib sheet: Cod

A.k.a. codfish. Bottom-dwelling fish of the North Atlantic and Pacific. Close relative of haddock and pollock; scrod is a young cod (or haddock) weighing less than 2 pounds, whereas an adult cod can reach 6 feet. Popular battered and fried in fish and chips, but also shows up in fish chowder and fish cakes (sometimes specified as "cod cakes," and good for a hangover).

Turk's Restaurant

425 Captain Thomas Boulevard, West Haven 203-933-4552 • Open year-round
BEST BITES: Fried soft-shell crabs, hand-cut french fries, lobster sauté, Black Forest cake

Turk's, like nearby Chick's Drive-In, owes its existence to Savin Rock Amusement Park, the seaside sensation that drew crowds from all over the Northeast for the first half of the 20th century. As Turk's kitchen manager Skip Ramadon tells it, his grandmother Josephine started the place in 1939 with her dad and her husband. It was right across the way, and you went there for fried clams or split hot dogs, and if you didn't, you went to Jimmie's or Phylliss's nearby (all three served basically the same menu, but people played favorites), and then you went to the stock-car races or tried to win a stuffed animal for your sweetie. They were institutions forced to figure out their future when the Savin Rock era came to a close in the late '60s, before an onslaught of redevelopment of the shore made log rides and penny candy a thing of the past.

The Ramadons, for their part, decided to stick it out. Turk's moved to its new spot in 1969, and it's still owned and operated by the family. Like much of that era's architecture, its new building is squat, beige, and unassuming, a blink-and-you'd-miss-it structure on the side of a busy road, with a plain, high-ceilinged dining room to one side and dark, wood-paneled booths and carpeting by the less-formal takeout counter on the other. Aside from a few touches like the red neon "Turk's" sign, the backlit takeout menu with the Coca-Cola logo (sample item: "Extra

DINNERS COME WITH FRIES
COLESLAW & A ROLL

ORDER		DINNER
9 95	SHRIMP	13 25
9 95	SCALLOP	13 25
9 95	CLAM	13 25
9 50	STRIP CLAM	12 75
9 95	SOFT SHELL CRAB	13 25
9 25	CALAMARI	12 75
8 50	FILET OF FISH	11 50
9 50	FISH N CHIP	11 50
8 95	LOBSTER ROLL	11 95
SEAFOOD PLATTER		19 25
+SHRIMP, SCALLOPS, CLAMS, FISH		
MARINER PLATTER		26 75
+A SEAFOOD AND A SHELL		
CHICKEN DINNER		9 50
EXTRA TARTAR		10¢

Tartar: 10 cents") or the bags of Terry's Caramel Corn for sale, if you weren't from the neighborhood, you'd never suspect you were standing in an almost 70-year-old West Haven institution that used to serve fried clams to roller coaster lovers. Compare this patch of Connecticut landscape to the framed black-and-white photos of the original restaurant hanging on Turk's walls, and it seems like the only thing that hasn't changed is the sea.

That, and the food. Skip Ramadon, whose father Eddie owns the place, started working at the restaurant when he was just 10 years old. While he admits that the parking lot used to be more whitewall tires than bumper-stickered Tauruses, he's never known a time when Turk's trademark dishes were prepared any differently from the recipes his grandparents used when they started out. "It's all very simple stuff," says Skip, adjusting the tie on a well-worn white apron. "Nothing's pre-made, nothing's pre-breaded–everything is cooked to order. It takes a little longer, but people seem to know that it's worth it." Behind him, trays are stacked four- and five-high with plain white bowls waiting to be filled up with chowder, as cooks make fast work of coating fish, clams, and calamari for the steady Saturday lunch crowd. The scene is as well-oiled of a machine as it gets.

Favorites on Turk's menu are the basics: Fried seafood is lightly battered and barely greasy; for a little taste of everything, try the Seafood Platter piled high with caramel-colored full-belly Ipswich clams, shrimp, haddock, and scallops. A few dollars extra will net you the Mariner Platter, the seafood version topped with a plump, deep-fried soft-shell crab. Chesapeake soft-shells may be Turk's most popular item: One bite, with the double-crunch of batter and shell and the smoky, tender center, explains why. Order soft-shells alone, too, paired with some of the restaurant's fries. The latter are homemade, a rarity at seafood shacks, simply because peeling and slicing potatoes is time-consuming; Skip points out that these fries have won statewide awards.

Try the Rhode Island clam chowder (even though this is Connecticut), a clear-broth kind with firm, diced potatoes and sweet bursts of clam; it's the only chowder on the menu and Turk's devotees are mad for it. And of course, there's lobster. The roll is simple, a griddled bun crammed with sweet lobster meat that's been tossed simply and perfectly in melted butter. You could also do away with the pretense of the bun altogether and order the lobster sauté: warm pillows of fresh-picked lobster, gently warmed with even more butter, and served with a spoon. Hummel hot dogs, a good burger, and fried mozzarella round out the menu with some offerings for the non-seafood crowd. And if, for some reason, you have room for dessert, get the Black Forest chocolate cake or the cheesecake with strawberries.

shack people:
Skip Ramadon, kitchen manager at Turk's

• *On praise:* "People tell us our seafood is the best they've ever had. We probably don't appreciate it as much as we should."

• *On love and coleslaw:* "We've had so many first dates here. One time a guy came back here to the kitchen—he was going to propose to his girlfriend and he had us hide the ring in the coleslaw. I'm pretty sure it was in the coleslaw. She said yes. Our coleslaw's really good—not vinegary."

• *On standards:* "You should try the fries. We cut our own—I think that makes a big difference. We've won Best French Fries in the State from *Connecticut Magazine.*"

• *On lobster rolls:* "Just a little unsalted butter on the meat. Do they do a lot of mayonnaise up north? Yeah, no—we don't do that. Butter."

• *On longevity:* "We've been here forever. That's not going to change."

Westfair Fish & Chips

1781 Post Road East (Route 1), Westport 203-255-3184 • Open year-round

BEST BITES: Fish and chips, fried belly clams, seafood bisque, hot lobster roll

*I*f you don't live in Westport, Connecticut, Westfair Fish & Chips is one of those places that you wouldn't know about unless someone told you. It doesn't trumpet its existence from the roadside (it's tucked away in a mini-mall, across the street from a Super Stop & Shop), it barely advertises, and the postage stamp–sized eatery is not much to look at, what with its handful of chairs and a Snapple case taking up half the room. There's exactly one table outside, and if you sat here, you'd have a view of the parking lot. Its general appearance is all the more out of place given the manicured allure of most of Westport: here a Restoration Hardware, there a Pottery Barn, everywhere antique dealers, most bearing fancy French names spelled out in gilded letters ("Parc Monceau," "L'Antiquaire").

And yet, Westfair should be on more people's radars, because it's been serving some of the most righteous fish and chips on the Connecticut coast for nearly 20 years.

The variety of seafood and fish on Westfair's menu is impressive. Few restaurants give diners a choice between bay and sea scallops, generally going with one or the other, but Westfair offers both (the bay are sweeter and slightly more expensive). The fish in the eponymous dish is scrod, but fried sole is available too. Nearly everything on the regular menu can be had fried or broiled, and the specials board next to the takeout window nearly doubles the offerings, calling out, on my visits, everything from Maine steamers and oysters on the half shell to blackened swordfish and mussels steamed in garlic. A tiny tank in the corner holds a few ultra-peppy lobsters (these suckers are fresh–a sign above them reads "Please do not put hands in tank"). Clam chowder lovers will find New England, Rhode Island, and even Manhattan versions up for grabs (the first is excellent), and the unusual seafood bisque is hearty and delicious.

Be forewarned: Seafood-frowners won't find anything on the menu other than french fries, onion rings, and coleslaw.

ten tasty pit stops off I-95

I don't care how good that Cinnabon smell is, highway travel is bad enough without having to waste your appetite on a fast-food meal. Starting in Connecticut and heading north, these places are all less than 10 minutes off I-95 (coastal New England's main artery, which breaks inland before mid-coast Maine), meaning that a quick detour won't carve time out of your journey—but will leave your stomach happy.

1. *Chick's Drive-In,* West Haven, CT (Exit 43)

2. *The Place,* Guilford, CT (Exit 58)

3. *Lenny & Joe's Fish Tale,* Madison, CT (Exit 61)

4. *Johnny Ad's,* Old Saybrook, CT Exit 69)

5. *Sea Swirl,* Mystic, CT (Exit 90)

6. *Lena's Seafood,* Salisbury, MA (Exit 59)

7. *Markey's Lobster Pool,* Seabrook, NH (Exit 1)

8. *Bob's Clam Hut,* Kittery, ME (Exit 1)

9. *Maine Diner,* Wells, ME (Exit 2)

10. *Cindy's,* Yarmouth, ME (Exit 17)

Additional Listings

Chesterfield

David's Place
1647 Route 85 • 860-442-7120

Look for the 30-foot fiberglass dinosaur: He presides over a nature shop across the street from David's, where the burgers are almost as good as the fried clam bellies.

Darien

Fisherman's Net
11 Old Kings Highway (Route 1)
203-655-0561

Sitting quietly in a Truman-era shopping center off the highway is this unassuming fish market with a short menu chalked onto a blackboard above the counter. Nearly everything is good, but the soft-shell crabs (in season) and the fried fish, both dark brown and crunchy, are magnificent.

Derby

The River Restaurant
656 New Haven Avenue • 203-732-2630

It's a heavily Italian spot, but the lobster roll is pure New England.

Branford

U.S.S. Chowder Pot III
560 East Main Street • 203-481-2356
www.chowderpot.com

Turn off when you see the giant lobster on the roof. The pot started nearly 30 years ago as a drive-in clam shack in Madison, and it's moved twice to accommodate the overflow of regulars. Vast menu of seafood favorites, from fried bites to a raw bar.

East Hartford

Mickey's Oceanic Grill

119 Pitkin Street • 860-528-6644

Stand at a powder-blue blue Formica counter (nope, no chairs here) and sink into a succulent blue crab roll with Key lime dressing or a bowl of peppery chowder.

East Haven

The Sandpiper

161 Cosey Beach Avenue • 203-469-7544

Cheery blue umbrellas dot the patio at this fish house (try the grilled swordfish or soft-shells, in season) overlooking Long Island Sound on Momauguin Town Beach.

Hampden

Glenwood Drive-In

2538 Whitney Avenue (Route 10)
203-281-0604

Most come to the Drive-In (which really isn't one) for the yummy charcoal-grilled burgers and dogs; you'll come–and keep coming–for the clam basket and the euphoria-inducing warm lobster roll, bathed in pale butter.

Milford

Bobette's Takeout

93 Boston Post Road (Route 1) • 203-874-9414

Bobette's is so well loved, there was a ribbon-cutting by the mayor when they unveiled their mussel chowder.

Legends

1492 Boston Post Road (Route 1)
203-874-0177

This place has straight burger-joint appeal (and excellent Angus beef to back it up), but there's also a 9-inch hot lobster roll and fresh clams, squid, and sea scallops, fried to perfection.

Milford Seafood

315 New Haven Avenue • 203-874-1753

For lovers of Rhode Island–style broth clam chowder, Milford's is a milestone.

Seven Seas

16 New Haven Avenue • 203-877-7327

Dare you to find a tourist in this homey dive, a cozy pub where fried food is king (and the lobster roll's not bad, either).

Mystic

Cove Fish Market

20 Old Stonington Road • 860-536-0061
www.covefishmarket.com

This unassuming bungalow is set apart from the Mystic Seaport mania (and Route 1 traffic), so you can enjoy a quiet moment with your delicious lobster roll or brothy clam chowder.

Kitchen Little

Route 27 • 860-536-2122

The tiny shop on the water hums in summer, ladling out quart after quart of its creamless clam chowder and serving possibly the definitive fried scallop roll. Popular breakfasts, too.

New London

Bank Street Lobster House

194 Bank Street • 860-447-9398

Two sights greet you when you enter this sweet clapboard shack on the Thames River: glass-domed, heavenly-looking cakes and pies, and a live lobster tank. All is right with the world. Butter-drenched lobster warmed on a torpedo roll confirms it.

Fred's Shanty

272 Pequot Avenue • 860-447-1301
www.fredsshanty.com

Order fried scallops and hot dogs at this sweet takeout counter with the bright blue awning and a smattering of tables overlooking New London's Thames River (pronounced soft, with the *H* in New London, not with a silent *H* and hard *T,* Old London–style). You'd never know it to look at it, but Fred's also rubs elbows with an important literary landmark. Right next door is Monte Cristo Cottage, the boyhood home of playwright Eugene O'Neill and the setting for *Long Day's Journey into Night.*

Captain Scott's Lobster Dock
80 Hamilton Street • 860-439-1741

Past the railroad tracks, the boat yard, the lumber yard, a couple of grassy knolls dotted with stray cats, and a Porta-Potty, there it is: an adorable shack frying and steaming New England favorites right on Shaw's Cove.

Niantic

Dad's Restaurant
147 Main Street (Route 156) • 860-739-2113

Dad's has a big fan base of locals and visitors, who flock here for the hot lobster roll.

Skipper's
167 Main Street (Route 156) • 860-739-3230

Lefty Tsiropoulos opened this straight-up clam shack just a couple of years ago, offering lovable fried plates and rolls. How often do you get to eat clams fried by a guy named Lefty?

Noank

Seahorse Tavern
65 Marsh Road • 860-536-1670

Worth a detour for the grilled mussels alone: The orange mollusks are steamed and half-shelled, then topped with garlic-parsley butter and a dusting of breadcrumbs and browned.

Norwalk

Rowayton Seafood
89 Rowayton Avenue • 203-866-4488

A cute by-the-marina seafoodery with a selection of straightforward New England dishes.

Sono Seaport Seafood
100 Water Street • 203-854-9483

Some come for the oysters and littlenecks (that lighthouse on the dock? That's the raw bar), others come for the lobster, and everybody enjoys the cooling breezes flowing right off Norwalk Harbor.

Old Saybrook

Dock and Dine
10 College Street • 860-388-4665

Folks flock to this cute waterside spot on Saybrook Point to chow on seafood standards with a stunning water view.

Southbury

Denmo's
346 Main Street South, Southbury
203-264-4626

Known for their monumentally tasty split and charred hot dogs, but you can get a good hot lobster roll and succulent fried clam bellies, too.

Stonington

Sea View Snack Bar
145 Greenmanville Avenue (Route 27)
860-572-0096

A cheery shake shack with blue awnings, red picnic tables, and the Mystic River bubbling along below. Great fish and chips.

Skipper's Dock

66 Water Street • 860-535-0111

www.skippersdock.com

Some frou-frou touches jar (valet parking? Is this Beverly Hills?), but the tasty seafood dishes, lively ambience, and crackerjack view (that's Fisher's Island in the distance) make up for it.

Stonington Deli

Route 1 • 860-535-9142

When owner Robert Ottaviano isn't serving up chowder and clam fritters beneath the red awning at the Deli, he's catering clambakes all along the Connecticut shore.

Westbrook

Bill's Seafood Restaurant

548 Boston Post Road (Route 1) • 860-399-7224

Beady gull eyes follow every crunchy clam from plate to mouth on the marinaside patio at Bill's, where you can fill up on reasonable, solid seafood while your toes tap to live jazz and blues.

Lenny & Joe's Fish Tale

86 Boston Post Road (Route 1) • 860-669-0767

www.ljfishtale.com

Westbrook outpost of the Lenny & Joe's in Madison.

Westbrook Lobster Market & Restaurant

346 Boston Post Road (Route 1) • 860-664-9464

Satisfying standards made with the freshest seafood, which you can also pluck raw from market cases on your way out.

West Haven

Jimmie's of Savin Rock

5 Rock Street • 203-934-3212

Detractors say it's nothing like its 1940s heyday, but the straightforward seafood (and famed split-top hot dogs) keep them coming back.

Woodbury

Carmen Anthony Fishhouse

757 Main Street South • 203-266-0011

Nutmeg Staters consistently vote the Carmen Anthony mini-chain to the head of the class for the creamy clam chowder and crabcakes.

rhode island

2

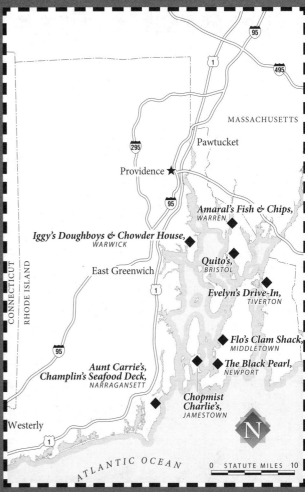

MASSACHUSETTS

Pawtucket

Providence ★

CONNECTICUT
RHODE ISLAND

Amaral's Fish & Chips,
WARREN ◆

Iggy's Doughboys & Chowder House,
WARWICK ◆

East Greenwich

Quito's,
BRISTOL ◆

Evelyn's Drive-In,
TIVERTON ◆

Flo's Clam Shack,
MIDDLETOWN ◆

Aunt Carrie's,
Champlin's Seafood Deck,
NARRAGANSETT ◆

The Black Pearl,
NEWPORT ◆

Chopmist
Charlie's,
JAMESTOWN ◆

Westerly

N

ATLANTIC OCEAN

0   STATUTE MILES   10

Amaral's Fish & Chips

4 Redmond Street, • Warren 401-247-0675 • Open year-round
BEST BITES: Fish and chips, fried scallops, fried smelts, clamcakes, "natural" clam chowder

Don't expect views or pristine clapboard at Amaral's. This tiny Portuguese diner tucked away in a nondescript business park in Warren is not about looks. But the name piqued my interest, and the food backs it up: This may be some of the lightest, crispiest battered haddock in Rhode Island, and the rest of the fried seafood–clams, shrimp, juicy, wonderful scallops, and totally addictive smelts–is just as winning; a couple of combo dinners let you mix and match. The "natural" chowder is a thick, pale gray-green version of the cream-less Rhode Island kind, full of hefty nuggets of clam; in the red chowder, tomatoes give the plain version a spicy kick. In a mystifying move, white chowder is served on Fridays only, but it doesn't taste as much like clams. What does is the clamcakes, smaller than some I've tasted, and salty and satisfying. "If the gods on Mount Olympus ate clamcakes," writes Quahog.org, a virtual shrine to the all-holy bivalve, "they'd buy them here."

lingo: Stuffies

Slang for stuffed clams. Quahog meat is chopped and combined with a host of ingredients such as onions, peppers, even linguiça sausage, bound with some breadcrumbs, seasoned with herbs, heaped back into the shell, and baked.

Clams even show up in a grinder, but try the chouriço instead. This and a few items like the marinated smelt dinner, along with broad, round loaves of dark-crusted bread for sale at the register, bespeaks Amaral's Portuguese roots.

The Great Clam Chowder Debate

"Tomatoes and clams have no more affinity than ice cream and horseradish."

—Eleanor Early, on the issue of tomatoes in clam chowder, *A New England Sampler*

In New England, you should never come between a man and his clam chowder—which is a completely different animal depending on where you are. The debate over which is authentic has been raging for nearly two centuries, and it's not about to stop anytime soon. While there's some overlap, these guidelines should help you tell them apart (so you can pick a team):

Rhode Island Clam Chowder (a.k.a. "clear," "natural," "Southern New England"): Broth-based, without milk or cream, thickened only with the potatoes' own starch, made with hard-shell clams and often flavored with salt pork. Can be thin or thick, usually a steely gray color. "Noank chowder" is a Western Connecticut variant. With the addition of pureed tomatoes and/or diced vegetables, it becomes Rhode Island red chowder.

New England Clam Chowder (a.k.a. "Boston," "white"): Usually made with chopped hard-shells against a cream or milk broth. Diced potatoes and flour to thicken are common. Usually started with salt pork, sometimes finished with a sprinkling of it. Considered by many to be the gold standard of chowders.

Maine Clam Chowder (a.k.a. "chowdah," "stew"): Dairy-based but thin and milky, with no thickening agents, but usually lots of butter pooling on top. May use soft-shell clams (this is sometimes called "steamer chowder") or hard ("quahog chowder"). Can include potatoes or salt pork.

Manhattan Clam Chowder (a.k.a. "Italian chowder," "red chowder," "a shame"): Clam chowder popularized by Italian restaurants in New York City. Usually thin-brothed and full of tomatoes and vegetables. Rarely seen in New England, for fear of being tarred, feathered, and run out of town.

Aunt Carrie's

Point Judith, Narragansett 401-783-7930 • Open April to September • BEST BITES: Clamcakes, Rhode Island–style clam chowder, steamers, rhubarb pie (in season), strawberry shortcake

Newport and Narragansett share twin histories as getaways for the wealthy who flocked here in the late 19th century. But if Newport's past has sometimes translated into ostentation for its own sake, Narragansett has settled into a laid-back elegance that's seemingly impervious to change–and nowhere is that clearer than at its most beloved eatery, Aunt Carrie's, which has overlooked the beach at the end of Ocean Road since 1920. Here, at the gray building with the green trim and the flagpole, change amounts to the recent replacement of a rooftop sign that had begun to fall apart.

If the quality of a clam shack's fare can be measured by the number of seagulls loitering on the eaves, Aunt Carrie's serves the best food in the universe. Perched up there, the little fellas have quite the view: salt marsh to one side, a patchwork of quahog beds off Galilee Escape Road, the two-tone lighthouse at Point Judith, where Narragansett Bay begins, and its perfect stretch of sandy beach below.

It's on this very beach, almost a hundred years ago, that Ulysses Cooper and his wife Carrie would bring their brood of six and camp out each summer. Ulysses always complained that there was no place to buy a drink of something cold nearby, and soon they started selling homemade lemonade out of an icebox. Corn-fritter clamcakes and chowder followed–the Coopers' lunches

AUNT CARRIE'S

Specializing in Sea Food
Since 1920

End of Route 108-S
(401) 783-7930

1240 Ocean Road
Narragansett, RI

Ms. Elsie Foy
Mr. Raymond VanHine

April — May
Open Friday, Saturday & Sunday

Memorial Day — Labor Day
Open Every Day But Tuesday

September
Open Friday, Saturday & Sunday

smelled so good that other families began asking for a taste. So Ulysses built a clam shack where the building stands today, and the rest is history, one that's very much alive in the black-and-white photographs that line the walls of Aunt Carrie's slope-floored old dining room with the screen windows.

The place is still in the family, turning out an expanded version of the menu that made those early beachgoers drool. Everyone in Rhode Island can tell you that Carrie invented that Ocean State specialty, the clamcake. It's not surprising that these puffy nuggets of dough, tasting of sweet cornmeal and dotted with shredded quahogs, are a bestseller. On a busy day, all over the beach, you can watch people dunking these into one of Aunt Carrie's three varieties of clam chowder: "milk, tomato, or plain"–the latter being the Rhode Island–style broth-based kind. If you'd rather your quahogs less fussed-with, you've probably come for the clams themselves, served up two winning ways that are hard to choose between. The Pan of Steamed Clams with butter and broth sets the bar high for all future steamers to pass your lips. This dish is hard to negotiate on your car hood, by the way; if the marshside picnic tables are full and you're eating on the go, get the fried clams instead, magnificent, craggy knots of pure crunch with a smoky center. These didn't have to try all

its fresh-baked pies; the rhubarb is heaven. When the rhubarb harvest is over, it becomes strawberry shortcake season at Aunt Carrie's. Or go for the apple pie–if you get there early enough you can peer into the kitchen and watch prep cooks peeling the apples.

clams casino:

Broiled littlenecks on the half shell, typically topped with a mixture of minced peppers and onions, herbs, and crumbled bacon. Said to have originated around 1917 in southern Rhode Island, in the kitchen of the late Narragansett Pier casino.

that hard to make my list of the best fried bellies on the seaboard. Big appetites or special occasions call for a seat in the dining room and the Rhode Island Shore Dinner: steamers, clamcakes, chowder, broiled fish (another house specialty; get the flounder), and fries, with a drink and dessert. The brave can add a whole boiled lobster to this feast and win the staff's respect. The side to get is the onion rings; Aunt Carrie's fries theirs in the same oil as the seafood, and that's a good thing.

Speaking of dessert, the kitchen does an authentic Indian pudding, musky-sweet with molasses and finished off with a scoop of vanilla ice cream. It's also known for

The Black Pearl

Bannister's Wharf, Newport 401-846-5264 • www.blackpearlnewport.com • Open year-round
BEST BITES: Clam chowder, mussels Black Pearl, seasonal-fruit bread pudding

By all reckoning, the Black Pearl doesn't belong in this book. After all, this is a place with tuxedoed waitstaff, bread dishes, and warm Brie. A place with a wine list—and not just any wine list: one that tops out with a $950 Château Mouton Rothschild '82. But Newport, Rhode Island, is a place of contradictions, a posh getaway town that draws as much from its history as a playground for the rich and richer as it does from the salty New England Tao that defines so many working waterfronts along the seaboard. Everything in the building's humble history, its atmosphere, its oldest recipes, and its cocktails—served strong enough to have you singing sea shanties before long—earns it a spot within these pages. The Pearl may be fancy, but I believe it has a shack's heart.

Besides, you can eschew the linens and silver of the Black Pearl's Commodore's Room for the more plebeian pleasures (and prices) of the Tavern or, in accommodating weather, the raucous outside patio, open-air bar, or Hot Dog and Chowder Annex. (This is about as in-the-rough as it gets in a town with regattas, golf clubs, and more than one place to buy a humidor.)

The restaurant is smack dab in the center of Newport's harbor district, a concentration of shops, bars, and restaurants on a few wharves off Thames Street. Bear left as you walk waterwards down busy Bannister's Wharf and duck—if you're over 5'5"—into the Tavern in the Black Pearl's main building. Low, low ceilings, creaky floorboards, glossy black trim, and spindle-back chairs all brew the sense that you've dropped in to share a pipe with a shipbuilder who calls his cook "Cook" and has a bellowing laugh that makes his spaniel stir from its spot by the fire.

This room with its elbow-shaped bar is especially inviting when the weather cools, and it's almost impossible not to stop in for a bowl of the clam chowder. It's famous and award-winning, and happily, not all hype. A

hearty veal-stock base and fresh, oceany quahogs set the tone for this delectable stuff, pale amber-colored where the butter meets the cream, and finished off with just enough dry vermouth. I've seen people order a second bowl when the first gets low. It's that good.

The terrific raw bar, the sandwiches, the gray sole, the rack of lamb—none but the most hardcore vegan will feel left out here. The menu is vast, varied, and verges on overwhelming, and so much is worthy that it's hard to recommend just a few dishes. But the mussels Black Pearl should be on your list. Served as an appetizer but big enough to be a main, it's a bowl that comes piled high with slick black shells harvested from nearby Narragansett Bay, each cradling a plump orange mussel, the whole shebang steaming with heat from a milky broth below. The silky liquid gets its kick from freshly torn basil and begs to be sopped up with a crusty baguette, but a bread roll will have to do. You'll want another for the lemon butter bathing a handful of pearly Nantucket Bay scallops or the lime and tequila marinade seasoning a grilled shrimp brochette. Much at the Black Pearl requires a roll, which may be why they charge for them.

Desserts, like the rest, are homemade, and the thing to get at the Black Pearl is the bread pudding, made with fresh fruit that changes with the seasons. The apple-raisin version is hard to beat. Even a Vanderbilt couldn't argue with that.

lingo:
Little Rhody

What natives fondly call Rhode Island, one of the original 13 colonies and the smallest state

lingo: ## Doughboys

A.k.a. fried dough, elephant ears. A Rhode Island specialty, traceable to the state's Italian immigrants. Hunks, usually square, of deep-fried pizza dough liberally coated with granulated sugar. Often available where seafood is fried.

Ten Great Scoops

New Englanders eat about 20 percent more ice cream than anyone else in America. Can you blame them? The region has some of the best frozen treats anywhere. These 10 spots should be must-licks on any ice cream lover's circuit.

1. *Four Seas Ice Cream* (360 South Main Street; Centerville, MA; 508-775-1394). Cape Cod's oldest ice cream shop handmakes 2,000 gallons a week. Legend has it Chocolate Chip was born in this former blacksmith shop, not long after it opened in 1934.

2. *Brown's Old Fashion Ice Cream* (Nubble Road, York Beach, ME; (207-363-1277). No jimmies or sprinkles, ever—as owner Steve Dunne says, good ice cream doesn't need it. This stand near Nubble Lighthouse is a favorite of Ben Cohen, of Ben & Jerry's fame.

3. *White Farms Ice Cream* (326 High Street/Route 133, Ipswich, MA; 978-356-2633). Grab a scoop of Key lime pie ice cream at this Clam Alley institution (open since 1953) and head back to your sandy towel on nearby Crane's Beach.

4. *The James Gallery and Soda Fountain* (2 Pennywise Lane, Old Saybrook, CT; 860-395-1406) The butterfat runs thick and good at this 1896 soda fountain (and, yes, art gallery). A cone here is the perfect topper to a pint of fried clams at nearby Johnny Ad's.

5. *Island Cow Ice Cream Co.* (Main Street, Stonington, ME; no phone). Ginger and Peach are locked in a dead heat for yummiest flavor at this main drag shack, which serves all-natural Smiling Hill Farm ice cream (made, as the sign says, "by happy cows").

6. *Lago's Lone* Oak (71 Lafayette Road/Route 1, Rye, NH; 603-964-9880). Coastal outpost of the famed Manchester, NH, makers of heavenly hard-packed, soft-serve, and sherbet. Try the Muddy Sneakers.

7. *Dr. Mike's Ice Cream* (158 Greenwood Avenue, Bethel, CT; 203-792-4388). Mind-blowing licks made with cream delivered from a farm in the next state every single day. The Rich Chocolate is a must.

8. *Gray's Ice Cream* (16 East Road, Tiverton Four Corners, Tiverton, RI; 401-624-4500). The proof's in the cows nearby. Famous for their homemade Ginger ice cream, they also serve wonderful, frothy cabinets.

9. *Mad Martha's Homemade Ice Cream* (20 Union Street, Vineyard Haven, MA; 508-693-5883). Since 1971, where islanders go for their last butter-creamy lick before hopping the ferry to the mainland (there are outposts in the Vineyard's other towns, too).

10. *Annabelle's* (49 Ceres Street, Portsmouth, NH; 603-436-3400). Fresh cream, ultra-rich texture, and no artificial anything have made Annabelle's a must for more than two decades. Try the Cashew Caramel Cluster.

Champlin's Seafood Deck

256 Great Island Road (on Galilee Harbor), Narragansett 401-783-3152 • www.champlins.com •
Open year-round • BEST BITES: Snail salad, fried flounder, fried calamari with hot peppers

There's a lot going on in Galilee Harbor. There are cottages to rent, shops to trawl, beaches with names like Scarborough and Salty Brine, the Block Island Ferry coming and going–and yet it's still, more than anything, a place with an awful lot of fish. It's always been this way: Throughout the late 19th and early 20th centuries, Galilee evolved into one of the

biggest fishing ports on the East Coast. Even today, some 10 million pounds of scales and shells pass through here on their way to markets, cans, freezers, and dinner plates across America.

Some don't have very far to go at all, because unsurprisingly, Galilee is also home to some terrific seafood restaurants. Champlin's is one of the oldest, though the building doesn't look it–the original 1920s shanty was razed by a hurricane that spared little of the shoreline itself. The Champlin family rebuilt their restaurant, adding on here and there as the business grew to occupy a sprawling structure that feels a bit like a cruise ship, with its decks, stairwells, tarps, and flags. On the upper deck, gray-blue walls are hung with photographs of fishermen who've dragged or trapped off Galilee, and the life preservers you see hung all over the place aren't throwaway nautical flair: Each bears the name of a boat that sells its catch to Champlin's. And of course, as you sit slurping your chowder, you can watch the boats come and go along the channel, with seagulls swooping in their wake.

Unless you get here early, you'll have plenty of time to soak up all this local flavor, as Champlin's takeout window boasts some of the longest lines in Rhode Island. Still, the staff here is crackerjack, and the line moves fast. Best to know what you want and be prepared to bark it out, Soup Nazi–style, when your turn comes. If you're not sure what to order, keep an eye on the trays lining up at the pick-up counter to your left: still-sizzling fried shrimp and scallops mounded onto paper plates, raw cherrystones by the baker's dozen, piles of golden, puffy clamcakes, and steaming red lobsters bought from the lower deck market and trotted up here for cooking–one or two to an order. Lobster is big at Champlin's. Sometimes 14-pounds big.

As good as all that is, there are a few rarities worth ordering here. Champlin's takes a noble stance on fried fish: First, the fish comes right off the boats into Champlin's, where it's filleted, batter dipped, deep fried, and on your tongue all within less time than it may have taken you to get to the front of the line. Second, they only serve flounder or yellow tail. I love cod and haddock, but there's something delicate and sweet about flounder, and it works majestically with the kitchen's special dry batter. Add these up, and you've got one of the best pieces of fried fish you'll ever eat. It takes a sanguine disposition to order the garlicky snail salad when there are so many fried and butter-dipped things to be had, but do it (see sidebar).

Champlin's also shows off its serious kitchen standards in the clam chowder, made with sea clams (the chowder standard) and quahogs (usually considered too costly and labor intensive for chowder). It's rare for a place with this kind of frantically high volume to use both; smaller and usually pricier restaurants tout quahog chowder because it's such a luxury item. All three chowder varieties are on the menu: white (New England–style), clear (the Rhody classic), and red. I'd urge even the most tomato-cursing chowder purist to try a spoonful of the red at Champlin's, because its peppery undertones and those sweet, briny quahogs make it a different beast from much of the Manhattan-style chowder I've been unlucky enough to sample. This is one of the

few items you can order at the Channel View Lounge downstairs, best suited to chillier days when you can pair a cup of chowder and a clamcake or six with an icy cold brew.

There's no dessert up here, but the Down Under shop on the lower deck sells ice cream, fudge, and, yes, saltwater taffy.

local specialty: Snail Salad

You'll see snail salad almost exclusively on Rhode Island menus, often mystifying visitors from outside the Ocean State—and no, we're not talking escargots, though the dish's point is similar to that of the French bistro staple: The sea snail (a.k.a. conch) is essentially a vehicle for prodigious amounts of garlic. You'll taste Rhode Island's Portuguese and Italian roots in every sliver of the shaved meat that's been marinating in it, along with cloves, onion, olive oil, herbs, and a few other things. This is served over tender lettuce with a lemon wedge on the side.

"My grandmother used to make snail salad. I used to hate the stuff, but I love it now. This place makes the best around."

–Victor Tennett, Galilee, Rhode Island, waiting in line at Champlin's

Chopmist Charlie's

40 Narragansett Avenue, Jamestown • 401-624-3100 • Open year-round
BEST BITES: Lobster bisque, stuffed quahogs, broiled striped bass, apple crisp

Chuck Masso answers his cell phone on the first ring and wastes no time informing me that he's in the men's room at a *Rhode Island Monthly* awards gala. "My restaurant just won Best of Rhode Island! When are you coming by? Do you need a place to stay? I can give you a tour of the town—hey, do you need a car?"

I politely decline Chuck's generous offers and write off his effusiveness as award-ceremony adrenaline, the kind that makes actresses forget to thank their husbands. I know Ocean Staters are friendly and all, but come on. A week later, as we're sitting at the bar at Chopmist Charlie's discussing everything from quahogs to former New York mayor Rudy Giuliani, I stand firmly corrected.

First, Charlie's has won more awards than anyone can count. Second, that's just how Chuck Masso is. Warm, funny and big-hearted, he loves his patrons, he loves his family and his dogs (the dogs have their own swimming pool), he loves his native Rhode Island (after spending 10 years in Florida, he's come home to roost), and above all, he loves good food. Especially seafood. And his restaurant is an accurate mirror of its owner.

To start with, there's the look of the place. Jamestown— a mile-wide island a stone's throw from Newport—is a movie set of a seaside town: its main street is dotted with houses in colors a paint chip might refer to as Scrimshaw White and Nantucket Red, and slopes gently down to the water. Standing here outside Chopmist Charlie's, you can make out sailboat masts amid snatches of blue where the street ends.

Seafood places tend to be imbued with the spirit of summer, but Charlie's begs to be a stop on your October leaf-peeping trip. (Chuck's wife has the summer thing covered just down the street with Tricia's Tropi-Grille, a sprawling eatery with Floribbean flair.) Inside, the low-lit room wraps itself around you like a blanket: dark wood, brass rails, lobster traps hung low from the ceiling and strung with twinkle lights (a precious touch that somehow works), thick rope, and fish lures for miles.

It's exactly as Chuck imagined it, growing up in Rhode Island's Chopmist Hill, so-named because when the fog rolls in (and it rolls in often) it's thick enough to chop with a knife. While his dad Charlie fished for a living, young Chuck got his start in the food business working at the Chopmist Hill Inn. When it went out of busi-

ness, its owner bequeathed the Inn's legendary secret recipes to Chuck, and he uses them to this day.

The menu has three settings: traditional shack fare, pub grub (including no fewer than eight Caesar salads), and fancier offerings (scrod in lobster sauce, seafood au gratin in a rich Mornay sauce, and plenty of seafood pastas). I focused on the first part. Rhode Island specialties abound, like the calamari, fried and tossed with spicy peppers, garlic and black olives. You'll want to try the stuffed quahogs, first-prize winners at the International Quahog Festival. Sweet minced indigenous clams get mixed up and baked with panko breadcrumbs, garlic, butter, parsley, bacon, and a jolt of Tabasco. Two of these is a meal for medium appetites, and might be topped with an order of beer-steamed peel-and-eat shrimp (in the same catego-

ry, the steamers are plump and sweet). Chuck's lobster roll is a big fat thing: The meat of a chicken lobster (about $1\frac{1}{8}$ pound) is chopped and tossed with Hellmann's mayonnaise, a little lemon juice, and minced celery, and piled into a butter-griddled torpedo roll.

Clamcakes should be reserved for the starving and the masochistic. These baseball-sized fritters, six to an order, loaded with quahog bits and deep-fried into caramel pillows, will kill your appetite for days. Pairing these babies with chowder (there's both clear Rhode Island quahog and New England cream–style) is a popular move. But if you're going to get a bowl of something, promise me you'll order the creamy, sherry-laced lobster bisque. I was going to pass until a customer tapped me on the shoulder and gave me a piece of her mind.

shack people:
Chuck Masso, owner and fisherman, Chopmist Charlie's

- *"I'm* Charlie! No, my dad's the original Charlie. He fillets all the fish. I catch it, bleed it, ice it, and bring it home to Dad."
- "It all comes down to fresh seafood and sticking to lots of old swamp Yankee recipes. Less is more, you know?"
- "We're the Cheers of Rhode Island. People tell us they try a lot of other restaurants, but Chopmist Charlie's is home."
- "We had a guy propose here once. He dropped the ring into the aquarium in a baggie, and when the right moment came, the waiter gave him a pair of tongs."

"Excuse me, have you tried the lobster bisque? You have to try it. It's unbelievable. People take it home by the quart and use it as a base for other recipes. It's that good. No, Chuck's not paying me to say this. The cream, the sherry—I'm serious, I'm not letting you out of here without a cup of that bisque. There's gonna be trouble. There. I'm done."

—JANET, EATING A LOBSTER ROLL (BUT LEAVING THE BUN) AT THE BAR AT CHOPMIST CHARLIE'S

If fins are your thing, you'll want to try some of Charlie's fish dishes. Chuck catches all the restaurant's fish himself, and he believes in keeping preparation simple. Try the broiled striped bass, his specialty, or go for the bluefish if he has any that day. There's no raw bar here, but Chuck—ever the good neighbor—suggests Jamestown Oyster Bar a few doors down. And if for some reason, you find yourself at Charlie's jonesing for turf over surf, the place roasts pork butts every day for their signature pulled pork sandwich, just as they make their own homey desserts. Try the warm apple crisp.

drink up, Little Rhody!

A primer to the quirky beverage options of the Ocean State:

Coffee milk

Just like it sounds: coffee and milk, sometimes written as a single word, coffeemilk. Served ice cold, traceable back to drugstores and soda shops of the '30s. Today two syrup brands, Autocrat and Eclipse, vie for coffee-milk supremacy on supermarket shelves. Official state drink of Rhode Island (does *your* state have an official drink?).

Cabinet

Milk, syrup, and ice cream blended together—a local name for the regional frappe, which, to non-New Englanders, is a milkshake. The name's thought to be a reference to the inventor's blender, which was kept in its own cabinet. Add ice cream to coffee milk and you get a coffee cabinet.

Del's Lemonade

A slushy, tart, utterly addictive drink tasting a bit like melting lemon sherbet. The recipe was brought to the new country from Italy, where lemons were mixed with snow. In 1948, the first Del's sold its first glass of the stuff in Cranston, Rhode Island. The company boasts a real lemon peel in each cup.

Awful Awful

Ice cream drink served at the Newport Creamery chain, made with flavored syrup and a secret frozen ice milk mix. As they say, "Awful big, awful good!"

Evelyn's Drive-In

2327 Main Road (Route 77), Tiverton 401-624-3100 • Open April to October
BEST BITES: Clamcakes, Rhode Island–style chowder, chow mein sandwich, Grape-Nut pudding

Evelyn's Drive-In is no stranger to kitchen-related disasters. Everybody in Tiverton knows that Evelyn Duponte, who started the place nearly 40 years ago, pencils in her eyebrows because her real ones were burned off in a Fry-o-lator accident.

But the latest disaster, an electrical fire that ravaged the place in July 2005, left Evelyn's closed and more than just Rhode Islanders heartbroken. On a sultry August day, cars–many with Massachusetts and Connecticut plates–paused at the famous Coca-Cola sign to take in the

wreckage before slowly moving down the bucolic road.

"We'll be back!" was spray-painted on a square of plywood nailed up over one of the red shack's windows.

"Of course they'll be back," said a woman lining up for coffee at the nearby Coastal Roasters, where I stopped on my way out of Tiverton. "It's just not summer without Evelyn's."

This is exactly what husband-and-wife team Jane and Dominic Bitto like to hear, especially after their 1987 purchase of the clam shack raised a few eyebrows–real ones– among the locals. The young couple was looking for a new life after a string of other jobs had left them uninspired. Dom had worked at a collection agency and New York–born Jane had been a model, briefly, and she promised herself she wouldn't take a job that required her to fake a smile ever again. En route to Cape Cod to look at a restaurant for sale, Dom took a wrong turn, got hungry, and happened upon the little shack. As luck would have it, it had just been put on the market. The place changed hands quickly, and Evelyn decamped to St. Cloud, Florida, where she still runs a joint called Evelyn's New England Seafood.

But people loved Evelyn's and they loved Evelyn herself, and just who did these hotshots think they were, coming in and taking over? In time, the Bittos won the customers' trust, mostly by not changing a good thing. Today, to the couple, the place is more than just a livelihood. It's home, the job they lucked into and can't imagine life without.

The big draws at Evelyn's are the dishes that have

been around since long before Dom and Jane. Batter-fried clam bellies, tight little clamcakes perfect for dipping in the excellent, creamless Rhode Island–style chowder, big quahogs stuffed with a savory mixture studded with chouriço sausage, an oversized cold lobster roll with plump flesh pouring out of a thick toast bun, Federal Hill–style fried calamari served with hot peppers and garlic butter for dipping, and fried clams–legendary fried clams (the fried shrimp are magnificent too). Many say there are none better in the Ocean State. Throngs of tourists line up on weekends for these shack favorites and a short list of more formal dishes, such as the grilled scallops (Bridgeport littlenecks simmered in a spicy tomato-garlic broth) or the crabcake dinner (herbed, crispy pucks sidelined by a delectable homemade horseradish sauce). Evelyn's more comfort-foody dishes have a staunch neighborhood following, so much so that some are served only from Monday to Thursday: meatloaf, chicken potpie (the crust is homemade), liver and onions (a Dom specialty), and a . . . chow mein sandwich? If you haven't tried this very local specialty, increasingly rare in Little Rhody, it's something like stir-fry on a bun: Crispy noodles and vegetables are piled on toast, napped with gravy and–despite the name–eaten with a knife and fork. Weird and oddly addictive.

The chocolate forest cake is a bestseller, but the only-in-New-England Grape-Nut pudding is the thing to get, a custardy goo spiced with cinnamon and nutmeg and topped with whipped cream. Order it warm.

The indoor dining room will be back, but unless the weather's lousy, grab a waterside spot under the long tin roof. Evelyn's Drive-In is also a boat-in, with docks separating the crushed-clam shell driveway from pretty Nanaquaket Pond, dotted with sailboats on a breezy day.

shack classic:
Grape-Nut Pudding

Sometimes called Grape-Nut custard, this unusual New England institution gets its name from the key ingredient, the Post cereal with its nutty nubbins made from whole-grain wheat and barley flour. The cereal gets softened with an egg-based mix of milk, sugar, and vanilla, and gently spiced with cinnamon or nutmeg—in some cases, even clove—before it's baked into the final product, heavenly with a dollop of freshly whipped cream. Try it at Evelyn's Drive-In in Tiverton.

Flo's Clam Shack

4 Wave Avenue, Middletown • 401-847-8141 • Open April to December
BEST BITES: Portuguese stuffed quahogs, littlenecks on the half shell, Rhode Island chowder, clamcakes

Flo's had me at its "$50 Special": a bottle of Moët and two hot dogs. The frou-frou touch of bubbly might give uninitiates the wrong idea about Flo's, and that would be a shame. It's the ballsy spirit of the thing that's so winning, the idea that this combo could be right at home next to that of "Chowda and Clamcakes, Soda or Beer" for $4.25, served up by gum-snapping teens through a cheery blue takeout window, in a joint that started out 60 years ago as a renovated chicken coop that sold clams.

Okay, so the history of Flo's is a little more complicated than that–especially since history's wiped it out twice. In 1936, the original owners dragged said chicken coop to the beach at Portsmouth's Island Park; just two years later it was leveled by the hurricane of '38. Its replacement lasted longer but met its match (and demise) in 1991's Hurricane Bob. Only the drive-in sign remained. Flo's rebuilt the same year, and the next opened this Middletown location right across the bridge from Newport, a stone's throw from Easton (a.k.a. First) Beach, in one of the few structures to survive the '38 hurricane.

Yet it doesn't look all that sturdy (words like "ramshackle" and "lopsided" come to mind), and that's part of the charm. The two-level shanty seems endless, comprised of what appear to be hastily added-on decks and porches, with two takeout windows, a courtyard patio peppered with checkered tablecloths and hula-skirted umbrellas, a vast, indoor-outdoor raw bar, and a ground-level dining room–the kind of place where you feel like wherever you're seated, you're missing the action some-

where else. If the restaurant is barely in its teens, you'd never know it. Everything in its scrappy, beachside decor makes the place feel like 1936 isn't so far away after all. (Rare touches like a plastic "Attack Quahog" sign pull you back, if briefly, to the present.)

The only real work involved in a trip to Flo's is deciding whether to go fried or not. A late afternoon spent perched on one of the stools at the Topside raw bar, sucking down littlenecks and oysters as the beach crowd thins and the sun falls past Ochre Point, is hard to beat. You can also get peel-and-eat shrimp by the pound up here, a lobster, and baked native fish; pretty much everything at Flo's is fished from local waters except the Alaskan king crab legs (and the prime rib, a Friday-night special last time I popped in.) The raw bar also boasts more than 90 varieties of hot sauce, though I think a squeeze of lemon works just fine.

Downstairs, Flo's is all about delicious food that's bad for you, a lot of it involving clams, the house specialty. A big, goofy cartoon clam with Groucho eyebrows stares up from their menu, where Flo's trumpets its awards and accolades. The restaurant's racked them up for everything from fried clams (crumb-coated for maximum crunch) to clamcakes (if they're your thing, Flo does one of the best versions I've had, a half-dozen to an order, dotted with tender quahog meat) to "fiery stuffed quahogs," based on an "ancient Portuguese recipe." These suckers are huge, packed with tangy herbed stuffing that's more brine than breadcrumb, and so full that they're served with a rubber band barely clasping the shells together.

shack classic: Clamcakes

- Also known as clam fritters; made from dough studded with chopped hard-shell clams, deep-fried into luscious pillows about the size of a baby's fist.
- May or may not actually taste like clam; with a good fritter, this is beside the point.
- Sold by the dozen, the half-dozen, and the piece.
- A Rhode Island specialty, where they're served with chowder.
- Carrie Cooper—who in 1920 founded über-shack Aunt Carrie's in Narragansett, Rhode Island—is widely recognized as the inventor of the clamcake.
- In Little Rhody, a bad clamcake is known as a "sinker," and the dim or cuckoo are said to be "one clamcake short of a dozen."

Get an order of stuffies to split, and add a chowder sampling if you're feeling adventurous. The kitchen does three: Flo's White, Rhode Island Red, and Classic Clear. The first is a tasty medium-thick New England mixture, the second a Newport cousin of Manhattan clam chowder. But it's fans of traditional Rhode Island–style chowder who'll win this one: Flo's version is packed with diced onions, potatoes, and clams swimming in a punchy clear broth. In summer, a baked fish derivation rounds out the chowder menu, starring baked cod, haddock, or sole instead of clams, and some baked green peppers for a kick. The whole thing is then baked some more. Finally, the clams casino come laden with fresh parsley tossed with diced peppers and onions, topped with a buttery cracker-crumb mixture (Flo's uses Ritz) and crisped bacon.

If you're clammed out, go for some other fried favorites, like cod, Campeche shrimp (another import, from Mexico), scallops, calamari–plain or "Italian style," tossed with peppers–or Chesapeake oysters (a Fisherman's Platter offers a taste of everything, clams included, but minus the oysters). All of it is an excuse to try Flo's genuinely yummy tartar sauce: creamy, homemade with more herbs than relish (I tasted dill), and very fresh. There's also that elusive Ocean State specialty, the Rhode Island Lunch: melted cheese on a bun with onion and pickle. Have it with onion rings.

"All our food is cooked to order. Thank you for your patience," reads a little plaque, Rhode Island-ese for "Relax, city folk. You'll get your clams." Another sign cau-

> "Flo's means summer to me. After a day at the beach, sitting on the deck with a beer and some clams . . . Life is good, you know?"
> —EDDY OLIVEIRA, WAITING FOR ORDER NO. 27 AT FLO'S

tions that they run out of items often, which is always a good sign; I'd rather see a place take this approach than stockpile product just in case, letting the seafood sit around for days just so they won't miss a sale. Order at the outdoor window near Flo's little bamboo grove or at its indoor counterpart; either way, customers waiting for food are handed rocks painted with their order number–perhaps because they'd stay put in a hurricane.

photo op: The Cliff Walk

If you're not headed back to the beach, don long pants and sturdy shoes and redeem your gut-busting Flo's lunch on the Cliff Walk. This 150-year-old path takes you about $3\frac{1}{2}$ miles—sometimes smooth, sometimes challenging—around the southern tip of Newport. Peek at private gardens on one side, gape at the 30-foot drop to the sea on the other, smell the roses lining the path . . . the trail gets a bit reedy and rocky at times, but it spits you out into Newport (and back in time) amidst turreted "cottages" and stunning Gothic mansions.

Iggy's Doughboys & Chowder House

889 Oakland Beach Avenue, Warwick • 401-737-9459 • www.iggysdoughboys.com • Open year-round • BEST BITES: Red chowder, doughboys, clamcakes, fried cod, sausage-pepper sandwich

"Is it wrong to dip a doughnut in chowder?" The woman at the takeout window has heard this before. "A doughnut, maybe," she deadpans, handing over a steamy white paper bag that's spotted with grease. "But these are doughboys. Totally different."

She's right. A doughboy, for anyone who hasn't spent the day on Rhode Island's Oakland Beach, clambering up the sand to Iggy's when hunger strikes, is a wallet-sized wad of dough, fresh from the fryer and liberally sprinkled with sugar—you'll need an ocean dip to fully remove it from your person. This Rhode Island delicacy may not

have been invented at Iggy's, but fervent followers insist it was perfected here, where the dough is made fresh every hour. The doughboy has won awards, and it comes 6 or 12 to an order (or, if you're a good customer, a baker's dozen). It's fairground food at its most irresistible and fattening. On the menu, the door and the T-shirts, the doughboy has eyes and a chef's hat. And it does taste good dipped in chowder.

As the eatery's name suggests, chowder–the clam kind–is the other thing that Rhody institution Iggy's is known for. "Don't bother asking" for the secret recipe. Also, don't bother looking for the trademark Ocean State clear-broth chowder here: Chowder at Iggy's comes in red or white, the latter thick enough to stop even the most eager of spoons. This creamy New England–style mixture, with its tender little clam bits and herb flecks, can have an overpowering saltiness that's nicely offset by the sugar from your doughboy. The red is an unusual take on Manhattan clam chowder, thicker than most, and peppery.

If dunking sweet into savory creeps you out, get the chowder-clamcake combo. The clamcakes, deep caramel on the outside, cornmeal yellow on the inside, and tasting faintly but unmistakably of clam, are puffy nuggets designed with a little tail for dainty dipping.

Beyond these three bestsellers, there's a full menu of cooked-to-order standards like huge, stuffed quahogs, seafood rolls, and the usual fried fare–get the fresh calamari or the cod, available with chips, as a soft-bunned sandwich or solo.

Iggy's was founded in 1989 by Gaetano and Sally Gravino, whose Italian roots are proudly served up in turf dishes like the sausage-pepper sandwich (New York–deli good), eggplant Parmesan, and the shaved steak and cheese on a roll, which is as close to Philly as you can get and still have saltwater nearby. The Famous Iggy Burger comes dripping with peppers and onions.

Head inside to a pink vinyl booth in the no-frills dining room, grab a chair on the patio and people-watch the throngs on Oakland Beach Avenue, or just carry your treats back to your beach towel. At sunset, the view is stunning, with both the Jamestown and Newport bridges soaring in the distance over Narragansett Bay.

This location, the original, is open year-round, seven days a week (but has limited winter hours); a second Iggy's in Narragansett is open from April to October.

five things to know about Iggy's

1. *Seaside pedigree:* Iggy's may only date to 1989, but it's housed in the oldest beach shack in Rhode Island. Gus's, which used to be in this spot, was built in 1924 and survived more than a few hurricanes. The man who founded Iggy's used to work for Gus.

2. *Iggy who?* Gaetano Gravino's license plate began with IG, so his kids called him Iggy. When his restaurant needed a name, this one stuck.

3. *The Classics:* When Iggy's opened, its menu was exactly three lines long: doughboys, chowder, and clamcakes. They're still the most popular items.

4. *No cutting!* How long is the takeout line on a summer Saturday? The place sells T-shirts emblazoned with "I survived the line at Iggy's!"

5. *Stars, stripes, and doughboys:* Locals know that Iggy's is the place to be on July Fourth, offering a plum view of the fireworks that light up Narragansett Bay. People start camping out well before the restaurant opens.

Quito's

411 Thames Street, Bristol • 401-253-4500 • Open year-round • BEST BITES: Clam fritters, steamed littlenecks in white clam sauce, fried calamari, seafood stew, homemade root beer

*I*t's hard to overemphasize just how postcard-perfect of a New England town is Bristol, Rhode Island. The paint seems not quite dry on the 18th- and 19th-century houses lining the narrow streets that wind down to the water. Every clapboard, dormer, pediment, gable, and knocker stands at attention, ready for inspection by Martha Stewart herself. Or a parade. Bristol boasts the oldest July Fourth celebration in the nation–along the two-lane road that serves as the parade route each year, the divider is actually three: Red, white, and blue.

All this oom-pah-pah can work up an appetite; for that, there's Quito's. It's not quite as old as the parade, but it does date back to 1954, when Al Quito's father Peter–a burly Sicilian who famously loves his shellfish raw–opened Quito's Shellfish in this spot. "It was just a seafood shop then, no restaurant," says Al, who grew up quahogging with his dad on Narragansett Bay. "Fishermen unloaded right on the dock. In 1962, my mother decided to put in a few tables." The formula of spanking-fresh fish, homey recipes, and hospitality caught on. The elder Quitos ran the place until the '90s, when Al took over full time. Some major renovations occurred recently, doubling the seating, adding a roof deck, and moving the market into a spiffy spot out front.

But the fishermen still tie up a net-toss away from your table, hoisting crates full of lobsters that'll all be steamed, rolled, wine-sauced, and Caesared within hours for a few lucky patrons.

The Italian influence is palpable at Quito's, a real find if your seafood tastes run more to flavors of the Med than to fried clams in a cardboard box. Buttery cod is baked with lots of garlic and fresh oregano. Fresh Maine steamers are available with butter and broth, but I love the appetizer of delicate steamed littlenecks, done up "red or white" in clam sauce made to be ladled over linguine, but here served with hunks of crusty Italian bread for sopping. And if you do want pasta, it comes heaped with steaming shrimp, clams, calamari, lobster; all scampi'd or zuppa'd (in a brothy tomato base) and almost impossible to finish in one sitting.

There's plenty on the menu in the cardboard box camp too, including whole clams, strips, and sea scallops, but the local calamari crosses over, as it often does in the Ocean State: A crunchy pile of tubes and tentacles comes crowned with rings of hot pepper and spicy olive oil on the side. Quito's does righteous justice to a couple of other Rhody favorites, like the peppery stuffed quahogs (though some may frown on the restaurant's practice of loading the mixture into plastic faux shells), and the clam fritters, keeping the size small, the dough light, and the bits of mollusk sweet and plentiful. The creamy New England clam chowder is good, made in small batches strictly with quahogs, but try the seafood stew, a not-quite-bouillabaisse made with scallops, shrimp, lobster, and whatever the day's catch yields on the fish front—often, it's swordfish. This ambrosial stuff is so popular, Al Quito just inked a deal to start selling it at the Whole Foods market chain.

You can see the water from the honey-hued indoor dining room, but if it's warm enough, why pass up the patio? A sunset over Mount Hope Bay and a clam fritter or two just taste better out here. Did I mention they make their own root beer?

shack people:
Al Quito, owner and cook, Quito's

• "The lobster rolls are big—we probably sell about 100 of them a day. We get the rolls from Bristol Bakery over on Wood Street, they're really good. We toss the lobster with just a little mayonnaise and some fresh dill. And butter on the bun, of course."

• "My wife and I never eat what we serve at the restaurant—only because we're always cooking up new concoctions at home. If we make something we really like, we'll add it to the menu."

• "I love food. I'm Italian! And I'm Sicilian, so I can eat a lot of seafood. It's in my blood."

Additional Listings

Block Island

The Beachhead
598 Corn Neck Road • 401-466-2249

The perfect open-air stop to put away a bellyful of fried scallops.

Dead Eye Dick's
Water Street, near Payne's Dock
401-466-2654

The logo is a shark with an eye patch, and the specialty is swordfish pulled right out of Block Island Sound.

Finn's Seafood Restaurant
Water Street, facing the Ferry Landing
401-466-2473

Fresher-than-fresh fare comes from the nearby seafood market, and the clam chowder has been an island favorite for more than 30 years.

The Oar
West Side Road • 401-466-8820

Get your fingers good and fishy on peel-and-eat shrimp as you watch the Montauk and New London ferries come and go.

Old Harbor Takeout
Water Street • 401-466-2270

Changeovers always have naysayers, but since the Dugan family gave up this shack with its famous lobster rolls, the menu hasn't changed all that much.

Spring House Hotel
52 Spring Street • 401-466-5844
www.springhousehotel.com

The island's oldest hotel has housed Ulysses S. Grant and Billy Joel. I bet they both had several bowls of the restaurant's life-giving New England clam chowder, packed with local mollusks and skin-on potato chunks, seasoned with bacon and chives.

Bristol

The Lobster Pot
119-121 Hope Street • 401-253-9100

The Pot, which has been in this plum spot on Narragansett Bay since 1929, used to be a fair bit smaller, grubbier, and shackier than its modern-day incarnation. If the current owner went upscale when he rebuilt, the menu retains some hearty, simple fare along with its more daring dishes—and more twists on lobster than you can count.

Tweets Balzano's

180 Mount Hope Avenue • 401-253-9811

Go for the name, the calamari, and a reminder that Rhode Island is home to *la famiglia* in New England.

Charlestown

The Hitching Post

5400 Post Road (Route 1) • 401-364-7495

Locals despair when this summer-only spot with its little fish pond closes for the season–they have to make do with someone else's fried seafood until next May.

Nordic Lodge

178 East Pasquiset Trail • 401-783-4515
www.nordiclodge.com

The average eater puts away half a dozen bugs at the Lodge's $65 Giant Viking Buffet, home of all-you-can-eat lobster (five words you don't see together nearly often enough). Can you do better?

East Greenwich

Harbourside Lobstermania

38 Water Street • 401-884-6363

It looks and sounds like pure tourist trap, but this sprawling eatery on the water is a homey, terrific find.

Jamestown

Jamestown Oyster Bar

22 Narragansett Avenue • 401-423-3380

A resolutely frills-free spot, centerpieced by a long bar that's always crawling with locals. Check out the blackboard for lots of goodies on the half shell, or try the lobster cakes Newburg.

Tricia's Tropi-Grille

14 Narragansett Avenue • 401-423-1490

Right down the street from Chopmist Charlie's, this Floribbean-themed spot is owned by the same couple. Have something jerked or coconut-crusted on the perfect little patio.

Little Compton

The Commons Lunch

On the Commons • 401-635-4388

A drive down to Little Compton is all cow-dotted green and wild-rosed fences, and this lunch spot is the perfect capper. Get your quahog chowder with a side of steamy-centered jonnycakes.

Middletown

Atlantic Beach Club

55 Purgatory Road • 401-847-2750

Boisterous bar scene with solid seafood on the menu amid the surf shops of First Beach.

Misquamicut

Captain Zak's Restaurant & Grille

137 Atlantic Avenue • 401-348-0885
www.captainzaks.com

Have some of the New England clam chowder. Pet the black lab, Max, whose predecessor, Zak, was the place's namesake. Then head back to the beach.

Sam's Snack Bar

301 Atlantic Avenue • 401-322-1432

Just what it sounds like: a shack with a takeout window facing Misquamicut Beach, the longest and one of the loveliest in the Ocean State.

Seafood Haven Restaurant & Fish Market

668 Atlantic Avenue • 401-322-0330

It's taken just a decade for this little white bungalow to earn a rabid following. Try the clamcakes.

Narragansett

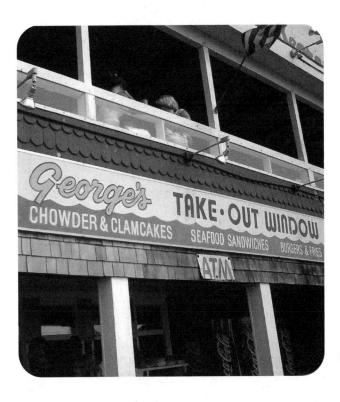

Concession stand

Roger Wheeler State Beach, 100 Sand Hill Cove Road

The takeout hut on Roger Wheeler State Beach (or Sand Hill Cove Beach, to locals) has no name and no phone, but it has some superior clamcakes and Del's frozen lemonade to wash them down.

George's of Galilee

250 Sand Hill Cove Road • 401-783-2306

This massive, nearly 60-year-old eatery near Champlin's Seafood Deck has dining rooms, takeout windows, and shack fare a-go-go.

Port Side Restaurant

321 Great Island Road • 401-783-3821

Come for the lobster sautéed in sherry butter, stay for the wonderful rough-hewn bar stools, each one depicting a salty fisherman.

Starboard Galley

190 Ocean Road • 401-782-1366

A towel over your bikini is about as dressy at it gets at the Starboard. Sip your chowder at one of the picnic tables tilting toward the water.

Newport

Christie's

351 Thames Street • 401-847-5400
www.christiesofnewport.com

Slurp down some of Christie's irresistible lobster bisque, smoky with sherry and roe, on a dock that's seen many an America's Cup champagne hosedown.

Dry Dock Seafood

448 Thames Street • 401-847-3974

Scrumptious fish and chips are worth braving the wharf-side crowds.

The Mooring

Sayer's Wharf • 401-846-2260

This restaurant right on the water is no shack (remember, this is Newport), but its scallop chowder is utterly worthy.

Rhode Island Quahog Company

250 Thames Street • 401-848-2330

Despite the old-school sign and vintage photos of clammers on the flats, things can get radical here–you might not expect quahog salsa. But the joint never sacrifices freshness or oceany flavor.

Scales & Shells
527 Thames Street • 401-846-3474

Billing itself "Newport's only 'only fish' restaurant," this place is nouveau-fancy with words like "mesquite" on the menu and tasty takes on the classics.

North Kingstown

Duffy's Tavern
235 Tower Hill Road • 401-295-0073

This sweet dive serves up fried seafood that's cheap, cheerful, and no greasier than it needs to be.

Pawtucket

Horton's Seafood Too
Slater Memorial Park, Newport Avenue
401-726-9222

Seasonal outpost of the East Providence seafood standby.

New England Fish Factory
271 Newport Avenue • 401-729-9600

I love that this place serves fried squid, the whole squid, crispy tentacles (the best part) included. There's also a solid raw bar, homemade pies, and tables outdoors.

Portsmouth

Sakonnet Fish Company
657 Park Avenue • 401-683-1180
www.sakonnetfish.com

Take shelter at this upscale spot near Bluebell Cove, amid the cottage-dotted landscape of laid-back Island Park. The owner buys fresh and buys native for everything on his inventive menu (try the lobster cakes).

Providence

Carrie's
1035 Douglas Avenue • 401-831-0066

Reliable neighborhood haunt with a menu that's Ocean State via Sicily. The seafood bisque—made with scallops, crab, and lobster—is worth a detour. Have the carrot cake for dessert.

Haven Brothers
Fulton and Dorrance Streets • 401-861-7777

Since 1888, this diner-on-wheels has been doing its thing. It rolls up just before 5 PM, plugs in to a nearby streetlamp, and starts serving comfort food to everyone from cops to TV anchors who come by for a lobster roll, cheese fries, or a Murder Burger, washed down with a frappe.

Hemenway's

One Providence Washington Plaza
401-351-8570

Head here for what's widely (and justly) considered to be the best lobster bisque in the city.

Horton's Seafood

809 Broadway, East Providence
401-434-3116
www.hortonsseafood.com

Horton's has been here year-round since 1945, serving up a shack menu packed with Rhode Island fare (clear chowder, stuffies, and snail salad), and award-winning lobster rolls and fish and chips. Come on a Tuesday for a real trip—it's classic-car night, and the sidewalk's lined with gleaming retro rides.

Providence Oyster Bar

283 Atwells Avenue • 401-272-8866

Warning: This place on Federal Hill has banquettes and martinis. But skip the latter, and get drunk instead on oyster brine from as far away as Oregon and as near as Watch Hill, courtesy of the raw bar's seductive, well-curated selection.

South Kingstown

Cap'n Jack's

706 Succotash Road • 401-789-4556

Word has it a Cape Cod restaurant once offered Cap'n Jack's a couple hundred grand for their clamcake recipe. They refused.

Wakefield

Surfin' Tacos

344 Main Street • 401-792-8226

For a taste of San Diego by way of South County, get a fish taco at this little spot. Three perfect bites and you're done.

Hanson's Landing

210 Salt Pond Road • 401-782-0210

An unassuming, screen-windowed spot on Salt Pond Marsh. Try the excellent codfish bites and the Portuguese-style clams and mussels.

Warwick

Cherrystones

898 Oakland Beach Avenue • 401-732-2532

Try the old-world calamari, batter-fried to a crunch and tossed with lemon, peppers, and olives.

Crow's Nest

288 Arnolds Neck Drive • 401-732-6575

This stubbornly local hangout has a roomy oak bar, beer for pennies, and a lobster sauté to write home about: fresh-torn meat drenched in butter.

Rocky Point Chowder House

1759 Post Road (Route 1) • 401-739-4222

It looks like a Dunkin' Donuts (and it's on a stretch of Route 1 that has about five of them), but it's a foolproof stop for chowder and good, greasy takeout.

7-Seas Chowder House

26 Palmer Avenue • 401-737-8368

Try the fish and chips and the red chowder at this breezy, weathered building with the wraparound deck, just inland from the cove at Warwick Neck.

Warren

Wharf Tavern

215 Water Street • 401-245-5043

This popular dock-and-dine spot has been around since 1965 and feels like it. Snatch a lobster from the tank or try the Nantucket scallops.

Watch Hill

St. Clair Annex

6 Bay Street • 401-348-8407

A cute-as-pie ice cream shop that also makes a seriously good lobster roll.

Westerly

Two Little Fish

138 Granite Street • 401-348-9941

A sweet spot on the Connecticut/Rhode Island border with yummy fried clams, and superior coleslaw and Rhode Island clam chowder.

Woonsocket

Ye Olde English Fish & Chips Restaurant

Market Square at South Main Street
401-762-3637

As the name implies: fish and chips served in a pubby room that's more East London than Woonsocket. But Woonsocket is more fun to say.

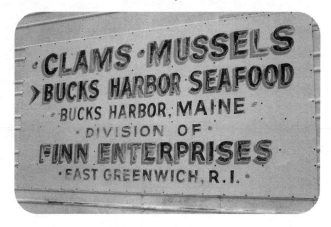

massachusetts

3

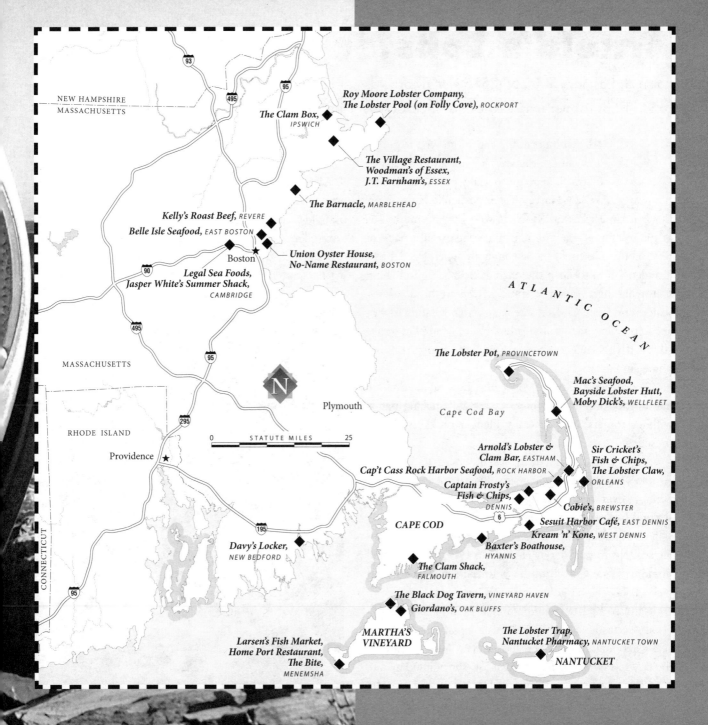

Roy Moore Lobster Company,
The Lobster Pool (on Folly Cove), ROCKPORT

The Clam Box, IPSWICH

**The Village Restaurant,
Woodman's of Essex,
J.T. Farnham's**, ESSEX

The Barnacle, MARBLEHEAD

Kelly's Roast Beef, REVERE

Belle Isle Seafood, EAST BOSTON

Boston

**Union Oyster House,
No-Name Restaurant**, BOSTON

**Legal Sea Foods,
Jasper White's Summer Shack,**
CAMBRIDGE

NEW HAMPSHIRE
MASSACHUSETTS

MASSACHUSETTS

RHODE ISLAND

Providence

CONNECTICUT

Plymouth

Cape Cod Bay

ATLANTIC OCEAN

N

STATUTE MILES
0   25

The Lobster Pot, PROVINCETOWN

**Mac's Seafood,
Bayside Lobster Hutt,
Moby Dick's**, WELLFLEET

**Arnold's Lobster &
Clam Bar**, EASTHAM

**Sir Cricket's
Fish & Chips,
The Lobster Claw**, ORLEANS

Cap't Cass Rock Harbor Seafood, ROCK HARBOR

**Captain Frosty's
Fish & Chips,**
DENNIS

Cobie's, BREWSTER

CAPE COD

Sesuit Harbor Café, EAST DENNIS

Kream 'n' Kone, WEST DENNIS

Baxter's Boathouse,
HYANNIS

Davy's Locker,
NEW BEDFORD

The Clam Shack,
FALMOUTH

The Black Dog Tavern, VINEYARD HAVEN

Giordano's, OAK BLUFFS

MARTHA'S
VINEYARD

**Larsen's Fish Market,
Home Port Restaurant,
The Bite,**
MENEMSHA

**The Lobster Trap,
Nantucket Pharmacy**, NANTUCKET TOWN

NANTUCKET

Arnold's Lobster and Clam Bar

Route 6, Eastham 508-255-2575 • www.arnoldsrestaurant.com • Open May to September

BEST BITES: Lobster roll, fried clams, fried oysters, clam chowder

"Come with me to the bathroom—you're gonna love this." Ordinarily it's not a good idea to follow strangers, especially ones who look a bit like Harvey Keitel, to public bathrooms. But Nathan Nickerson III–Nick, who's giving me a tour of his restaurant–has the infectious energy of a pack of Boy Scouts: He could be selling anything, and you'd buy it and tell him to keep the change. So it's a good thing that what he's selling is some of the freshest, tastiest seafood on Cape Cod's Route 6. And that he stops shy of accompanying me into the ladies' room, where I'm greeted by a sequence of hand-painted sandpipers on the porcelain tile.

"Cool, right?" And he's off again, showing me the raw bar, introducing his daughter, talking and shaking hands with customers, and generally filling Arnold's with his presence.

With Nick at the helm, it's not hard to see why Arnold's has lived through nearly 30 years of trends, competition, even a decimating 2002 fire, to be the bustling seafood beacon it is today. He's comfy in his restaurateur skin now, but he didn't exactly grow up dreaming of serving scallops to summering families. In 1977, Nick returned home to Cape Cod from the Navy and had a career to pick. "I sure wasn't going to be a doctor or a lawyer," he says, and so he snapped up an icon from his own childhood: Gertrude's Beach Box. "This is how I remember it," says Nick, handing me a scallop-edged '50s postcard of the tiny restaurant, its takeout window surrounded by tan, flip-haired beachgoers who could be extras from the Frankie and Annette bikini movies.

And once he'd bought Gertrude's, it's exactly that bobby-soxer spirit Nick decided to play up. Blame it on the Fonz. "*Happy Days* was big then, so we called it Arnold's, had car-side trays, and the staff delivered food on roller skates," he says. Over the years, retromania faded, surrendering the spotlight to the menu. Out with roller skates, in with clambakes. Nowadays, with the

exception of some gourmet forays like wasabi-encrusted salmon, Arnold's menu is happily old school and seafood heavy.

Nick's motto? "Keep it fresh, keep it clean, keep it friendly." He concedes that the fresh part comes at a price. He fries local oysters into delectable submission, never ridding them of their briny flavor. If his fried scallops taste sweeter than most, it's because they're sea scallops but harvested from the local bay. It's a rare combination that costs more, but with scallops as with everything else, Nick's perfectionism comes in to raise the bar. "They're the best," he says. "I eat 'em raw." He's equally demanding with his clams. Like at many restaurants in the area, the ones served here are dug less than a mile away, but Nick adds a step that his competitors often skip: The clams are dumped in a basin of water where they work out any sand, ensuring your fried bellies or steamers are served without a side of grit. And batter-fried or steamed with butter, their flavor is unstoppable. They also shine in the New England–style chowder, which gets its consistency– just short of creamy–from potatoes, "not flour or, God forbid, cornstarch!" he says, throwing up his hands.

If the sheer math of Arnold's onion rings is hard to wrap one's brain around–the restaurant uses two tons of onions a week–after one taste, these numbers make perfect sense. Thinly sliced, fried just long enough for the batter to crunch, and nearly as sweet as those scallops, they demand a rapt audience. The lobster roll keeps it simple: lettuce, mayonnaise, lemon juice, and sweet lobster meat, in a top-loaded toasted bun. Arnold's patrons gobble up about 12,000 of them each season. If you still have room, Arnold's is also known for its ice cream. The frozen stuff comes from a small dairy that keeps its own cows in Milton, Massachusetts.

In the evening, Nick serves up beer, booze, and a full raw bar from the "shucking shack" he built himself, a lean-to encased in weathered wood shingles recycled from a condemned house nearby. Ask and he'll tell you why the Andy's Raw Bar sign is a nod to his son, that the mural was painted by a friend, the story behind the mounted 80-pound bass caught by his builder–and, of course, about the sandpipers in the bathroom. "I love all the little details," he says. "But those are the coolest."

"happy as a clam"

What do clams have to be so happy about, anyway? *World Wide Words* editor (and *Oxford English Dictionary* consultant) Michael Quinion responds: "Even the most comfortable of clams . . . can hardly be called the life and soul of the party. All they can expect is a watery existence, likely at any moment to be rudely interrupted by a man with a spade, followed by conveyance to a very hot place. The fact is, we've lost its second half, which makes everything clear. The full expression is *happy as a clam at high tide* or *happy as a clam at high water*. Clam digging has to be done at low tide, when you stand a chance of finding them and extracting them. At high water, clams are comfortably covered in water and so able to feed, comparatively at ease and free of the risk that some hunter will rip them untimely from their sandy berths. I guess that's a good enough definition of happy."

The Barnacle

141 Front Street, Marblehead 617-631-4236 • Open year-round
BEST BITES: Mussels with honey, fish and chips, fried scallops, steamers

The meticulously preserved pre-revolutionary buildings in Marblehead's Old Town—one of the greatest clusters of them anywhere—make for a dazzling, history-filled late-morning stroll, and such things build up an appetite. In this tiny wooden house that juts over the water near Fort Sewall, the bar always hums with locals, the kitchen churns out fresh, frills-free favorites, and the view is simple and serene: rocky Marblehead Harbor, where gulls bend and swoop, and where fishing boats and pleasure craft alike go about their daily rounds.

The mussels are a must, steamed in a broth dreamed up by head chef John Walker, who punches up a standard

white-wine-and-garlic broth with torn basil leaves and honey. Also from the steamer, Ipswich clams are sweet and tender, even if they do require the broth bowl and some dedication on your part to rid the mollusks of grit. The Barnacle's fried haddock, a dish of small, dry-breaded, utterly greaseless nuggets sided with fries that can't possibly compete, will become your new standard against which all future fish and chips will be measured (with the exception of the English chip shop kind, whose puffy beer batter is a whole other story). The clam chowder here is tasty, though it gives a new meaning to the word thick, with an almost puddinglike consistency. I'm not sure turning a bowl of this stuff upside down would necessarily empty it.

If you're very lucky, you may snag one of the seats on the slender deck wrapped around the building, right over the water. But the counter that runs under the harborside windows is a fine second choice. Here you can dine to the hubbub and gaze up at the Barnacle's old hand-drawn menu, where the grilled cheese is a wallet-busting 30 cents.

Baxter's Boathouse

177 Pleasant Street, Hyannis 508-775-4490 • www.baxterscapecod.com • Open Memorial Day to Labor Day • BEST BITES: Fish and chips, fried scallops, crabcake

Baxter's was built on an old fish-packing dock in 1955, and it's been a Hyannis landmark ever since. It's what you do while you're waiting for the ferry to Nantucket, or what you do when you've just come off the ferry and want to squeeze in a last bite of the sea before driving home. Either way, pad your trip to include a good hour spent on the harborside patio here, inhaling the heady vacation smell of diesel fumes from revving boat engines and devouring some expertly fried scallops, a crabcake laced with lobster chunks, or a half-dozen somethings from the raw bar. Service is counter-only, and eating is in the rough. If you have longer to linger, slip into the Boathouse Club next door for live music and a well-mixed martini. Legend has it that over Memorial Day weekend in 1972, three guys had one too many here and decided to race to Nantucket in their sailboats, and thus the Figawi—one of the largest regattas on the East Coast—was born.

"You haven't lived until you've had fried scallops at Baxter's. If they're good enough for the Kennedys, they're good enough for me."
—RODNEY FULLMAST, LIFELONG NANTUCKET VISITOR AND BAXTER'S PATRON

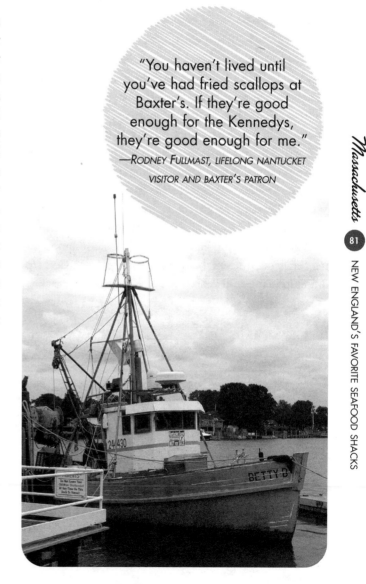

Bayside Lobster Hutt

91 Commercial Street, Wellfleet 508-349-6333 • www.lobsterhutt.com • Open Memorial Day to Labor Day • BEST BITES: Shore dinner, sea clam pie

When a bright red, 8-foot lobster statue disappears from the side of a barn, people tend to notice. Which is why, at this writing, the tiny town of Wellfleet was abuzz with rumor: What was going on with the Bayside Lobster Hutt? Its doors had remained shuttered clear into June, and even its trademark roof display hadn't reappeared: The red skiff remained, but the sou'westered fisherman who'd occupied it for years, dangling the giant lobster in a net, was missing. Was it closed for good?

Landowner Jerry Parent assured me that the Hutt, as it's fondly known around here, was just under renovation—and as of Memorial Day 2006, it would resume serving the shore dinners that have made it a Cape Cod tradition for almost 30 years.

I can only assume that when it does, protocol will be similar to the old days at this scruffy spot: Order your lobster at the counter, specifying size and sides (corn, coleslaw, and such), cart your chow over to a communal table, and put your pick, bib, and melted butter to work. You can also gorge on fresh, famed Wellfleet oysters (the owner comes from a family of oystermen and is one himself), as well as an unusual sea clam pie, sort of like a chicken potpie filled with chowder. Grossed-out kiddies will appreciate the hot dogs and burgers. Bring your own booze to the Hutt.

shack classic: Steamers

No disrespect to the majestic fried clam, but to really savor a bivalve's connection to the sea, many say steaming is the only way to go. Steamers—soft-shells steamed plain and served in the shell, usually sided with some of their own broth and drawn butter for dipping—can seem daunting to the uninitiated, as they require a little prep work before eating and are often gritty with sand unprocessed by the clam. First, use your fingernails to peel off and discard the light sheath on the dark foot protruding from the shell. Now grab that foot, tug the clam from its shell, and swirl it vigorously around in the bowl of broth provided—this helps remove any sand that's left. The next dunking is into the butter, and you're ready to eat.

Belle Isle Seafood

1267 Saratoga Street, East Boston • 617-567-1619 • Open year-round
BEST BITES: Grilled swordfish sandwich, fried smelts, lobster pie

*Y*ou won't come across Belle Isle unless you make a wrong turn on your way to Boston's Logan Airport, but if you miss your flight, take solace in the exquisite seafood turned out by this shoebox of a fish market on the bridge to Winthrop. Just inside a gate centerpieced by a wrought-iron lobster, the room is a few stools and feet of counter space on one side, and gleaming glass cases filled with fresh fish and prepared eats on the other (like their lobster pie, a jackpot of juicy lobster meat with butter and breadcrumbs that you can reheat at home). The menu is long: Belle Isle fries, bakes, stuffs, blackens, teriyakis, and grills pretty much anything caught, dug, or otherwise harvested off these shores (and some chicken).

Everything from jumbo shrimp to tuna steaks is available as a side order or a full dinner (served with both fries and onion rings; skip the former and concentrate on the latter), and some items show up in a sandwich (try the swordfish kind). Be sure to check the specials board and order whatever the kitchen recommends that day—sometimes it's fried oyster sandwiches, sometimes it's a mound of delectable, crispy fried smelts that you won't want to share with anyone.

photo op: JawsFest

In 1974, a bunch of guys arrived on Martha's Vineyard with cameras to make a movie about a killer shark. One protruding fin, 30-plus years, and millions of box office dollars (and swimming nightmares) later, *Jaws* is a celluloid landmark, fêted once a year in June as the Vineyard turns itself back into fictional Amity all over again—right down to the storefronts and signage (looking for Quint's home port? It's in Menemsha). The fin never stops at this three-day affair, with screenings, contests, and a monster bash where you can swap trivia with rabid fans from Japan and Romania, and hobnob with original cast members. Just don't go in the water.

The Bite

Basin Road, Menemsha 508-645-9239 • Open May through October
BEST BITES: Fried flounder, clam chowder, potato salad, pickled beets

It's said that once you head to the western reaches of Martha's Vineyard—or up-island, as they call it around here—you never go back. Here, life is a little slower and brass door-knockers are a little less polished. In Menemsha, a salty fishing village in Chilmark, you'll see fewer yachts, more rusty lobster boats. And dining up-island generally means trading the linen tablecloths and wine lists of Edgartown for a paper plate of oysters balanced on a crate (or your knees) while you watch the sun set over Vineyard Sound, glowing pinky-orange off the bricks of Gay Head Lighthouse.

Sunsets are such a big deal in Menemsha that you can call up The Bite and ask them when tonight's is scheduled to happen. That's because the end of a day on the Vineyard is best enjoyed while munching on something fresh from the fryer at this shingled hut on Basin Road. It had a couple of previous lives, first as a snack bar and then as a dress shop, but by the late 1980s when Karen Flynn bought it, the place had found its niche: fried seafood. It even says so on the blue-and-white sign with the shark on the side.

The Bite is also known for its excellently creamy New England clam chowder and zesty side dishes, but the first order of business once you get in line—and there will be a line—is to choose what you'd like to have fried today. Go for the quarter-sized scallops, the gushy clam bellies, oysters or fresh squid, the chicken wings if you really must, or my favorite, the flounder. This flounder is so dazzling (and so straight from the oil) that you'll burn your tongue, refusing to wait for it to cool. Lots of places choose cod

or haddock for their fried fish as these are hardier and easier to work with, which is what makes fried flounder so special. The delicate fish is delivered to The Bite daily, dry-dipped and crumb-coated to order, and sizzled in vegetable oil, giving the double-whammy crust a perfect crispiness. French fries here are hand-cut, skin-on chunks of potato with an almost butterscotchy flavor, but if you're going to have potatoes at The Bite, you'll want them in the exalted form of the salad, one of Karen's mother's specialties. Barbara Flynn spends her summers making huge batches of the stuff, going through bag after bag of red bliss potatoes and sweet Spanish onions, and spiking the lightly mayonnaised mixture with fresh dill by the handful and plenty of cracked black pepper. As with the fries, the skins here stay on and the salad is served perfectly chilled, a fitting antidote to the piping-hot batter encasing that flounder. It's hard to choose between a cup of this stuff, the crunchy coleslaw (made from a "famous secret recipe"), and the pickled beets (a nod to Karen's Lithuanian grandmother), redolent of sharp cider vinegar and enemy of clean white T-shirts the island over.

Fudge brownies and cookies are perfect, fresh-baked, one-bite desserts.

On a practical note, come between meal times to lessen those lines; as for seating, if the first and last picnic tables are both taken, perch on the dock nearby or stroll for a few minutes to the pristine white sands of Moshup Beach.

crib sheet: Scallops

Bivalve mollusks mostly caught off the Eastern Seaboard, they generally show up on New England menus deep-fried, grilled or broiled, in seafood stuffings, and in chowders. A few rarified raw bars will serve their subtle, sweet flesh raw. It's common for companies that ship scallops inland to soak them in a preservative, which futzes with the flavor—one reason why they're best eaten at the source. (Tip: New Englanders pronounce the word *skaw-lop*.)

Sea scallops

A.k.a. wild scallops, the most common variety. These are usually dragged in deep waters (though found in shallows off Cape Cod) and account for more than two-thirds of the U.S. scallop supply.

Bay scallops

Smaller, sweeter, rarer, and more prized than their sea counterpart, these are gathered in bays from Long Island to Nova Scotia in the colder months, and because they're so delicate, rarely leave the northern East Coast.

Diver scallops

Large sea scallops harvested by hand (as opposed to being dragged with a net along the ocean floor), a method that's more ecologically friendly and results in less gritty meat.

Day-boat scallops

Scallops caught by fishermen who go out for a single day (instead of staying at sea until their holds are full), returning with fresh, untreated mollusks. Raw "day-boats" are an ivory color, while scallops that have been soaked in preservative are blindingly white. No surprise that these are some of the most expensive scallops around

The Black Dog Tavern

Beach Street, near the ferry dock, Vineyard Haven • 508-693-9223 • Open year-round
BEST BITES: Clam chowder, stuffed clams, blueberry bread pudding

Locals think back wistfully on a time not that long ago when the Black Dog was a tavern, *their* tavern, a rough-hewn little box with creaky floorboards where you could get a good cup of chowder or a gooey wedge of pie–even in winter, when the fireplace crackled–and gaze out at the moorings and the blue beyond.

Then one day, somebody got back on the ferry wearing a T-shirt stamped with the silhouette of a white-footed black Lab, a nod to the wooden dog on the Tavern's sign (itself a nod to the founder's beloved pet, whose name was actually Black Dog–see sidebar). And so the epidemic began: The shirts shot the Black Dog logo

around the world, suggesting the wearer's inside track on the good life, Vineyard-style: days at the beach, flapping sails, the proximity of Kennedys, "summer" as a verb. Soon, it wasn't just T-shirts–it was mugs, mousepads, golf balls, baby bibs. Then Bill famously stocked up on Black Dog merch for Monica, and the eight or so people who'd been living under a rock were let in on the secret. Today, Black Dog is more than a dozen businesses strong and extends well beyond the island, with stores in Falmouth, Provincetown, and Chatham–even Newport, Rhode Island. For many, a trip to the Vineyard without a stop at the Black Dog is like a Pisa vacation with no leaning Tower.

Many grumble that all this branding has made Black Dog's once-great food an afterthought, and an expensive one at that (prices can reach the $30 range for the more ambitious entrées). If some of the dishes seem to be coasting on hype, you can still get a good cup of chowder here, and the view remains wonderful, just a stone's throw from the beach in Vineyard Haven. (Beat the crowds if you can and nab a spot on the porch.) And as old-world Yankee island ambience goes, it's true that nothing much has changed since Robert Douglas served his first customer in 1971 but the length of the lines to get in.

Breakfast is the biggest deal at the comfort food-driven Black Dog: The tavern opens at 7 AM and by 9 has run through enough eggs to feed an army. And that's before the brunch crowd hits (when even the waiting list has a line), mewling for the Dog's eggs benedict or something off its vast omelet menu. Lunch and dinner are heavy on the seafood, with the creamy quahog chowder such a

standout that the company sells it in bulk online. Stuffed clams are good too, getting their tang and saltiness from a hefty helping of garlic and bacon. The smoked bluefish appetizer may be too fishy for some, but its intense flavor is simple and perfect on a piece of buttered bread. Things get fancy on the high end, such as stuffed cod with lobster sauce, a thick slab of white fish crowned with a plump lobster claw and swimming in buttery goodness. Moving from surf to turf, the pecan-crusted chicken is a favorite, coming topped with a ginger sauce, and the lamb chops are simply char-grilled on the outside, juicy within. There's also a dependably good burger.

You could make an entire meal out of desserts here– try the better-than-homemade blueberry bread pudding. If you want a sip of something alcoholic with your meal, remember to BYOB, as Vineyard Haven is a dry town. Also, a warning to the warm-blooded: The Tavern hasn't conceded to patrons begging them to install air conditioning, and it can get a little swampy in the dark dining room on an August afternoon. And if you must buy one of those T-shirts, the Black Dog General Store is right next door.

the black dog behind The Black Dog

Before the T-shirts, before the stores, before the chowder over the Internet, there really was a Black Dog. In 1958, Chicagoan Robert Douglas left the Air Force with a three-step plan: to build a ship (and not just any ship, but a pitch-perfect reproduction of an 1849 schooner), to sail it to Martha's Vineyard, and to get a dog to sail by his side (the restaurant came later). By 1967, he had the boat, he'd settled on the island, and he got wind of a just-born litter of black Labrador retrievers— "Whitefoots." He named the black dog Black Dog, and when the restaurant idea came to him, he named it Black Dog, after Black Dog. And the rest is history.

Cap't Cass Rock Harbor Seafood

117 Rock Harbor Road, Rock Harbor (Orleans) • No phone • Open late June to mid-October
BEST BITES: Lobster roll, broth-based clam chowder, crabmeat salad

Cap't Cass is one of those places that you don't know about unless you do: The gray-and-white shanty isn't really on the road to anything, it doesn't advertise, it has no phone, it's open four months a year for three days a week (Friday, Saturday, and Sunday), and it sits at the end of a residential street next to a little boat ramp mostly used by locals. Small wooden signs out front, painted with a shaky hand, advertise native clams and a lobster roll that's "all meat–no filler." There are

more buoys dangling off the shingles outside than place settings within, a small room with a few tables on one side and a soda-shop-style counter with blue vinyl-topped stools on the other. Walls are scattered with framed black-and-white photos of fishermen displaying their catch.

Food is plain here–you'll find no smoothies or jicama salad on the menu. What you will find is the granddaughter of the couple who started the place, picking a fresh-boiled lobster out if its shell for your roll. Clam chowder

shack staple: Cocktail Sauce

Who knows, really, where cocktail sauce—that zingy mating of ketchup and horseradish—came from? Some claim Native Americans prepared something like it to season meat and fish, but it's questionable whether they had access to tomatoes or anything like horseradish, a root brought to these shores from southeast Europe. Others call it the brainchild of Henry J. Heinz—and while he may not have invented it, the sauce's popularity can probably be chalked up to his company's legendary marketing genius. All I know is it tastes good with a bucket of peel-and-eat Maine shrimp (which, let's face it, don't need any sauce at all).

is brothy, reminiscent of Rhode Island–style and an unusual find on Cape Cod. Order a crabmeat salad and you may find juicy wedges of homegrown tomato posing as garnish. Wash it all down with pink lemonade squeezed in the back, or BYOB.

Sadly, Cap't Cass does lunch only, but now that you know how to get here, come back in the early evening: Nearby Rock Harbor is known for having some of the most spectacular sunsets on the Cape, and it's not uncommon for a steel-drum band to set up on this little crescent of beach and serenade the sun as it melts into the water.

Ten places *to stop in fall*

Come Labor Day, the summer crowd scatters, and most of the region's shacks shut tighter than—you guessed it—a clam. But a fall trek to New England is rich with rewards: few tourists, brilliant colors, and tastier seafood (pulled from colder waters). These 10 spots are open in October, offering the perfect fuel for a crisp afternoon of hayrides, cider, and pumpkin-patch cruising.

1. *Chopmist Charlie's*, Jamestown, RI

2. *Scales*, Portland, ME

3. *The Clam Box*, Ipswich, MA

4. *Brown's Seabrook Lobster Pound*, Seabrook Beach, NH

5. *Johnny Ad's*, Old Saybrook, CT

6. *Maine Diner*, Wells, ME

7. *Lenny's Indian Head Inn*, Branford, CT

8. *Sir Cricket's Fish 'n Chips*, Orleans, MA

9. *Barnacle Billy's*, Ogunquit, ME

10. *The Barnacle*, Marblehead, MA

Captain Frosty's Fish & Chips

219 Main Street (Route 6A), Dennis • 508-385-8548 • www.captainfrosty.com • Open April to September
BEST BITES: Lobster roll plate, fried cod, grilled salmon sandwich, sundaes

There are plenty of 1950s diner–style eateries on Cape Cod that are really children of the 1970s–born of the same nostalgic verve that spawned *Happy Days* and *Grease*–but Captain Frosty's is the real deal. It opened shop as a dairy bar a half century ago and looks it, right down to the hand-painted ice cream menu. If Doris Day were summering at the seashore in a screwball comedy, she'd bring her freckled brood here for a shake, a float, or the eponymous Frosty.

These days Frosty's is better known for turning out crisp, golden fried seafood. Place your order at the counter, where you'll be handed a clam box with a number scrawled on the side. While you're waiting, try not to rubberneck at what everybody else is scarfing down: massive, paper-plated portions of day-boat scallops–sometimes quartered and then battered, they're so big–or tender Gulf shrimp, brittle fried clam bellies or strips, nuggets of crumbed haddock, or all of the above, served up as the Captain's Plate. There's also a lobster roll dinner, its sandwich made with hand-torn tail and claw meat, served up with fries and a few golf ball–sized clam fritters. These salty, satisfying cakes are also available as a cheap and cheerful mini-meal ($5.99 in '05) with creamy New England clam chowder and a mound of crunchy-sweet slaw. The clam bellies here are big buggers available by the pint or half-pint, hefty knots of crunch that manage not to weigh you down or induce a fried-food coma, because they're done in a simple flour dip and plunged into lighter canola oil. Frosty's also serves the fried fish sandwich of your dreams. Tucked into a chewy bun is a battered chunk of cod that's especially wholesome-tasting because it's hooked, not gill netted. Smaller portions of the fried goods can be ordered as rolls to fill smaller stomachs.

On the non-fried side, pretend you're in Maine with the crab roll–sweet, savory shreds of meat caught off those shores to the north and lightly dressed before being heaped into a buttery bun. There's a tasty grilled salmon fillet loaded into a sourdough bun that's seasoned with a spread that's half mayo, half Dijon mustard. And the Captain also knows his beef: The Black Angus is one of the best burgers on the Cape.

Hit the dairy window for a frappe (that's a milkshake), a sundae, or a simple soft-serve cone. And that's just the beginning: The dessert menu's longer than the menu of mains, so ordering may take a while. Or you could save dessert for a mid-afternoon snack, when you return after nosing around the many antique shops that have earned this stretch of 6A the nickname Antique Alley.

Clam Box

246 High Street (Route 1A), Ipswich 978-336-9707 • Open March to mid-December
BEST BITES: Fried "native" clams, fried scallops, onion rings, haddock and chips

"The Clam Box? Just keep going and you can't miss it." That's because the Clam Box was built as a 30-foot-high version of an actual trapezoidal cardboard pint box, the kind fried clams have always been packed in for takeout, top flaps and all. But don't let the architectural gimmickry (or the line, which starts forming even before the restaurant opens on summer weekends) scare you off. Behind the gray clapboard exterior and red-and-white striped awnings, they've got what you want. The crack of the clam world. The seafood equivalent of Lourdes. Miraculous, worth the pilgrimage, and definitely a religious experience. The menu remains largely unchanged since the first meal was served here in 1935, and Marina "Chickie" Aggelakis, who bought the place 20 years ago–and whose father Louis Galanis founded the Agawam Diner in nearby Rowley–is fond of quoting a line printed on the back: "Though we don't claim to have invented the fried clam, we believe we perfected it."

The secret? First, the clams served here all come from less than 10 minutes away, harvested from the legendary mud flats of Ipswich. "There's really only one kind of frying clam, and it's known as an Ipswich," says Chickie. Then, there's the cooking technique, a meticulously calculated sequence of events that proves–better than anything but the first bite–just how high the standards are in this kitchen. The clams are first dipped in evaporated milk, then tossed in a mixture of yellow corn flour and pastry flour. And each clam is fried twice: Dropping it in one Fry-o-lator for 15 seconds seals the mixture and removes any excess flour– "that's what makes 'em so good and crispy," says Marina's son Dimitri, who works in the kitchen–and it's then transferred to a second fryer, where the cooking process is completed. The ratio of crunch to briny goo is about as perfect as fried clams get. Belly clams, identified on the Clam Box menu as "native clams," are available as a platter with sides, in small or large boxes, as a "mini-meal," or on a roll. (They're also available in strips, but then you're getting more batter than clam and, frankly, you're disappointing the Clam Box staff.) There's more than clams, of course: The same treatment's applied to all the usual suspects (get a

Fisherman to sample it all), and there's also a well-seasoned, thick, ultra-clammy clam chowder. As far as sides go, don't deny yourself the creamy homemade coleslaw or the excellent onion rings. Yes, it's fried stuff with a side of fried stuff, but the large, thickly cut rings pop with sweet, oniony flavor and a slightly peppery aftertaste–in my opinion, a Top 10 contender on the New England onion-ring circuit.

The Clam Box doesn't serve dessert, but if you're still hungry after polishing off a full, colossal portion of pretty much anything they serve, I doff my hat to you. (Sumo wrestlers and women carrying quintuplets can head down Route 133 to the Village Restaurant for a gooey bowl of Indian pudding to cap their meal.)

Eat in the dining room or, in fair weather, grab a seat at one of the picnic tables off the parking lot–the better to admire the Box's boxiness in all its glory. Just be warned: Those standing in line will be very, very jealous.

The Clam Shack

277 Clinton Avenue, Falmouth 508-540-7758 • Open mid-March through Labor Day
BEST BITES: "Ipswich-style" fried clams, onion rings, fried haddock sandwich

Jim Limberakis learned to fry before he learned to do a lot of other things. He started in the Clam Shack's kitchen at 12 years old, working alongside his father Leo, who founded the Falmouth eatery in 1962. Today, Jim spends seven days a week here, 10 to 10, from mid-March until the last bite's been swallowed on Labor Day. The man may not get a lot of hammock time in the summer, but he knows his way around frying a clam.

The Clam Shack, at the head of Falmouth Harbor, is exactly what a place by that name should be: a wind-and-salt-weathered hut, with minimal but nautical decor, that serves satisfying fried eats made to be consumed harbor-side, as boats glide by. Crunchy, briny, and irrepressibly fresh, the clams are the thing to get here: Jim usually buys his clams from The Clam Man in Falmouth, and they tend to be on the medium side. If you like them whole, order them "Ipswich style," but strips are also available for the belly-squeamish. The fried fish sandwich is a runner-up to these clams, a steaming slab of crispy haddock on a soft, warm bun. Or go for the straightforward lobster roll or fried scallops, with a tangle of onion rings on the side. There's also a battery of diner favorites like hot dogs and grilled cheese sandwiches for the kids.

Order at the little counter and carry your tray out to a red picnic table on the dock or up to the roof deck, where the view gets even better. On a clear day, you can see Martha's Vineyard in the distance. But get here early: Jim closes up shop around 8 PM.

clamheads of the world, unite!

Everybody likes lobster, and oysters have a following of their own, but no seafood inspires quite the rabid cult following as the clam—and no one loves clams quite like Michael N. Marcus, who founded United Clam Lovers of America so clamheads of all creeds could gather in virtual mollusk worship. Even if these bivalves aren't your bag, you have to admire the staggering treasury of trivia housed at UCLA's site, www.weloveclams.com. Read how mobster Jimmy "The Clam" Eppolito was whacked, why Prozac makes clams horny, and what everyone from Bette Midler to Glenn Close has to do with clams—or stop by the Clammunity Forum to rant and rave on the half shell.

Cobie's

Route 6A, Brewster 508-896-7021 • Open Memorial Day to Labor Day

BEST BITES: Fried clams, lobster roll, fish and chips, steamers

Folks from Brewster who were around in the '60s know two things about the late Coburn Emery: that he served some damn fine seafood, and that he saved himself a trip to the doctor.

"Story goes that Cobie got up one morning and wasn't feeling well," says John MacKenzie, a local cabinetmaker. "Apparently he said, 'If I'm still not feeling well tomorrow, I'll go see the doctor.' Next day, he didn't wake up."

Rob Slavin knows a little more about Cobie. Rob was teaching high school English and journalism in 1986 when he and his dad put a bid on the white clapboard structure tucked away on a leafy curve of Route 6A. As Rob tells it–a pencil tucked behind his ear–the restaurant came into being when Emery, a textile manufacturer, was looking for a small business to keep his wife occupied during the summer. He opened Cobie's in 1948. And while Rob and his father are the fifth owners of this pristine roadside shack, it hasn't changed much besides hands.

"People think of us as an old-fashioned clam shack. They want to see things unchanged. We just replaced this," he says on the first day of the season, pointing to a sign above the takeout window, "but we made it identical to the old sign." The new waxy, checkered green tablecloths also look just like the tablecloths always have. In fact the whole restaurant–shaped a bit like a key, with the kitchen and takeout windows at one end, and a long, roofed-in deck peppered with a dozen or so picnic tables jutting out to the side–would be hard to place time-wise in a photograph, as long as you didn't look too closely for details like the Red Sox helmet ice-cream cups, or the beepers that let you know when your order's up.

And the menu–with a few exceptions–is the same. "We've added paninis and salads the past couple years," says Rob, who's a vegetarian. "But our bread and butter is clams. People can't get enough. Fried bellies, fried strips, steamers, they just love 'em. That and lobster rolls." The Cobie's roll is a toasted top-loader with lobster meat, finely chopped celery, a sprinkling of parsley, and just enough mayonnaise to bind it all together without overstaying its welcome. Also good are the fish and chips: a delicious slab of cod or haddock–whatever's freshest that day–battered and bubbled to perfection. But I can't get away from those fried clam bellies, which come in a fat mop of crispiness with a side of ubiquitous Cape Cod Potato Chips. You may not be right on the water, but each belly's briny center more than makes up for the lack of ocean view (Cobie's does overlook the bike-lovers' Cape Cod Rail Trail, which runs within sniffing distance of the kitchen–"We get a lot of cyclist customers that way," says Rob). And Cobie's slaw is no throwaway. Chopped instead of slivered, sweet, tangy, and light on the sauce, it ends with a little heat, courtesy of horseradish.

One thing is different, Rob says. "The season runs longer now. More people stay through September, more are here year-round. We close after Labor Day, but by the time May rolls around, boy, we're raring to go. See that?" he asks, pointing to a large, red-and-white wooden sign advertising "Lobsters!" that's leaning against the wall in his office. Two brass eyehooks jut from its weathered top edge. "That's just itching to be hung."

try this at home:
The New England Clam Shack Cookbook

The very thought of trying to fry clams in my own kitchen has me reaching for the takeout menus, but *Bon Appétit* columnist Brooke Dojny is a better woman than I—she penned *The New England Clam Shack Cookbook,* a compendium of seaworthy Yankee recipes from 25 places up and down the coast, from B.G.'s Boat House's baked stuffed haddock to a foolproof version of Harraseeket Lunch & Lobster's lobster roll.

Davy's Locker

1480 E. Rodney French Boulevard, New Bedford • 508-992-7359 • Open year-round
BEST BITES: Fish chowder, steamed mussels, English-style fish and chips, grilled swordfish, Key lime pie

Davy's Locker has the kind of New England fish house vibe that was probably upscale and sophisticated when it opened in 1966, and now feels pleasantly old-fashioned, like you and a small Shriners' convention could co-exist peacefully here among the porthole windows, fish tanks, and rice pilaf.

Most of the time, a gigantic restaurant menu doesn't bode well—especially one that hops around between genres, putting jambalaya next to Italian shellfish pastas next to . . . Chinese food? It's a pretty simple equation: In order to offer such a wide array of choices, the kitchen needs to keep a lot of ingredients on hand at all times. Are more than a dozen shrimp dishes really necessary? How can it possibly all be fresh (much less good)? The answer, at Davy's, is high turnover. A half-hour wait for a table on a summer's evening isn't uncommon, but generally worth it. The place has been serving its hearty, mostly unfussy, spanking fresh seafood dishes for nearly 40 years out of a boisterous outfit on the water overlooking busy Buzzards Bay in New Bedford, former whaling center of the universe. With a cocktail in hand and a spot in the lounge, you won't mind the wait.

As for the multi-culti menu, unless you're feeling adventurous, leave the "Jamaican Me Crazy Filet Mignon" to other diners, and go simple. Get the fish chowder; it's

"Davy's Locker"

An expression used by sailors as early as the 1800s to mean the ocean's bottom—to conjure "Davy Jones" was to speak of the ocean's spirits, and to be sent to Davy's Locker was to perish at sea.

won awards, and for good reason: It's creamy, pungent with fresh dill, and overflowing with hunks of perfectly cooked local fish. (Most of the fish and seafood is local–though when I stopped by, they were using oysters from Florida.) Other big sellers at Davy's include classics like oysters Rockefeller, clams casino, and seared scallops wrapped in smoky bacon. Specials of the day might include a small but satisfying order of steamed mussels bathed in a garlic-butter broth. The fried items are tops: The thick-battered English-style fish and chips (also available Cajuned, with jerk spices) or the same hunk of flaky fish served up in a sandwich are worth a try. Entrées get more complicated, but tasty standouts include the Crabfish, a crabmeat-stuffed flounder with lobster sauce, simply broiled native scallops, and a spectacular grilled swordfish. The Lazy Man's Lobster, a platter of lobster meat topped with buttery seafood stuffing, is just like the restaurant itself: big, a bit of a throwback, very New England, and totally satisfying. Key lime pie is served in summer; and fried cheesecake? Maybe next time.

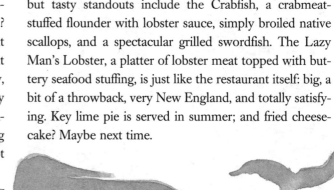

walk off the meal: New Bedford Seaport

After a bowl of superlative fish chowder at Davy's Locker, head down to the stately Seaport Historical District for a Herman Melville moment. In the 1830s, New Bedford was one of the richest cities in the country, thanks to whale oil, the only lamp fuel around. More than 170 whaling ships called it homeport, pulling in nearly half the American supply of oil, and Melville—who set out not far from here on the 1841 voyage that would inspire *Moby-Dick*—describes the still-standing Whalemen's Chapel (Seaman's Bethel) in the book. Whether he'd approve of the fridge magnets and bumper stickers ("New Bedford: A Whale of a Time!") littering souvenir shops along the docks nowadays is another story.

Giordano's

107 Circuit Avenue, Oak Bluffs 508-693-0184 • Open Memorial Day to Labor Day
BEST BITES: Fried clams, fried haddock, onion rings

This may be the only place on Martha's Vineyard where you can follow clams with cannoli. New and old worlds collide at Giordano's, which, strictly speaking, is no seafood shack. Since 1930, generation after generation of the Giordano family has served up simple, winning Italian fare on red-checkered tablecloths to townies and the summer crowd alike. But while folks flock here for oozy slices of Neapolitan-style wood-fired pizza and hefty portions of baked manicotti and veal cacciatore, they also clamor for the fried bites at Giordano's Clam Bar–the first clam stand on the island. It's the belly clams that win local awards, but Gio's also fries scallops, haddock, shrimp, oysters, and calamari in their own mixture of coarse crumbs, done to a light crisp in oil you won't taste for hours afterward. Order your poison in half-pints, pints, and quarts, and get some of the hand-cut onion rings on the side.

crib sheet: Red Tide

An algae bloom that's deadly to humans and carried by clams, scallops, or mussels (but not lobster, shrimp, crabs, or the part of the scallop that winds up on your plate). The toxins don't harm the mollusks and are naturally flushed out in time. In 2005, the worst plague on record closed clamming flats throughout the Northeast, and in some places the cost of a pint of fried clams almost doubled.

Home Port Restaurant

512 Basin Road, Menemsha 508-645-2679 • www.homeportmv.com • Open mid-April to mid-October • BEST BITES: Lobster dinner, broiled scallops, Key lime pie

Lovers of up-island Martha's Vineyard agree on two seemingly contradictory things: that you won't have the greatest meal of your life at the Home Port, and that you absolutely have to go. On your first visit, this makes perfect sense–you wouldn't want to pass up a boisterous evening amid the mounted fish in this fanfare-free 1930s mess hall, pitched over the harbor in the cheery, scruffy fishing village of Menemsha. Prices seem steep if you don't know what's going on, which is that your 1.5-pound lobster dinner is part of a package deal that includes an appetizer (steamed mussels or hearty quahog chowder are favorites), a salad, the standard shore sides, a fat wedge of home-

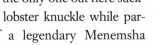

lingo:
Fannie Daddles

Largely out-of-use Massachusetts slang for fried clams.

baked pie (blueberry or Key lime? Tough call), and a beverage (a virgin one; BYO if you're feeling boozy). You'll need reservations to eat in (the Home Port is dinner-only), but last-minute cravings can be handled at the backdoor takeout window, where the prices are lower. Carry your meal around to the patio; I guarantee you won't be the only one out here sucking on a lobster knuckle while partaking of a legendary Menemsha sunset.

The Home Port is such quintessential Vineyardia that when Will Holtham threatened to sell in the early '00s, locals raised a ruckus and he reconsidered. At this writing, the restaurant was about to go on the market.

Jasper White's Summer Shack

149 Alewife Brook Parkway, Cambridge 617-520-9500 • www.summershackrestaurant.com
Open year-round • BEST BITES: Lobster corn dog, Rhode Island calamari, soft-shell crab BLT, raw bar

Can we all cut Jasper White some slack? His celebrity toque is well earned. He revolutionized American cuisine at the Bostonian Hotel, took it even further at his own landmark restaurant Jasper, and brought it to the masses as the executive chef of the Legal Sea Foods eateries. He's also authored a handful of insta-bestselling seafood cookbooks–his *50 Chowders* is sitting on my shelf right now, cream-splattered with use. And his wildly successful Summer Shack mini-chain elevates casual shoreline fare to gastronomic heights, without the stuffy surroundings that often go with upscale seafood. Yet he still gets flak– most if it, predictably, from New Englanders. Some call it a clam shack on steroids. Others sneer at its saucy slogan (*Food Is Love*™),

printed on everything from menus to T-shirts and chanted, mantralike, by the staff. Many denounce the faux decor, all repro-driftwood and weathered signage, and cackle at the sometimes breathtaking prices. Why pay through the nose for a lobster dinner when you can drive 20 minutes to a bona-fide shack and get the same thing for two-thirds the price–with a harbor view?

This is understandable–especially from Yankees, known for sniffing at put-ons and not paying more for anything than is strictly necessary– but it's a little misplaced. Sure, a real shack uses butcher paper for tablecloths and plastic buckets for condiments because they're cheap and easy to clean, while White uses them referentially, because he can. But his concept is to actual shoreline shacks what the Venetian Las Vegas is to Venice: so obsessively authentic that it bears no relation to the real thing, and comparing the two misses the point. It's no stretch to imagine the Summer Shack *in* Vegas, at a Nantucket-themed resort with an

lingo: Clam Alley

Slang. Name given to Route 133 in northeastern Massachusetts, home to some of New England's most legendary clam shacks (e.g. J.T. Farnham's, the Clam Box, Essex Seafood, and Woodman's of Essex, birthplace of the fried clam). Bivalves served at these restaurants all come from flats nearby, generally considered to yield the best clams anywhere.

indoor wharf, imported seawater, and lobstermen singing sea shanties on the half-hour as a fog machine pumps out mist nearby. (It could happen–there's already a Summer Shack outpost at Connecticut's Mohegan Sun Casino, along with a smaller one in Boston's Back Bay.) The truth–sad for the West, lucky for the East–is that you simply could never get seafood this fresh in Las Vegas.

And it is very, very fresh, and wonderfully inventive without losing sight of tradition, as is the Jasper White way. The menu is massive, ranging from simple, cheap, and sandwichey to high-end and lavish, like bouillabaisse. Try the lobster corn dog, his yummy perversion of the lobster roll (though you'll also find a classic lobster salad roll here–and a terrific straight-up corn dog, for that matter), or the garlicky Rhode Island calamari. The menu flags these as "spicy and greasy," and they're both, batter- instead of dry crumb-fried and topped with a hot pepper relish that's not for the weak. In season, a soft-shell crab BLT pops up as a special. It's a sizeable, crispy, meal-fried critter on a soft toasted bun, dolloped with tartar sauce and garnished with a few strips of toothy bacon. If squirmy things on the half shell are your idea of heaven, prepare to meet your maker at the Shack's raw bar, whose staggering selection of oysters from as close as Duxbury, Massachusetts, and as far away as Washington state, may be prepared for you by championship shucker Tien Van Tran. Check the blackboard for the day's fish specials and get something wood-grilled, like fresh anchovies. I've heard tell of tomalley toasts, which aren't on the menu but which the kitchen will whip up for you from a lobster if it's just been served to someone else (there's plenty of whole lobster at the Shack, and it's expensive). You could make a whole meal of the sides here, like the griddled brown bread, which is like twisted french toast, or the

heavenly corn fritters, which you dip into a dish of real maple syrup.

The kitchen does its soft-serve ice cream from scratch, making any dessert served with it a must-try (have it atop a steaming swirl of Indian pudding, redolent of molasses, or added to the homey, old-fashioned blueberry buckle).

J.T. Farnham's

88 Eastern Avenue (Route 133), Essex 978-768-6643 • Open March through November
BEST BITES: Fried clams, fried squid, coleslaw, broiled scallops, haddock chowder

As North Shore shacks go, Farnham's is pretty low-key: no star-spangled bunting, no gift shop, none of the fanfare of nearby Woodman's. All the better to bliss out on seafood at this affably grubby cabin, where a meal feels a bit like Sunday lunch at Grandma's house, if Grandma had a king-sized Fry-o-lator and an industrial tartar sauce pump.

The Celluccis bought Farnham's in 1994, but it's been here for nearly 60 years, one of the establishments—along with the Clam Box and Woodman's—to earn this stretch of Route 133 the moniker Clam Alley. The restaurant's expanded a fair bit since the changeover, but the original yellow-and-blue Farnham's sign bolted to the building's corner remains, a roadside landmark in itself. So does the genially old-world counter when you enter. There are stools here for eating in, and wooden booths in the dining room, but the best seats in the house are out back, dotting a reach of gravel that overlooks the endless blue-and-green patchwork of Essex Salt Marsh. It's a party for the senses out here: The smell of sun-warmed seaweed mixes with the fish-fry aroma pumped out of Farnham's workhorse of a kitchen, and you're surrounded by nesting egrets, swooping cormorants, and impudent seagulls. The gulls have turned the other sign into surveillance HQ, so stay alert—they're fat for a reason, and they can smell a newbie.

> "I've been coming here for 22 years. Woodman's has the legend, and the [Clam] Box has the building, but Farnham's has the clams."
>
> —ROBERT, ROWLEY, MASSACHUSETTS

There's also more to Farnham's menu than there used to be, but fried seafood is still the house specialty. Haddock, squid, shellfish from scallops to oysters, and the celebrated clams are all given the same egg wash and a corn-flour dip before hitting the fryer, where they acquire a tawny, brittle shell that's never heavy. Farnham's tends to leave the behemoth bellies to other buyers; their clams are medium-sized and more about maximizing the surface of crunch without sacrificing any clammy flavor within.

Coleslaw's no afterthought at this shack; it's crunchy-fresh and zested up with pineapple, a recipe the Celluccis brought with them to the restaurant. If you can get past the fried seafood (it's hard, but not impossible), the kitchen has a deft hand with the broiled kind, too (try the scallops). And treat yourself to one of the luscious award-winning chowders—not surprisingly, the clam is popular, but the haddock, abounding with nuggets of buttery fish and nubs of potato in a milky broth, is too good to pass up.

Kelly's Roast Beef

410 Revere Beach Boulevard, Revere 781-284-9129 • www.kellysroastbeef.com
Open year-round • BEST BITES: Lobster roll, roast beef sandwich, fried scallops, onion rings

When Bostonians who've moved away hear you mention Kelly's in Revere, they tend to well up. They'll ask you if the wall clock is still broken, and what you got with your sandwich. If you didn't get onion rings, they'll scold you genially, saying you have to get them next time, because the best part is running the rings alongside your sandwich to sop up the salty-sweet barbecue-style sauce dripping from the rosy shavings of beef. And if you don't seem to rhapsodize about Kelly's quite as fervently as you should, they'll tell you it's a Boston thing—you wouldn't understand.

There are four Kelly's restaurants around Boston, but this location across from Revere Beach is the original, dating to 1951: a sprawling building with shamrocks on the roof plopped on the corner of a stretch of boardwalk housing Krispy Kreme, Bianchi's Pizza, bars, and state police barracks. The takeout-only place is all kitchen, with nearly a dozen ordering windows—and yet lines still snake down the sidewalk on a summer day, when bikini-clad locals leave their towels unattended for a taste of Kelly's soft, juicy roast beef or a double-fisted handful of perfectly fried scallops. On busy days, the strip of sidewalk

fronting the restaurant is like a subway platform at rush hour. The chaos lets nonnatives brush up on their shore lingo: At Kelly's, if you want something carbonated, ask for a tonic; if you're in a milkshake mood, order a frappe. But it's late at night that Kelly's finds its true niche: This may be one of the only places along the coast where you can satisfy your lobster roll jones until 2:30 AM, breathing in the ocean's scent and watching a staffer empty all 37 trash bins. The same crowds rush Kelly's in the wee hours, coming from parties and clubs and dressed to the nines. "It's called a Kelly's Kraving, with a K," says one loyal customer. "If you have one drink too many, you need to go to Kelly's so the next day's not so bad."

The famed sammies are fat, sloppy piles of beef on a sesame-seed bun, oozing with the aforementioned sauce (and eye-watering with horseradish if you order them right). Landlubbers also laud the chili dog, a gargantuan thing made with a satisfying Kayem's deli frank. Lobster rolls at Kelly's can be pricey, but that's because they're big enough to split (though you may not want to): There's a full quarter pound of buttery meat–from two whole 1-pound lobsters–in each roll, tossed with mayo and celery nubs. And you can't go wrong with any of the fried seafood here, especially the fish sandwich, scallops, and clams. The kitchen turns out crunchy, dense batches of fried clams from Chesapeake Bay, delivered every day and a little smaller than their Ipswich counterparts.

Trek your bounty across the busy boulevard, grab a bench under the pavilion or a foot of breaker wall, and dine with a view of the jet traffic from Logan Airport and the first public beach in the U.S. It was created in 1898 and changed Boston summers completely, especially for those who'd just arrived in the country and didn't have much money to spend on entertainment. Even today, it's a heavily Italian spot. Mangia!

lobster for life

Life was rough in Massachusetts in the 1700s. Sure, the witch hunt was finally over—no more of this burned-at-the-stake-if-the-town-elders-thought-you-looked-at-them-funny-in-church business—but if you committed a crime that landed you in jail, you could still be subjected to cruel and unusual punishment beyond your worst nightmares: lobster at every single meal.

Lobster for breakfast. Lobster for lunch. And guess what's for dinner? Lobster. Always lobster. (And probably not with drawn butter, either.)

"Too much lobster?" you're saying. "Isn't that kind of like having too much money?"

Today yes, but it wasn't always so: In the late 17th and early 18th centuries, lobster was not the drooled-over delicacy it is in the 21st. Quite the contrary, it was so seasonlessly plentiful that it was considered fit only for feeding to pigs or fertilizing crops. Diaries kept by the pilgrims contain references to countless meals of the stuff, considered stringy and tasteless. Records documenting the Boston Massacre describe how the insult "you bloody lobster" was hurled at the Redcoats, on a par with such put-downs as "scoundrel" and "bastard."

And so legend has it that one crisp day in the late 1700s, inmates incarcerated on an island in Boston Harbor lined up for their meal. Realizing they were being served lobster once again, they snapped—and began one of the bloodiest prison riots in American history. In the aftermath, the prison directors realized they'd have to suck it up and start varying the menu a bit.

Kream 'n' Kone

527 Main Street (Route 28), West Dennis • 508-394-0808 • www.kreamnkone.com • Open Memorial Day to Labor Day • BEST BITES: Fried clams, fried haddock, lobster roll, ice cream

There's one thing Kream 'n' Kone owner Angelo Argyriadis wants to make very clear: His restaurant is not, I repeat, not, affiliated with the Kream 'n' Kone in nearby Chatham.

"People go there, they have a disappointing meal, and then they come here with the leftovers and ask for their money back," he says. His eyes narrow as he wipes his hands on his grease-spattered white apron. "What can you do? Let's just say we don't quite have the same standards."

In the beginning–which is to say in 1953, when two men named Haitas and Brokam opened the Kream 'n' Kone–the two were very much connected. But business partnerships being what they are, things changed over the years, and now they share only a name.

It also started out, as the name suggests, as an ice cream place. Over the years, when clams became more abundant and area restaurants began doing a booming seafood business, the menu changed. Angelo bought the place in 1989, when it was still about a mile down the road from where it is now, before a fire decimated the building.

Standards are a big deal for Angelo. When I ask if anything surprised him about going into the seafood restaurant business, he takes a slightly jaded turn and talks about seafood purveyors who sell to establishments such as his. "It's hard. Prices go up, they go down . . . and it's amazing what some people will try to sell to you," he says, chuckling and shaking his head. He acknowledges that his prices are slightly higher than at some other places in the area. "But we pay more for our seafood, and it's well worth it. People know that."

And they remember it, too. Angelo recounts taking his family on vacation to San Diego a few years ago and striking up a conversation with diners at the next table. Turns out they were talking to a California transplant who'd grown up in Dennis. "He just lit up. It was amazing how fondly he remembered his meals here. That's one of the best compliments I've received." Then there was the bride-to-be whose father showed up at the restaurant with an unusual request: batter, seafood, and all the materials necessary to recreate a Kream 'n' Kone dinner for the wedding reception.

Big, clean, and airy with a happy, high-school-cafeteria vibe, the Kream 'n' Kone offers a menu of fast-food

standards at the center of which are the legendary clams. Big fried whole clams are the main draw here, the dish that keeps people coming back year after year, but the other fried staples–from scallops to shrimp–are just as good, the batter perfectly crunchy (for the best value, order your seafood by quantity instead of as a platter). Even the fried clam strips get my vote; they're not a compromise, and they're great for younger palates, which can often find the whole clams a little scary (here the bellies are removed, leaving mostly the neck, which still manages to be wonderfully tender). While they don't serve whole lobster dinners, those hankering for a bug can sink their teeth into a wonderful hand-torn lobster roll with no fuss and few extras–"We even got away from the butter," says Angelo.

The other thing the Kream 'n' Kone is known for–aside from the 24 flavors of soft-serve ice cream–is its onion rings. Not too thin, not too thick, sliced from chubby Spanish onions and fried in the same light batter as the seafood, they're excellent. Wash them down with a frappe, suggests one patron waiting in line for lunch.

In fact, the only thing locals and vacationers seem to dislike about the Kream 'n' Kone is the fact that it closes for the winter. "I've been here for 16 years, and people come in every year in the last few days of the season," says Angelo, "They order up all this food. Then they take it home and put it in their freezer so they can have some Kream 'n' Kone in the winter, when we're closed."

shack staple:
Cape Cod Potato Chips

Pint of fried clams, check. Little waxy container of coleslaw, check. Mini-bag of Cape Cod Potato Chips, check.

Yeah, the "old-fashioned kettle cooked" chips are just that ubiquitous. It's rare for a single brand to blanket a region quite as exhaustively as Cape Cod Chips has, but in just 25 years, the original indie chip has become the gold standard of seafood shack pre-made sides even in this age of über-trendy gourmet/artisanal chips. Here's a little background on this famous snack:

- The company was officially born on July 4, 1980 (a fitting birth date for an all-American snack) when Steve and Lynn Bernard started frying Maine-grown taters in their 800-square-foot Hyannis, Massachusetts, factory.

- An intense local following, um, followed. Don't believe me? Head to www.capecodchips.com, where testimonials border on religious fanaticism. (One likens tasting a jalapeño and aged cheddar chip to meeting a soul mate: "You just know.")

- Steve and Lynn made about 200 bags of chips a day when they started out. Today, 150 staffers produce more than 150,000 packages every day, still cooking them by hand, one batch at a time.

- About 250,000 die-hard chip heads tour the factory each year, sampling the goods and stocking up on chip-branded merch (golf balls! puzzles! chip clips!) at the gift store.

Larsen's Fish Market

56 Basin Road, Menemsha 508-645-2680 • Open year-round
BEST BITES: Raw littlenecks, lobster roll, smoked fish selection

The fish markets and restaurants of Menemsha have an understanding. Larsen's doesn't fry anything, and The Bite agrees not to angle for a piece of Larsen's lobster or raw bar action. (Sometimes, they even help each other out: The Bite buys the base for its famous clam chowder from the Home Port restaurant.) As a result, Menemsha is the perfect place for the seafood lover with ADD of the taste buds–you could plan a whole food crawl here, pinballing back and forth until your belly begged for mercy.

The Larsen name has been synonymous with the catch of the day on Martha's Vineyard for generations: There are lots of Larsens around, and most of them peddle fish (the Menemsha Fish Market and the Net Result Market and Takeout in Vineyard Haven are two other Larsen-run businesses). At this cottage on Dutcher Dock–whose Larsen is a Stanley, owner of Edgartown Seafood–you'll find not only inspiration and materials for a homemade dinner, but a short and sweet list of goodies for the harborside picnic of your dreams. Grab a plate of freshly shucked littleneck clams or locally farmed Tomahawk oysters, served with a pair of lemon wedges and some straightforward cocktail sauce. Follow that with a cool, filler-free lobster roll, some crabcakes, or a hunk of smoked fish. If you're feeing energetic, pick out a snappy lobster and they'll boil it for you. Find a trap to sit on outside and contemplate the fishing boats while you chomp, dunk, and chew your way through the most satisfying of lunches.

Legal Sea Foods

20 University Road, Cambridge, and 16 other New England locations 617-491-9400
www.legalseafoods.com • Open year-round • BEST BITE: Clam chowder

Legal Sea Foods needs about as much of an introduction as Starbucks. The New England institution started in the 1950s, with its famous Cambridge fish market, out of which the first restaurant grew in 1968. Today, it's a fishy empire 33 eateries strong, and seafood lovers from Braintree, Mass., to Boca Raton know it as a consistently dependable choice for straight-up, fresher-than-fresh goods from the ocean. You'll find all the standards here, done classically and updated with a cioppino here and a walnut-crusted bluefish pâté there (and its signature clam chili, which you're welcome to fall in love with, but which just doesn't float my boat). I'm mentioning the chain here because of its incredibly good clam chowder. With a consistency that strikes the right balance between milk and cream, and a stock rich with the flavors of onions, garlic, salt pork, and Cape Cod clams, it's become something of a New England legend and a yardstick by which cream-based clam chowder is measured. It's won more awards than anyone can remember, it's been served at every presidential inauguration since 1981, and it's a concession-stand favorite at Red Sox games. Legal Sea Foods sells more than 2,500 gallons of the stuff every week. Have some.

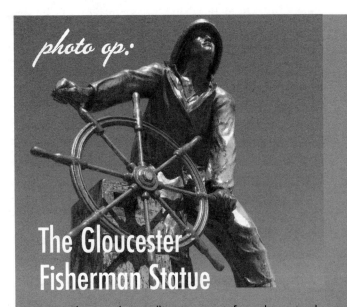

photo op:

The Gloucester Fisherman Statue

Pop culture junkies will recognize it from the episode of *Bewitched* where Serena turns Darrin (the Dick Sargent one) into its likeness while Samantha's off at a Salem witch convention. But the fishermen's memorial strikes a far more somber note with the locals: More than 10,000 Gloucester fishermen have lost their lives at sea trying to earn a living—Sebastian Junger's novel *The Perfect Storm* (and its big-screen adaptation) focused on those who went down on the *Andrea Gail.* Sculptor Leonard Craske created the figure in 1923 for the town's 300th anniversary; the plaque dedicates it to "They that go down to the sea in ships." (Western Avenue, Gloucester, Mass.)

The Lobster Claw

Route 6A, Orleans 508-255-1800 • www.lobsterclaw.com • Open April to October
BEST BITES: Clambake, lobster club sandwich, fried lobster, raw bar items

The Berigs, who've owned and operated this Orleans standby for more than 30 years, understand children. More importantly, they understand parents. Frazzled moms and dads drag their brood to the Claw for its toddler-pleasing touches, which include early-bird specials from 4 to 5:30 PM, crayons provided for placemat-coloring contests on the turquoise tables, huge (read: shareable) portions, and a full and cheap kids' menu that covers all of Junior's greatest hits. (Deep-fried lobster, rare on the shack circuit because of the widely held belief that the dish is a waste of perfectly good lobster, is available here–a consideration if your child's squeamish about lobster, but loves fried food.) Besides, the decor alone–sort of fishing-shack-meets-funhouse, with more than the usual quota of nautical-themed eye candy–is more than enough to keep the little darlings entertained. They'll probably want to take home one of the cute claw-shaped menus, and the accommodating staff will be happy to oblige. Despite the down-home look of the place, diners looking for lighter fare (or who've simply maxed out on the fried stuff) can find items like locally harvested cherrystones and oysters on the half shell, poached haddock, or a heavenly broiled native bluefish that's a bargain at just about $10. And the lobster club sandwich makes a nice change from the standard roll. The upstairs of this sprawling eatery is more geared towards adults, with a large bar and TV. While the Claw doesn't offer much in the way of picturesque views, perched as it is right on Route 6A, the structure itself–a great lobster-red barn of a building with clapboard, striped awnings, and a giant crustacean bolted to the side–will prompt Americana lovers to dig out the camera. You may not have the bite of your life at the Claw, but you'll have a fresh, tasty, and reasonably priced meal served to you by chipper staffers in a casual, boisterous atmosphere, and at the end of a long day of sun and sand, sometimes that's just what the doctor ordered.

photo op: The Jonathan Young Windmill

Cape Cod is teeming with windmills. One of its oldest, the Jonathan Young, has been moved three times since it was first built in 1720, and now sits in a round park overlooking pretty Town Cove in Orleans, not far from the Lobster Claw. If the weather's good, skip the indoor seating and carry your meal over to this well-loved little landmark. Its handful of benches are perfect for a picnic.

The Lobster Pool (on Folly Cove)

329 Granite Street (Route 127), Rockport 978-546-7808 • www.lobsterpoolrestaurant.com
Open April to October • BEST BITES: Fried oysters, the Boston Whaler, lobster dinners, zabaglione

I f you're suffering from seaside quaintness over-load and can't face another second among downtown Rockport's sightseeing throngs, rescue your car and head just beyond Halibut Point to a rusty-colored bungalow pitched over Folly Cove.

The Lobster Pool has changed hands but not much else since it opened in 1954. Here the eats are reasonable, the view of Ipswich Bay incomparable, and tipping strictly prohibited. The Tedesco family keeps the menu simple: Munch on "no nonsense, no celery" lobster and crabmeat rolls with Cape Cod potato chips, upgrade to boxes of fried clams and oysters, or get a baked fish or full shore dinner with a side of thin, crunchy onion rings. The Boston Whaler sandwich, a thick, fried slab of haddock on a lettuce-draped bun, goes well with a cup of the velvety seafood chowder, crowded with more haddock, scallops, and shrimp. Fido will be warmly greeted at the outdoor dining area, which turns into a real scene on weekends: As the sun sinks into the water beyond Plum Island, patrons tipsy on brine and beer (their own; hit a package store before you come) burst into rowdy applause.

Check the dessert board when you arrive. The end of the meal is one of the best parts of the Lobster Pool, but the offerings change. Pies ooze with tangy filling, blueberry and strawberry shortcakes are homemade, and the zabaglione (a rich Italian custard dish) gets its zing from fresh fruit (ask for raspberries) and a napping of cool, heavy cream.

lingo: Spat

The spawn of an oyster, clam, or other bivalve mollusk, especially when it settles to the bottom and begins to develop a shell

The Lobster Pot

321 Commercial Street, Provincetown 508-487-0842 • www.ptownlobsterpot.com • Open Mid-February through December • BEST BITES: Clam chowder, sopa do mar, pan-roasted lobster, berry-stone cobbler

The Lobster Pot just celebrated a quarter century in this plum spot overlooking Provincetown Harbor, on a busy stretch of Commercial Street where food can be faddish and many chefs are keen to ditch the town's ties to fishing history. Not so at the Pot, as locals call it. You may find some radical items on the menu like blackened tuna sashimi and pesto-broiled oysters (divine, by the way), but for the most part the fare is as refreshingly old-school as the twin-lobstered neon sign outside, a little slice of 1950s Atlantic City at the tip of Cape Cod.

This is the place to come for smoky-baconed clams casino, tender, corn flour-dusted calamari, and a bowl of thicker-than-thick clam chowder that's taken ribbons at chowder fests all over Massachusetts. The Pot is also one of P-Town's best bets for a taste of the region's Portuguese past: Try the Portuguese soup, a savory mixture with buttery kale leaves, earthy kidney beans and cabbage, and chunks of spicy sausage. A special occasion or impressive appetite calls for the mind-blowing sopa do mar, a seafood stew reminiscent of bouillabaisse that gets its fishy intensity from a stock made with flounder, white wine, leeks, and a few threads of saffron. The broth comes piled high with a smorgasbord of local catch: mussels, shrimp: scallops, clams, squid—even oysters from nearby Wellfleet.

And then, there's the Pot's raison d'être: lobster. I dare you to think of a variation on lobster that's not somewhere on this menu. Executive chef Tim McNulty's lobster comes boiled, bisqued, baked, scampi'd, and stuffed, it's served in and out of the shell, it's piled in under-mayonnaised chunks into a toasted roll, it's chilled with zippy cocktail sauce on the side. I happen to like the Pot's lobster tipsy: with sherry (and scallions) in a lusciously creamy take on the classic Newburg, or pan-roasted with brandied butter. Love.

Sweet tooths should consider the warm berry-stone cobbler, drowned in a fast-melting vanilla scoop, or a homemade ice cream sandwich that packs about a quarter-pint of frosty mint chocolate-chip between two devil's food cakes.

Lines are fairly common at the Pot when peak season rolls around, and only the luckiest few will snag a spot on the outdoor deck. No matter: Almost every seat in the house offers perfect views of Macmillan Wharf and the pretty harbor. Lazy late afternoons in P-Town were made for cocktails and raw cherrystones upstairs, at the loungey Top of the Pot.

The Provincetown Seafood Cookbook

Ever since saucy chef Anthony Bourdain lauded it in his bestselling backdoor tell-all *Kitchen Confidential,* it's been nearly impossible to get one's paws on a copy of Howard Mitcham's (out-of-print) *Provincetown Seafood Cookbook.* But beg, borrow, or steal one, because aside from being one of the best (and least fussy) seafood cookbooks around, it's a delicious, down-and-dirty valentine to Cape Cod's humble fishing roots, told in quasi-memoir form by the ultimate cook's cook, by all accounts a maddening, mercurial Mississippi native who moved east and worshipped all things sea. When he wasn't cooking, singing

(though a fireworks accident left him deaf at 16), or bashing around Provincetown in a drunken fog, he was writing; there are other books (*Creole Gumbo and All That Jazz* covers Cajun cuisine's way with seafood), but the *Provincetown Seafood Cookbook* remains the definitive work. In it, Mitcham evokes the town's Portuguese heritage in wonderful linguiça-laced dishes, sings the praises of trash fish like sea robins and conger eels, and canonizes the humble quahog. He also slings anecdote after salty anecdote: Here, a dog masters the art of clamming; there, one bad bivalve is slipped into a vat of chowder to exact revenge. And the whole thing is illustrated with Mitcham's own delightfully naïf pen: wisps of steam curl above squat crocks of squid stew, anthropomorphized clams glance around for imminent danger.

The Lobster Trap

23 Washington Street, Nantucket Town 508-228-4200 • www.nantucketlobstertrap.com • Open May to October • BEST BITES: Bacon-wrapped Nantucket bay scallops, steamed littlenecks, lobster dinner

Nantucket has no end of fine dining options—a spoiled Manhattanite or San Franciscan could spend weeks here and not miss the sushi- and tapas-addled comforts of home. Yet oddly, unlike Martha's Vineyard or Cape Cod, it doesn't have much in the way of down-and-dirty shack fare. "For an island surrounded by an ocean full of fish," a long-time Nantucket visitor told me, "it's sad that you have to pay through the nose to get the good stuff."

There used to be a shanty, I'm told, a stone's throw from the ferry landing, where weary travelers just arriving for a blissful week of R&R would get in line to pick up steaming, grease-spotted bags of fried clams and scallops on their way home. That takeout is no more, and opening-night honors have shifted over to the Lobster Trap, which may be the closest thing Nantucket has to a laid-back fish house.

Make that a fish house-cum-sports bar. The Trap has almost as many TVs as it has beers on tap, and they're usually turned to the big game, which tends to involve the Red Sox (rumor has it one of the bartenders is a Yankees fan and takes liberties with the remote control, though I haven't experienced this firsthand). The TVs may come in handy, as you'll probably need to bide your time for a table, a not-unpleasant circumstance involving a tarped-in patio and cocktails (try the Elbow Bender, a Cherry Herring-laced rum punch that the Trap's owner tasted while sailing through the Abacos). And if men in jerseys leave you cold, there's plenty more vying for your attention at the Trap. The lobster tanks, for instance, which the

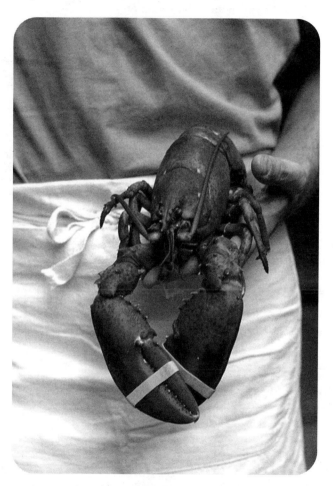

restaurant claims can hold up to 2,000 pounds of lobsters on the average summer night.

The menu is short and the offerings strictly no-frills, another anomaly on the island—the fussiest items here are lobster fettuccine (the sauce is a sort of Alfredo-bisque hybrid, with chunks of lobster meat tossed into the pasta) and scallops wrapped in bacon, which aren't even that fussy and are particularly good. They use Nantucket Bay scallops, local as it gets. You can also fill your bacon quota with a starter of stuffed shrimp wrapped in the stuff or a fiver of clams casino. Steamers—the usual full-bodied Ipswich Bay soft-shells—are hugely popular here,

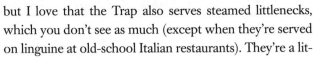

but I love that the Trap also serves steamed littlenecks, which you don't see as much (except when they're served on linguine at old-school Italian restaurants). They're a little smaller than an old silver dollar, juicy, and wonderfully sweet.

There's also a list of fish done simply (swordfish, flounder, salmon, and scrod, broiled or grilled), some turf for the naysayers (heralded on the menu as "Non-seafood offerings," to make you feel even more sheepish ordering a filet mignon in here), and then there are lobsters. Fly solo with a small one or order a monster to split (3 to 5 pounds officially, but if even that won't do, try a discreet inquiry). The restaurant bakes its own bread, something to keep in mind if there's any drawn butter left after you've put away all that lush lobster meat. Finally, kids with burgeoning taste buds might like the seafood combination platter, starring half a lobster and supported by fried clams, shrimp, scrod, those bay scallops, and calamari (if not, there's a full children's menu on hand).

If you can't bear the crowd cheering on the Sox or the inevitable half-hour wait for a table on a Saturday night, do what some of the more seasoned vacationers do: Dial-A-Lobster. The Trap's Meals on Keels program will run shore dinners over to your door, whereupon you can haul your bug, oysters, chowder, steamers, mussels, and whatever else to the beach (the Trap includes everything you need for a picnic—drinks are up to you) and chow down as the sun eases into the water. Sure, there's no "Sweet Caroline" in the eighth inning here, but did you really come to Nantucket to watch baseball?

Mac's Seafood

Wellfleet Town Pier, Wellfleet 508-349-0404 • www.macsseafood.com

Open Memorial Day to September • BEST BITES: Wellfleet oysters, crabcake sandwich, clambake

Don't be scared by the sushi chef. Or the guy rolling burritos. Purists will take one look at them and want to run for their lives, but have no fear: The bottom line, at this young takeout shack, is unstoppably fresh saltwater fare, a byproduct of Mac's lucky location right on Wellfleet's (working) harbor. See the boats across the pier from Mac's? Your seafood probably came in one of those boats a few hours ago, and the owners also operate a terrific fish market in Truro Center, so you know they know what they're doing.

If you're jonesing for standards, go for the raw bar (including so-local-it-hurts Wellfleet oysters), anything from the fried menu, one of the homemade chowders or seafood sandwiches (from the crabcake to the grilled tuna), or a clambake, one of Mac's specialties. For the latter, select your lobster size (anything from a 1$^{1}/_{2}$- to a full 2-pound beast), corn on the cob or red potatoes, and mussels or steamers–and then wait, while you watch the gulls circling. Or stray from the New England menu and sample the aforementioned sushi. The usual maki menu is available, but ask about the specials instead–sometimes there's sashimi or nigiri, using whatever fish impressed the cooks that morning. Or try something you're not likely to find elsewhere: a grilled scallop burrito, a codfish quesadilla, or spicy calamari stew. Mac's turns these into genuine winners that don't smother the seafood's freshness with too many other flavors. (Those who avoid seafood will find burgers, pulled pork and, incongruously, a falafel sandwich.)

And then there's Mac's location. The harbor's nearby, full of the kinds of rusty, barnacled fishing boats that

offer a nice change from the sparkling pleasure-craft marinas you're more apt to see on Cape Cod. And, Mac's isn't just on the water–it's the kind of place that gets erosion theorists hot under the collar trying to calculate roughly how much longer it has before the whole thing washes out to sea. If the swath of shore were any less out of the way, the place would be constantly mobbed, but as it is, the people-to-nature ratio tends to be manageable, despite proximity to popular Mayo Beach. If there's no room at one of the few indoor seats or picnic tables surrounding the small building, hold your lobster roll in one hand and your flip-flops in the other and wade into the water.

Moby Dick's

Route 6, past the Truro town line, Wellfleet 508-349-9795 • www.mobydicksrestaurant.com •
Open May to September • BEST BITES: Lobster roll, Outer Cape Onion, Nantucket Bucket

Order a lobster dinner at Moby Dick's, and it just might come with a husband. At least that's what happened to Manon "Miggs" Barry when she visited Provincetown in 1995, a Kansas native on leave from a nursing career in New York. "I asked the locals where I should go to get a lobster," she says. "They sent me to Moby Dick's, and my future mother-in-law delivered my food." Maternal instinct being what it is, Todd Barry came out of the kitchen shortly thereafter—on his mother's orders—to "buy that girl a cup of coffee," and now, one wedding and 10 years later, the pair co-run one of the Cape's most beloved restaurants.

If Miggs Barry seems to embody the place's casually polished spirit, Moby Dick's had been around long before that cup of coffee. Opened in 1982 by the Barry family, the original Dick's was a 35-seat operation. It's since been expanded to accommodate more than 120 diners—and yes, the gift shop one door down is also a Barry production.

Next to some of the ramshackle half-barns and tool sheds serving seafood up and down the Cape—especially in wonderfully laid-back Wellfleet—Moby Dick's seems at first to be relying heavily on The Experience, from the gewgaws lining the walls (obligatory whale motif, vintage lobster claw–base lamp, and nets, nets, nets) to the framed snapshots of folks decked in "Moby wear," posing by foreign monuments. It all makes you wonder if the food's going to be an afterthought.

Luckily, it's not. Order up front by the blackboards, then take a seat in either the big, screened-in porch of a dining room or the older wing with its cozy nooks and crannies. Once the lobster roll arrived, I barely noticed the sizeable wooden cod hanging from tiny hooks over my head. Just-out-of-its-shell lobster comes in a slightly buttered toasted bun, glistening with a whisper of mayonnaise and a dusting of paprika. There's lettuce, too, just a bit. If you're not in the mood for lobster, order the Nantucket Bucket: A pound of native mussels ("native" is almost redundant here; the Barrys buy from local fishermen whenever possible) and a pound of Monomoy steamers are flanked by corncobs in a pail. The kitchen does an excellent job of the standards (and a twice-daily oil change ensures that fried items taste fresh), but there's one dish you likely won't find elsewhere: the "famous Outer Cape Onion," advertised on the chalkboard menu as "A bloomin' delight!" If you can swallow the pun, your reward is a super-colossal Spanish onion—"It's a two-handed onion," says Miggs—that's flower-cut, battered, and deep-fried into one giant, magnificent onion ring.

On our way out, Miggs is enunciating slowly and

loudly, asking a large group of Japanese tourists huddled in front of the menu if they've had lobster before. Moby Dick's has definitely found its way into international guidebooks, and–superlative dining aside–the Barrys are happy to give the tourists their authenticke ye olde lobster shacke money's worth, right down to a gold whale tail pendant dangling from a chain around Miggs's neck. "I don't have my lobster pins on today," she laughs. "I can't really wear both–it's overkill."

great debates:
Whole Clams vs. Clam Strips

If you're squeamish about whole fried clams—also called belly clams—you're not alone. "The full bellies can be a bit overwhelming for some people," says Larry Woodman at Woodman's of Essex, birthplace of the fried clam. That said, you won't find many coastal New Englanders among the naysayers. They tend to favor the heady experience of piercing a juicy belly through a brittle crust, releasing all that full-bodied, oceany flavor. Good news for the squeamish is that most restaurants serve clam strips, made from just the siphon or foot, usually from surf clams harvested in deep Atlantic waters. The flavor's much milder, tasting more like a miniature, slightly fishy chicken tender.

the big questions:
Oysters—Aphrodisiacs?

Aphrodite, goddess of love, sprang forth from the sea on an oyster shell. Frisky Casanova famously breakfasted on 60 oysters a day. Coincidence? Scientists overwhelmingly pooh-poohed the idea of oysters as aphrodisiacs, calling it a myth—until early 2005, when a team of American and (of course) Italian scientists pinpointed amino acids in the mollusks that were found to boost sexual hormone production in some very well fed lab rats.

"If you don't love life, you can't enjoy an oyster."
—Eleanor Clark, *The Oysters of Locmariaquer*

Nantucket Pharmacy

45 Main Street, Nantucket Town 508-228-0180 • Open year-round
BEST BITE: Lobster roll

*I*n a town where old often gets replaced with new-old-fashioned and genuine makes way for genteel, it's heartening that you can still stroll into the Nantucket Pharmacy (not to be confused with Congdon's Pharmacy right next door), perch on one of nine stools at the soda fountain, and order a lobster roll for lunch. Cool chunks of lobster are moistened with a little mayo-based dressing and tucked into a soft, toasted bun. Wash it down with a strawberry or chocolate frappe (that's a milkshake to landlubbers), and ask if anyone remembers when the place was Mac's

Drugstore and used to host barbershop-style sing-alongs out on the sidewalk.

Get an ice cream cone to go, pay your tab (one of the cheapest on the island), brush the crumbs off your poodle skirt, and head back to the beach.

No-Name Restaurant

Boston Fish Pier, off Northern Avenue, Boston 617-423-2705 • Open year-round
BEST BITES: Broiled seafood plate, lazy man's lobster, No-Name chowder, strawberry-rhubarb pie

Of all the stories told over the years about the No-Name Restaurant, a landmark on Boston Fish Pier since 1917, the one people can't seem to nail down is how the place got its name—or lack thereof. But the version you hear most often goes like this:

It started out as a restaurant with 11 seats, catering to famished fishermen who called the pier home, and making good, hearty meals out of whatever came in on the boats that day. Word leaked beyond the fishing community of a waterside spot with simple fresh fish dishes, and others started stopping by. Nobody knew its name—it didn't have one—so they called it the No-Name, and that was that.

The other debate that rages over the No-Name is whether this place is past its prime, or if it ever had a prime. These days, disgruntled diners—many of whom come from out of town, having read about the place or heard Emeril Lagasse bellow its praises on the Food Network—point to uninspired sides, poor service, and cramped quarters. On a busy evening, things can indeed get uneven at the No-Name. But it remains a boisterous favorite, a colorful bit of Boston seaside history and a place where you can get a piece of fresh fish, simply done and cheaper than almost anywhere else in the city, and wash it down with an icy cold beer while you watch the fishing boats come in to the harbor.

Skip the downstairs if you can, and grab a spot in the upper room to really appreciate the place. On your way up, take note of the restaurant's framed history lining the staircase walls, where you learn that everybody from

movie stars to religious figures to John F. Kennedy has rubbed elbows with the wharf rats who've called the place home. Up here, the dark wood, tile floor, and no-nonsense bar are an object lesson in how a complete lack of atmosphere, given 80-plus years of patina, delivers atmosphere in spades. The "How to Eat a Lobster" place-mats seem almost out of place.

Everything comes from the docks below into the dining room, with a short layover in the kitchen so it can be fried, baked, or broiled. A broiled seafood plate is the way to go if you want to sample and share, offering swordfish, scrod, scallops, salmon, and some unspectacular fries. For fried fans, there's golden-crusted shrimp, scrod, scallops, and clams; get the platter for a taste of everything. Sole and bluefish lovers can order separately; bear in mind that everything at the No-Name is supersized, a nod, perhaps, to the gargantuan appetites of guys who haul fish out of the ocean for a living. There's a nice version of lazy man's lobster, delicately sautéed in white wine and butter. Like the fries, the vegetable sides are negligible, but easily forgiven. Whatever's left from the catch or not pretty enough to serve solo goes into the No-Name chowder. There are no discernible vegetables in this chowder, no potato cubes pretending to serve a purpose. Instead, mounds of fish and seafood—flaky haddock, tender scallops, sweet lobster—shimmer in a milky broth with a slick of butter up top. A giant serving of this stuff is criminally cheap (less than a fiver in '05), and with a piece of chewy bread for dunking and a frothy draft, it makes a satisfying pause on a bracing November day. In season, get the strawberry-rhubarb pie for dessert: It's made from Greek-born founder Louis Contos's own recipe. He died at 106 years old, which I think makes a compelling argument for eating fresh fish every day.

By the way, the No-Name's lunch menu isn't much different from the dinner menu, but its prices are a fair bit lower, so it's the perfect spot to grab a midday bite if you're strolling around the city.

shack classic:
Lazy Man's Lobster

"The two mysteries of the East that remain beyond the reach of an expatriate Midwesterner are the New York subway system and the proper eating of a lobster."
–Calvin Trillin, *Alice, Let's Eat*

It's cheating, in a way—after all, the best things in life require a little hard work. And it's almost always the most expensive item on the menu. But for those days when you simply can't face all that cracking and extracting, there's Lazy Man's Lobster (called lobster sauté on some menus), the premise of which is simple: bug made easy, its meat removed from the shell, usually tossed with butter (and sometimes a little sherry), and nothing left for you to do but eat.

Roy Moore Lobster Co.

37 Bearskin Neck, Rockport 978-546-6696 • Open April to Columbus Day
BEST BITES: Clam chowder, lobsters, smoked fish

A few decades ago, Rockport was still a hamlet at the tip of Cape Ann trying to hawk its quaint, winding streets and listing fish-scaling shacks to tourists as a rustic getaway. The plan worked; so much so that now, on the average July day, it's hard to see past the fudge shoppes and wind-chime emporia–not to mention the hordes of tourists eating it all up–to the real town underneath.

"There's not much left," says Corey Tevan, who remembers pre–travel brochure Rockport. "But there is one place you can go to see it the way it used to be."

This is how I wind up making my way to busy Bearskin Neck–Rockport's harborfront epicenter of sightseeing–to a gray-shingled one-room structure held up almost entirely, as far as I can tell, by the buildings on either side. A huge plywood lobster done up with red paint and those hardware store peel-and-stick letters dangles off an iron pole out front. Inside, every inch of wall and rafter is grown over, moss-style, with stuff: newspaper clippings, buoys, boat prints, shells, and police patches, dozens of them, from squads as close as down the street and as far away as California. There's a stainless steel scale and some glass cases filled with fish, and that's about it.

Roy Moore Lobster Company is a gritty, fast, and real little place that's been around since 1918. It's not technically a restaurant, but a fish market that'll cook your groceries for you and give you everything you need to eat them (picks, wet naps, butter, horseradish sauce for dipping), making it one of the best lobster deals around. One of the only pre-made dishes here is the clam chowder. It's creamy-rich, packed with sweet nubs of meat, and ladled out of a kettle that you sidestep on your way to what passes for a dining room: a narrow, wooden rear deck littered with decommissioned lobster traps. Carry your still-steaming lobster out here in its red-checkered cardboard boat, or bring out your shrimp, steamers, and sometimes even crabs, or a chilled slab of smoked salmon or oily, intense mackerel. Sit yourself down on one of the

upturned crates, spread out your food on another, and make the most satisfying of messes as you peer down at the water below. Back here, the informal, cramped seating combined with the bustling activity through the open door to the market—not to mention the reward of such fresh, unfussy seafood—makes things convivial: Some eat standing up, some lean on the railing, some are invited by strangers to share a "table." Tucked far away from the foot traffic, it could be now or half a century ago.

"Roy Moore is right on Bearskin Neck—you can't miss it, it's in a building that's a little slanty, like maybe one day it's just going to fall over. Which I think is the sign of a place that serves good seafood."
—COREY TEVAN, ROCKPORT, MASSACHUSETTS

You're forgiven for thinking that the apple-cheeked man with the lumberjack beard who's ladling your chowder or pre-cracking your lobster for easy access is Roy Moore himself. He seems like a Roy, but he's really a Ken, and he looks the same now as he did in a photo taken 20 years ago that's tacked over the lobster scale. Ken Porter and his wife Karen own this place and two other restaurants in Rockport, the Fish Shack (which used to be housed above Roy Moore) and Dock Square Market.

One thing to remember is that this non-restaurant keeps store hours: The last cooking, the blackboard out front informs you, is at 5:45 PM—one more reason to pick up some fish of the day for later.

Sesuit Harbor Café

357 Sesuit Neck Road (Northside Marina), East Dennis • 508-385-6134 • Open April to September
BEST BITES: Fried scallops, mussel chowder, lobster roll, clam chowder

Bottomless cup of chowder. Do I have your attention? That's right: bottomless cup of chowder. As gimmicks go, it's a doozy–owner J.C. Cuchetti happily ladles out free refills on his signature clam chowder, full of slips of smoky mollusk and firm potato cubes, at least until you pass out from the cream. It's good, too; milky-brothed in consistency, and more typical of chowders up in Maine or New Hampshire, where J.C. heads for the winter.

It's not like Sesuit Harbor Café even needs a gimmick–it already has one of the best restaurant locations around. Plopped on a spit of land that houses the Northside Marina boatyard, it's not much to look at from the front, and the dining room has something of a community rec room feel. But duck out onto the back patio, and you'll find a dozen or so picnic tables perched at the water's edge, some right on the rocks, overlooking a tiny beach and the narrow channel where boats come and go. Because the marina is off the beaten path and its moorings are open to local residents only, the Café remains largely undiscovered by tourists.

The big blackboard of a menu is mostly sandwich-board fare, running the gamut from juicy Virginia ham to a corned beef reuben (and some vegetarian options), but check the specials board for surf. A delectable mussel chowder pops up occasionally; it's thicker than the clam, and sadly, not bottomless. Sea scallops are king here: Get them coated in a light seasoned-crumb batter and fried, or in a salad, where they're seared and nestled into fresh greens with a simple tangy dressing. Shrimp, oysters, and belly clams get the same frying treatment, with apologies to the belly-squeamish: You'll find no clam strips on the premises.

There's no straight-up lobster on the menu either, but if you can flag down J.C. (he's the charismatic guy with the ready grin and dazzling suntan), ask him about his special-event clambakes, which crop up every so often. He slips a lobster and some steamers into a net with corn and hunks of linguiça, then boils the whole affair in pots set up on the rocks out back. Hard to imagine a more ideal setting for a clambake (or a casual seaside wedding-rehearsal dinner, which is also popular here).

The Café is open for breakfast, so come by, sip some coffee, nibble on fluffy pancakes as morning breezes carry off the ocean, and watch the boats head out to sea.

Sir Cricket's Fish 'n Chips

Route 6A, near the windmill, Orleans 508-255-4453 • Open year-round
BEST BITES: Fried scallops, fried clams, clam chowder, onion rings

This fish-fry hole in the wall had me at its sign: a dapper cricket with top hat and monocle, sort of like Mr. Peanut's enigmatic cousin. I'm not sure what a cricket dressed for a debutante ball has to do with fried clams, and no one who works here ever seems to know, which just adds to the place's mystique.

I also love this restaurant because of its chairs and wall menu, proof that art can happen in the unlikeliest of places. Tiny Sir Cricket is designed for takeout, but the handful of seats come straight from the imagination of local artist Dan Joy. On-Cape and off, he creates whimsical, otherwordly set designs for the stage, and here he's brought snatches of Cape Cod history to life in color-saturated trompe l'oeil so exquisitely detailed that customers do double-takes—on my first visit I paused mid-sit, thinking I was about to tear my shorts on a rusty fish lure. Joy also painted Sir Cricket's huge menu mural, dotted with coils of rope, slabs of driftwood, and a ruddy fisherman presiding over the entire affair.

Sir Cricket fries pretty much its entire menu, using the same light crumb-based mixture to coat everything from onion rings to oysters, and letting the freshness of the seafood come through. You know batter's good when you've eaten far enough down your pint box of clams that you can see the bottom, but you don't feel like you're carrying a bag of cement mix in your belly. Whole clams or strips, oysters, scallops, shrimp, and cod (which the place is known for) can all be ordered as a roll or sandwich, as a side order (in three sizes; the large is eminently splittable), or mixed up and piled high on the Fisherman's

Platter. Clam fiends will be happy here, but I go straight for the fried oysters, same-day fresh and pungent with brine inside their crunchy shell, or the chubby scallops, barely coated at all so the pearly flesh is what you taste. This kitchen also turns out some epic onion rings, greaseless and sweet, and improved only with a single dash of malt vinegar.

On the non-fried side, there's an okay cold lobster roll, but try the crab roll instead. These aren't easy to find south of Maine, and Sir Cricket does a great version, with sweet shreds of crabmeat dressed lightly in a mayo-based mixture and stuffed into a soft, chewy bun. Rainy September days on the Cape call for some of the kitchen's straightforward New England clam chowder, medium-thick and lusciously complicated with flavors beyond clam. Lobster bisque pops up sometimes as a special; try a cup.

On your way out, slip into the Nauset Fish Market & Lobster Pool next door and pick up a slab of their peppery smoked bluefish for dinner. I like it on Triscuits, with a dot of Dijon mustard.

Patti Page and "Old Cape Cod"

One of the chairs at Sir Cricket features a painted tribute to the Singing Rage, Miss Patti Page. When the girl from a railroad shack in Muskogee, Oklahoma, recorded the song "Old Cape Cod" in a Hollywood sound booth in 1957, she'd never even set foot on the Cape—and yet her croons about ocean views and lobster stew roused seashore wanderlust from Buffalo to Boise. Covered by Sinatra, sampled by Groove Armada, the song remains the unofficial anthem of the elbow-shaped getaway, and Patti herself the Cape's unlikely ambassador.

Crib Sheet: Clams

Learning about all 2,000 clam varieties would cut into valuable clam-eating time. For the purposes of chowing your way up the seaboard, you really only need to know about two basic families.

Hard-shell clams

So called because their rounded shells are sturdy. Littlenecks are the smallest and sweetest, usually eaten raw or steamed until they pop open (in old-fashioned Italian restaurants, these are often garlicked and nestled in curls of pasta). A little bigger, cherrystones are sometimes served on the half shell, but also show up cooked in dishes like clams casino. All of the above are in the quahog (ko-hog) family, but if you specifically ask for quahogs, you'll get the largest of the bunch. These are generally minced for sauces, stuffies, and chowder—though unless a restaurant specifically refers to quahog chowder, you're likely getting a chowder made with surf or sea clams, which are different. These can be found chopped, canned, and sitting on your supermarket shelf.

Soft-shell clams

Fans of soft-shell crabs may be misled by the terminology here—you can't pop the whole thing into your mouth. These clams have white, elongated shells that are a fair bit thinner than quahog shells and so brittle, you can usually snap them in two. As a result, soft-shell clams are fragile and don't travel well. They're harvested from Labrador to North Carolina, but the conditions off Massachusetts' North Shore—combined with the region's storied clam history—have made the ones clammed in these mud flats most prized among bivalve aficionados. So much so that soft-shell clams are often called Ipswich clams, after the Cape Ann town of the same name. Other monikers include manninose, piss clam (because they squirt at you from beneath the sand), long neck, and just plain steamer and belly clam, because they're the only ones used for steamers and fried whole clams, respectively.

Union Oyster House

41 Union Street, Boston 617-227-2750 • www.unionoysterhouse.com • Open year-round
BEST BITES: Clam chowder, lazy man's lobster, shore dinner, raw bar items, homemade gingerbread

At Union Oyster House near Boston Harbor, for something in the vicinity of $20, you'll be served the Ye Olde Seafood Platter, a smorgasbord of crunchy clams, squid, white fish, and shrimp—and onion rings, because you need to eat your vegetables. In general, the more "ye olde" claims a restaurant makes, the better the odds that it's been around since cell phones, maybe Chia pets.

"I will not eat oysters. I want my food dead—not sick, not wounded—dead."
—Woody Allen

Union Oyster House actually gets to use this appellation, however: It's the oldest continuously operating restaurant in America. The Oyster House's first bowl of chowder cost 5 cents, and in those days (1826), that was kind of steep. When John F. Kennedy was a regular, he talked about how Daniel Webster had been a regular 100 years before him. When the original Oyster House opened, replacing Capen's Dry Goods Store, the building it occupied was already old—built around 1715, it had housed the first paymaster of the Continental Army. King Louis Philippe once stayed on the second floor. And yet since the Union Oyster House served its first meal, it's changed hands only twice.

Yet the pomp and circumstance are kept to a minimum—a bronze plaque flagging JFK's favorite booth is a subtle touch—and you'll find similar tradition and understatement on the menu. Chef William Coyne's kitchen is refreshingly free of cheffy flourishes, offering good broiled fish, lobster, the aforementioned fried platters, and oysters cooked in a few traditional ways (stewed to Rockefeller). Don't look for tilapia or sea bass here; all the fare is determinedly local, with just a couple of exceptions (sometimes the lobsters are Canadian). The lazy man's lobster is extravagant, with butter, sherry, and toasted breadcrumbs not really concealing spoon-sized bites of lobster meat. The gut-busting shore dinner might be renamed the

Last Request—it seems to come with one of everything on the menu (lobster, steamers, chowder—even Indian pudding or spicy gingerbread for dessert, dolloped with freshly whipped cream).

The patronage seems cleaved between those who come for the restaurant's history and old-world elegance, and those who come for the raw bar. If you're among the latter, take a seat at the demi-lune bar downstairs, select your enhancer—lemon? cocktail sauce?—and hoist your oyster fork. In a year, the restaurant turns out about 60,000 plates of oysters on the half shell. Lore has it that Webster himself used to polish off up to six plates in a sitting, with a brandy chaser.

The other standout here is the chowder, which in the early days was topped by a bowl-sized "common cracker," potpie-style. It's gone up to around $5 (though on the restaurant's 175th birthday, they rolled the prices back to that nickel), and the crackers are the standard-issue oyster kind now, but the basic recipe hasn't changed. Thicker-than-thick and rife with clams, a crock of this stuff on a cold day is like slurping a little bit of Boston history off a spoon.

"There is another well-worn controversy among chowder-lovers as to which is correct, the kind made with milk or the kind made with tomato and water . . . Who knows? Furthermore, who cares? You should eat according to your tastes, as much as possible, and, if you want to make a chowder with milk *and* tomato, and crackers *and* potatoes, do it, if the result pleases you (which sounds somewhat doubtful, but possible)."
—M. F. K. Fisher, *How to Cook a Wolf*

Village Restaurant

55 Main Street (Route 133), Essex 978-768-6400 • www.wedigclams.com • Open year-round
BEST BITES: Baked haddock, fried clams, lobster pie, Indian pudding

Admittedly, there's a special place in my heart for any restaurant whose Web site address is www.wedigclams.com, but luckily there's a lot more to love at the Village. For starters, a near-half century ago–when it was a five-booth diner–there was no lock on the restaurant's door. That way, regulars could stop in before the place opened, cook themselves breakfast, and deposit a fair payment into a cigar box on the kitchen counter.

Today, the Village is a proper restaurant (though not too proper, in the fancy-pants sense of the word). There's a lock on the door, seating for more than 200, and all meals are prepared by the staff, but little else has changed at this family-run spot. Kathleen Ricci still handles the floral arrangements, as she did the day it opened, and clam chowder is still prepared according to a recipe perfected by her grandmother, who supported her family through the Depression with her culinary expertise. Every town deserves a place like the Village–it's a casually elegant joint that caters to the locals but maintains world-class standards in the kitchen.

Modern and landlubber options abound on the multi-page menu (vegetarians and meat-and-potatoes people will have plenty to choose from), but it's the classics built on the local catch–comfort food from the sea–that are so satisfying here. Some dishes go back as many as four generations, like the sumptuous baked haddock, which Kathleen's son Mark Ricci (who runs the restaurant these days) reports is their most popular menu item by far–and the recipe of which is a well-guarded secret.

Ditto for exactly what the Riccis use to season the brittle golden shell on their transcendent fried clams (though the fact that they're fried in lard, a throwback technique less popular in these heart-healthy times, may have something to do with it). There's also an unfussy lobster pie, extravagantly rich with buttery shards of tail and claw meat beneath a toasted crumb topping, and a delectable Indian pudding, served with a scoop of high-buttercream vanilla ice cream.

On your way out, take a minute to scope the menus and other framed paraphernalia from the Village's earliest days, hanging in the foyer. A lobster dinner listed for mere dollars may hamper digestion, but it's a heartwarming thing to see the same dish you just finished listed here on a menu from 1956.

There's seating for every season at the Village. The little leaf-shaded patio is perfect in warm weather, and icy months call for a booth in one of the dark-wooded dining rooms (or even a cup of chowder at the cozy bar). But it makes an especially nice stop on a Cape Ann leaf-peeping weekend: The high-ceilinged greenhouse in the back lets you slurp and crunch your way to a full belly while gazing up and out at Essex's spectacular fall colors.

shack classic: Indian Pudding

It's easy to assume that Indian pudding was a Native American dish adapted by New England's colonists, but Boston's Durgin-Park restaurant—where the hearty dessert remains a perennial favorite—sets the record straight: It's so-named because "early settlers considered virtually anything made with corn to be Indian in nature." And corn is what it's all about. Mushy meal is gooped with molasses, then whisked with eggs and milk to form a deliciously dark, caramelly mixture that's often spiked with autumnal flavors like nutmeg and ginger. At the Village Restaurant in Essex, Massachusetts, you can order it hot or cold—either way, it's perfected with a lush scoop of vanilla ice cream.

Woodman's of Essex

121 Main Street (Route 133), Essex 978-768-6057 • www.woodmans.com • Open year-round
BEST BITES: Fried clams, quahog chowder, steamers, onion rings

Clamheads know that the best fried clams in the world are found in New England, and the best of the best are served on a short stretch of Massachusetts' Route 133 between Ipswich and Essex, otherwise known as Clam Alley. Whether Woodman's of Essex actually fries the best clam on Route 133–and therefore on earth–is a topic of endless heated debate, but it's somewhat beside the point. What really matters is that Woodman's fried the *first* clam.

The bivalve met bubbling lard here on July 3, 1916, in a happy experiment (see sidebar) that would change the face of New England cuisine and the cholesterol count of generations to come. Since then, the Woodman family has grown Bessie and Lawrence "Chubby" Woodman's roadside donut and potato-chip shack into a staggering empire of the clam.

Consider the numbers: On an average week in July, some 20,000 hungry patrons pass through these doors, for whom the kitchen has been known to fry some 60–100 gallons of local soft-shell clams a day. And it's not all about clams, either. On a summer afternoon, there's a lot going on at Woodman's: Multiple lines are forming at the ordering counter inside for everything from crab rolls to the award-winning chowder; lobsters are being piled into pounds or cookers by the roadside as cars slow for a look; oysters are being shucked at the raw bar upstairs (pronounced "shocked" in Essex-ese); tourists are loading up on souvenirs at the marshside gift shop; someone's in the office taking orders for a wedding clambake; and in the middle of it all, nine of the largest Fry-o-lators known to man are pumping out seafood, fries, and lip-smacking onion rings. And keeping all this humming are the cheeriest of staffers, most of whom are Woodmans by blood or marriage: Last year Larry Woodman, Chubby's grandson, sent out W-2s to no fewer than 52 members of his family.

So what to eat besides those clams? Some love the pillowy clamcakes, filled with Ipswich nubs. Others like Woodman's New England–style clam chowder (made mostly with quahogs), thin-brothed and slightly sweet.

The lobster roll is a hearty standout, the buttery toast of the bread doing justice to lightly mayonnaised meat—nothing else. If you want a whole lobster, head outside and ask whoever's manning the cookers to boil you one fresh (the massive volume of patrons can sometimes mean pre-cooked bugs are given a plunge into heat just before serving, which changes the flavor). You can also order steamers out here, light and tender, perfectly briny, and crying out for a quick dip in that ramekin of butter. Larry Woodman orders his steamer clams bigger than his fryer clams, about $2^1/_2$ to 3 inches long (fry these, he says, and the bellies can get overwhelming). All the fried seafood, clams included, is done in a mixture of flour and cornmeal, but the onion rings get their own puffy batter, which browns to a much darker crunch.

Wait for your number to be called, carry your cardboard tray (usually the bottom half of a Miller beer carton) out to the sea of tables, and chow down on history. And hoist your pint to Chubby Woodman, without whom clams and crunch might still be strangers.

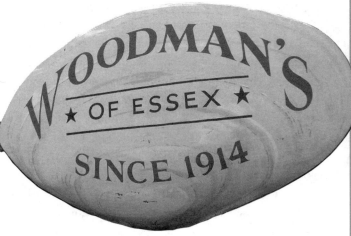

shack lore:
Chubby Woodman and the first fried clam

Some have contested Woodman's boast of the first fried clam, saying they have proof it happened in some other kitchen. It's possible, but when it comes right down to it, are you really going to dispute the claim of a man named Chubby? Here's how it went down, in the words of Chubby's grandson (and namesake) Larry:

"My grandfather loved being out on the water. He opened a shack here in 1914; he dug clams on the flats of the Essex River in the morning, sold them in the shell. He fried donuts and potato chips, too, but his profits weren't quite what he'd hoped. One day, a fisherman named Tarr—no one remembers his first name—came in from West Gloucester and ordered some potato chips. He told my grandfather they were so good, he should try frying one of the clams. So he did, and it was good. He fried more the next day—July Fourth—and for the first time Chubby ran out of clams halfway through the day. He made thirty-five dollars, and that was that. Ever since then, the Fourth has been our busiest day of the year."

Additional Listings

Aquinnah

The Aquinnah
27 Aquinnah Circle • 508-645-3867

There are charter fishing captains and oyster farmers in the Vanderhoop family, which owns this more than 50-year-old landmark. In other words, this is some seriously fresh seafood, served with incredible views of the Gay Head Cliffs off the open porch.

Boston

B&G Oysters, Ltd.
550 Tremont Street • 617-423-0550

There may be track lighting at this sexy South End spot, but the point of the place cuts through its chichi allure: spanking-fresh fish and shellfish, served by a staff that seriously knows (and loves) its stuff. Worship at the raw bar or try the lobster BLT.

The Barking Crab
88 Sleeper Street (Northern Avenue Bridge)
617-426-CRAB

The food has its frowners, but as far as ambience and location go, the Crab has Boston's other seafood eateries beat claws-down. Enjoy breezes off the water in the outdoor tent, which becomes one big wharf party on summer weekends.

Durgin-Park
Faneuil Hall Marketplace • 617-227-2038
www.durgin-park.com

Their motto? "Established Before You Were Born"—more than 130 years ago. Settle family-style at long tables and dig into a big menu with a small but stalwart selection of old-fashioned seafood favorites. Finish with an apple pan dowdy, just to say you did.

Jimbo's Fish Shanty
42 Northern Avenue • 617-542-5600
www.jimmysharborside.com

Created as a mellow, shack-food alternative to the adjoining Jimmy's Harborside Restaurant on historic Fish Pier.

Bourne

Bourne Lobster Trap
290 Shore Road • 508-759-6400

Tuck into a full menu of laid-back shack goods as you take in the water traffic on Buzzards Bay.

Brewster

Brewster Inn and Chowder House
Route 6A • 508-896-7771

This sweet, old-fashioned cottage has a loyal following for its chowders, but bigger appetites call for some snowy broiled Chatham scrod or the homey Yankee pot roast.

Chatham

Impudent Oyster
15 Chatham Bars Avenue • 508-945-3545
www.impudentoyster.com

Casual seafood can be hard to find in tony Chatham, but this lively pub delivers. Try Yesterday's Quahog Chowder, so-named because it steeps a day for flavor.

Cohasset

The Olde Salt House
40 Border Street • 781-383-2203

It proves the rule that if they call it Olde, it's really Newe—but I still like the seafood at this mellow, sophisticated waterside pub.

Eastham

Eastham Lobster Pool
Route 6 • 508-255-9706

When you've thrilled to the freshness of your grilled, broiled, fried, stuffed, poached, or rolled seafood, swing by the fish market to ogle the 1,000-foot lobster tank.

Edgartown

Edgartown Seafood Market
138 Cooke Street • 508-627-3791

Pick up a swordfish slab for dinner and a little something—like a tasty lobster roll—to eat on the spot.

Navigator Restaurant & Boathouse Bar

2 Main Street (on the harbor), Edgartown
508-627-4320

Quick bites downstairs, fuller plates topside, and a wonderful view from both of Edgartown Harbor.

Essex

Essex Seafood

143 Eastern Avenue (Route 133)
978-768-7233

Blink and you'll miss it—a tragedy, because this unfrilly fish house-cum-lobster pound maintains the highest of standards.

Fairhaven

Fairhaven Chowder House

1 David Drown Boulevard • 508-996-4100

Fish chowder, smoked seafood chowder—you name it, the Fairhaven chowders it, usually with a thick cream base. The Maine crabcakes, all sherried up in Newburg sauce, are supreme.

Gene's Seafood

146 Huttleston Avenue (Route 6)
508-996-5127

Platters overflow with excellently fried seafood at this unobtrusive restaurant, tucked away in a shopping plaza on the eastern side of New Bedford Harbor.

Gloucester

Amelia's Subs & Seafoods

78 Thatcher Road • 978-281-8855

Generous golden seafood plates and broiled fish dinners. Try the fried fish cheeks.

Boulevard Ocean View

25 Western Avenue
978-281-2949

Shack standards with a Portuguese touch rule here, and there's a good halibut chowder. Snag a deck seat for sweeping views of the harbor, or get your goods to go from the takeout window and wander to a bench near the Gloucester Fisherman statue.

Hyannis

Spanky's Clam Shack & Seaside Saloon

138 Ocean Avenue • 508-771-2770
www.spankysclamshack.com

If clams had arms, the Red Sox cap–wearing cartoon bivalve on the sign at this Hyannis Harbor newcomer would be cradling a can of Bud.

Marblehead

Flynnie's at the Beach

Ocean Avenue • 781-639-3035

The seasonal Devereux Beach outpost of the original Flynnie's on Marblehead's Atlantic Avenue serves a menu that's pure sandside shack.

Mashpee

The Raw Bar

252 Shore Drive • 508-539-4858
www.therawbar.com

The Raw Bar calls its shore dinner the Lobster Feed Bag: bug, chowder, steamers, corn, and kielbasa. There's also a mayo-and-meat lobster roll so huge, they use an ice cream scoop to garnish it.

Mattapoisett

Oxford Creamery

98 County Road (Route 6) • 508-758-3847

The Creamery serves a solid lobster roll (and a good lin-guiça roll) and some of the best ice cream around. Get it to go and head to nearby Ned's Point Lighthouse.

Turk's Seafood

83 Marion Road • 508-758-3117

A recently added sushi bar raised some eyebrows, but don't be fooled: This place is all about seafood classics, fried and boiled.

Menemsha

The Galley of Menemsha

515 North Road • 508-645-9819

The Galley hasn't closed since the 1950s, and it's known around here for serving a doozy of a lobster roll and scooping excellent cones.

Menemsha Fish Market

54 Basin Road • 508-645-2282
www.menemshafishmarket.com

Like Larsen's next door, this straight-up fish market—formerly Pooles—cooks some of its wares on the spot.

Nantucket Town

The Galley

54 Jefferson Avenue • 508-228-9641

It's been an island favorite since 1958, but these days chic chefs give claws and fins a sophisticated mien at this otherwise unassuming waterside cottage next to the Cliffside Beach Club.

Sayle's Seafood

99 Washington Avenue • 508-228-4599

Local fisherman Charlie Sayles short-orders just-caught seafood at this wee takeout shack outside of town.

Newburyport

Michael's Harborside

One Tournament Wharf • 978-462-7785
www.michaelsharborside.com

A sweeping double-decker eatery right on the water with low-key dishes and lively, liquored-up evenings.

Orleans

Land Ho!

Route 6A at Cove Road • 508-487-1811

Don't be fooled by the "Snappy Attire" sign outside–this salty pub is casual in the extreme, with a menu of seafood dishes scrawled in chalk over the bar. Try the broiled bluefish or some local oysters on the half shell.

Liam's

Nauset Beach Road • 508-255-3474

Most of the standards are lovable at this Nauset Beach snack shack, but it's the delicately battered onion hoops that earned Liam's its nickname: Lord of the Rings.

Young's Fish Market

Rock Harbor Road • 508-255-3366

Grab a lobster roll too good to be this cheap out of a one-room hut plopped in a parking lot next to Rock Harbor.

Plymouth

Lobster Hut

Town Pier • 508-746-2270

Under the green-striped canopy out back, nosh through your lobster, steamers, and fried bites while you watch boats bob in Plymouth Harbor.

Wood's Seafood Restaurant

Town Pier • 508-746-0261

www.woodsseafoods.com

This market-cum-shack serves classics, done well, with no frills whatsoever. Ask them about the blue lobster.

Provincetown

Clem and Ursie's

85 Shankpainter Road • 508-487-2333

www.clemandursies.com

Provincetown's Portuguese roots are showing at this wildly popular hangout—Dad's squid stew and catfish vinho dahlos share the menu with the Hot, Lazy Lobster Roll.

Napi's

7 Freeman Street • 508-487-1145

You'll need a year to read the menu at Napi's, which calls itself "Provincetown's most unusual restaurant." Very good fish and seafood dishes, many with a Portuguese flair.

Quincy

The Clam Box
789 Quincy Shore Drive • 617-773-6677

Not to be confused with the legendary Clam Box of Ipswich, this little restaurant nevertheless does right by the bivalve, served up golden and crunchy in a no-frills, Formica'd atmosphere.

Tony's Clam Shop
861 Quincy Shore Drive (on Wollaston Beach)
617-773-5090
www.tonysclamshop.com

Good, creamy clam chowder, thick skin-on fries, and a popular fried lobster plate are all fuel for an afternoon of rays at Wollaston Beach.

Rockport

Ellen's Harborside
1 T Wharf • 978-546-2512
www.ellensharborside.com

A throwback dining room where hungry patrons tuck in to cheap bowls of sultry chowder, made the same way by three generations of Balzarinis since 1954.

The Fish Shack
21 Dock Square • 978-546-6667

The owners of nearby Roy Moore Lobster Company moved the Shack from the cramped quarters the two eateries shared to this roomier spot. Lots of casual seafood favorites on deck here.

Portside Chowder House-n-Grille
7 Tuna Wharf • 978-546-7045

You'll find good chowder at this crusty old place on Bearskin Neck. Stop by Helmut's Strudel Shop next door for dessert.

Rowley

Agawam Diner
Route 1 at Route 133 • 978-948-7780

Not a shack, but a shiny throwback that serves seafood chowder alongside diner classics; they bake their world-famous pies–the kind that make you cry–right in the back.

Salem

Bob's Famous Fried Clams

429 Highland Avenue (Route 107)
978-744-9366

It's a dowdy bungalow on a decidedly un-picturesque stretch of road, but the fried clams became famous for a reason.

The Lobster Shanty

25 Front Street • 978-745-5449

When you're all witched out from your tour of Salem's unsavory past, gather fuel on the little brick patio at this casual seafood spot.

Salisbury

Footes Ice Cream

159 Beach Road • 978-462-7376

It's the double coating of batter that's earned Foote's fried clams a loyal following.

Lena's Seafood

131 Rabbit Road • 978-465-8572

Turn in at the giant whale for light-as-can-be fried seafood plates and dining-hall charm.

Vineyard Haven

John's Fish Market / Sandy's Fish & Chips
State Road • 508-693-1220

As the name says, it's all about the fish and chips here–though the fried clams aren't bad, either. Call in your order to avoid the line.

The Net Result
79 Beach Road (at Tisbury Marketplace)
508-693-6071

www.mvseafood.com

Another excellent fish market–this one recently expanded–owned by one of the Larsen family (this one's Louie) and offering fantastic, fresh takeout.

Westport

Handy Hill Creamery
55 Hix Bridge Road (at Route 88)
508-636-8888

Look for the blue-striped awning in a clearing and an old diner car in the parking lot, and get in line for satisfying seafood rolls, stuffed quahogs, and ice cream any way imaginable.

Way Back Eddy
Bridge Road (at Horseneck Beach)
508-636-9055

Unlike the elegantly casual Back Eddy across the street, where sophisticated seafood is the norm, this shacky spinoff will serve you in your swimming trunks. Try the fried fish or pulled pork sandwiches with some dirty chips on the side.

West Yarmouth

Captain Parker's Pub

668 Main Street (Route 28) • 508-771-4266

Colorful, noisy alehouse on Swan Pond Marsh known for two things: being a local cop favorite (just look at the patches on the walls) and winning more ribbons for its thick clam chowder than anyone can count.

Jerry's Seafood & Dairy Freeze

654 Main Street (Route 28) • 508-775-9752

Clamheads are especially excited when they learn that Jerry's, a hole in the wall that fries a milestone bivalve, is open year-round.

Wellfleet

The Beachcomber

1120 Cahoon Hollow Road • 508-349-6055
www.thebeachcomber.com

An 1897 lifesaving station-turned-party zone, the 'Comber is perched atop a dune that slopes 75 feet down to Cahoon Hollow Beach. The food takes a back seat to live music and dancing, but it's fun to slurp down some raw bar bites before hitting the dance floor.

Bookstore and Restaurant

Kendrick Avenue • 508-349-3154
www.bookstorerestaurant.com

Paw through box after box of bargain-priced old books, and then settle in for a terrific lobster roll or a hunk of grilled swordfish.

PJ's Family Restaurant

Route 6 • 508-349-2126

A Cape Cod favorite for their extra-reasonable, grease-less fried seafood platters and family-friendly cafeteria ambience.

Woods Hole

Fishmonger's Café

56 Water Street • 508-540-5376

Have a heavenly crock of fisherman's stew and a slice of banana cheesecake by the water.

Shuckers

91a Water Street (down Cobble Way)
508-540-3850

Grab a waterside seat and pair a few goods from the raw bar with the house's own brew, the Nobska Light–as in lighthouse, not low-calorie.

new hampshire

4

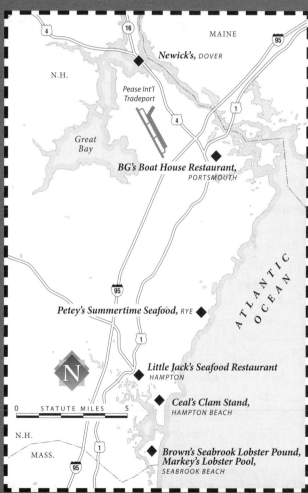

MAINE

N.H.

Newick's, DOVER

Pease Int'l
Tradeport

Great
Bay

BG's Boat House Restaurant,
PORTSMOUTH

A T L A N T I C   O C E A N

Petey's Summertime Seafood, RYE

N

Little Jack's Seafood Restaurant
HAMPTON

0   STATUTE MILES   5

Ceal's Clam Stand,
HAMPTON BEACH

N.H.

MASS.

Brown's Seabrook Lobster Pound,
Markey's Lobster Pool,
SEABROOK BEACH

BG's Boat House Restaurant

191 Wentworth Road, Portsmouth 603-431-1074 • Open mid-March to October
BEST BITES: Fried smelts, fried oysters, Portsmouth seafood chowder, baked stuffed sole

Tucked away in cozy, brick and ivy-filled Portsmouth–said to have more eateries per capita than any town in New England–BG's is the kind of place that makes you want to own a boat. If you did, you could wake up on a Saturday morning and decide to rev your engine or shake down your sails and head over to BG's, where you could order a pile of fried saltwater smelts, zest them with a drop or two of juicy lemon, and dip them in Jeff Graves's homemade tartar sauce, all while watching the world go by from your deck. These tiny, succulent fish get a milk bath before being dipped into a dry breading and tossed into the bubbling fat. The result is superbly crunchy with a hint of brine: the potato chip of the sea. Frying also does justice to sweet oysters from the shores of Maine at the nearly 30-year-old restaurant.

No boat? No problem. Grab a spot on one of the decks, from which you can still enjoy the bustle of BG's own marina, and ask for some plump steamed mussels, and maybe a cup of the Portsmouth seafood chowder. In a sublime and frustrating twist, this magnificent stuff is never exactly the same twice, because the kitchen makes it with whatever looked good and stew-worthy at the market that morning. Generally speaking, the chowder gets a hefty helping of haddock and scallops, and a smoky, peppery kick from bacon and Old Bay–that, a few other magical ingredients, and enough cream to leave you comatose.

If you're feeling fancier, try the baked stuffed sole, where the fish's pearly flesh is paired with a mixture that seems effortlessly simple but is really a labor-intensive medley involving fresh vegetables (mushrooms make it earthy), sea scallops, little shrimp, and a generous coating of buttery Ritz crumbs.

There's also a full battery of pub grub–mozzarella sticks and jalapeño poppers and the like–and one hell of a burger.

Ten Meals with a View

A day-old Pop-Tart would taste pretty good if you ate it on a wharf in Maine. These 10 spots already serve excellent eats; factor in their plum waterside location and the result is seafood shack nirvana.

1. *Larsen's Fish Market,* Menemsha, MA
Shop here for your picnic, then pop around back to suck down your oysters or lobster roll while watching rusty lobster boats bob in Vineyard Sound.

2. *The Lobster Shack* (at Two Lights),
Cape Elizabeth, ME
So-nicknamed because you crack your claws right on the water, with a lighthouse to your left and another to your right.

3. *The Black Pearl,* Newport, RI
More than 9,000 boats call lovely Newport Harbor home. Start counting as you sip the Black Pearl's legendary chowder.

4. *Abbott's Lobster in the Rough,* Noank, CT
Get lucky and you might land a glimpse of the antique Mystic Whaler schooner gliding by from your dockside picnic table.

5. *Tidal Falls Lobster,* Hancock, ME
Reserve the Captain's Deck, a one-table overlook, and have the spectacle of the roiling, reversing tide of Frenchman Bay (and the occasional baby seal) all to yourself.

6. *BG's Boat House,* Portsmouth, NH
You can dock (or drive) and dine at this sweet fish house with its own marina in Portsmouth's Sagamore Creek.

7. *Five Islands Lobster Company,* Georgetown, ME
From this working wharf, gawk at the five islands of Five Islands, a vista that inspired artists from Marsden Hartley to Gaston Lachaise.

8. *Lobster Pool* on Folly Cove, Rockport, MA
This place really hops just before sunset, when locals and visitors flock for the Pool's rare view west over the ocean on Ipswich Bay.

9. *The Dip Net,* Port Clyde, ME
Definition of the good life: bouillabaisse downed on a wharf in quaint Port Clyde before you hop the ferry to Monhegan Island.

10. *Eaton's Lobster Pool,* Little Deer Isle, ME
This ultra-remote spot has a stunning view of Penobscot Bay and the Camden Hills, a fireplace for chilly evenings, and fresh, simple shore dinners.

Brown's Seabrook Lobster Pound

Route 286, Seabrook Beach 603-474-3331 • www.brownslobster.com
Open year-round (weekends only Nov. to April) • BEST BITES: Boiled lobster, steamers, fried shrimp

The vast shore-hall dining room was a beautiful sight. To my left, a few clusters of families had arrived straight from the beach, with kids in bathing suits and sunburns, racing each other to the lobster tanks. To my right, an entire wedding party had just settled in–guys in tuxes loosened their bow ties as women in satin kicked off their heels under the picnic table, and the bride wound her veil around one arm so it wouldn't get covered in butter. And everywhere you looked, people pulled their liquor out of brown paper bags (there were crates of champagne near the newly-weds) as they tore into fat, steaming red lobsters.

That's the score at Brown's Lobster Pound, a drafty, butter-yellow restaurant with red trim on a salt marsh, right across the border from Massachusetts. It's about as fancy as the cafeteria at your son's sleepaway camp. It's big, it's boisterous, and it thrums to the constant cooking, serving, and eating of fresh seafood, simply prepared and gobbled in the rough. Within these walls, not much else matters, and that's how it's been since Bruce Brown started the place (he and wife Cynthia still run it) more than 50 years ago. There's work involved: steamers must be ordered from one station, lobsters by the pound from another, and fried foods from a takeout window outside. Drinks (the nonalcoholic kind) are procured still elsewhere, and after all this you still need to stake out one of the premium-demand picnic tables. But it's all part of the fun, and Brown's is one of just a few lobster pounds that stay open all year (in the colder months, Brown's cuts back to mostly weekend service, so be sure to call ahead). From November to April, things are considerably less frenzied, and the seafood is even tastier.

Brown's took the blue ribbon for its lobster roll at the Hampton Beach Seafood Festival up the coast, but very little beats a plain, boiled-to-order lobster here. To start with, these aren't lethargic lobsters. Watch the snapping fuss your bug kicks up—an excellent sign of freshness— when the guy manning the cookers fishes it out of the tank. (This explains why the kitchen also turns out a pretty good lobster bisque, rosy and creamy, bobbing with tiny nubs of meat.) The steamers are equally winning. Extra large-sized, the clams were clutching on to a few grains of sand that washed out with a swirl in the broth, leaving nothing but a sweet mouthful of tender, briny mollusk. You'll run out of steamers before you run out of melted butter, which will have absorbed the clammy flavor by the time the last empty shell hits your tray—you'll be tempted to just upend the rest like a shot.

The fried menu is extensive and solid, and everything from the basics (native clams, haddock, scallops) to the more unusual (small, juicy oysters, and nuggets of lobster claw and tail meat) comes in three portion sizes (the large is mammoth). The shrimp's a standout: firm curls in a light, crispy-dry batter that doesn't overwhelm the shrimp-ness of the meat. You'll also find burger-and-dog fare for the picky child.

shack staple: Tartar Sauce

Fried fish without tartar sauce? Perish the thought. It's named for the Tatars, who hung out in Mongolia around the 5th century A.D. and created all sorts of fun culinary traditions, like tenderizing raw meat by tucking it under their saddles before heading off somewhere far (and thus, steak tartare was born). In its simplest form, tartar sauce as Americans know it is a mix of mayonnaise and pickle relish, and most seafood shacks serve perfectly good commercial versions (Heinz's is popular). Others make theirs from scratch—capers, minced green olives, and spices from thyme to tarragon sneak into twists on tartar along the coast.

Ceal's Clam Stand

22 Ocean Boulevard (Route 1A), Hampton Beach 603-474-3150 • Open Memorial Day to Labor Day
BEST BITES: Fried clams, lobster rolls, milkshakes and frappes

Growing up in Newburyport, Massachusetts, Cecelia Littlefield–Ceal–crossed the New Hampshire border to spend her summers here at Seabrook Beach. In 1948, after she'd been uninspired by a string of jobs (including bookkeeping for Singer Sewing Machines), she turned pleasure into business and opened a small seafood shack on Route 1A, where she served the kind of food she wanted to eat at the beach: haddock and fries, onion rings, and clams.

When she wasn't tending to her rose garden, Ceal was in the kitchen of this tiny white building with the snappy red trim, running it for more than 50 years until she died in 2000. Today, the lines are long at this local landmark, an old-fashioned oasis of great fried seafood and lobster rolls at the end of a busy boardwalk strip where pizza, fried dough, and thongs are more the norm. Veal cutlets and Syrian subs round out the menu of clam-shack fare at Ceal's, where you can wash it all down with a thick strawberry shake, a mocha frappe, or an icy pineapple slush, then pop next door to Ceal's Cold Creations for a lick of Maine-made Gifford's ice cream.

crib sheet: Soft-Shell Crab

A blue crab fished along the Gulf and Atlantic coasts during molting season (from May to early fall). It's caught less than 12 hours after shedding its hard shell, and its new one is thin enough that you can eat the whole crab, shell and all. Usually served lightly floured and fried, often in a sandwich; sometimes grilled.

Little Jack's Seafood Restaurant

539 Ocean Boulevard (Route 1A), Hampton Beach 603-926-8053 • Open May to October
BEST BITES: Daily Catch specials, prime rib, fried sole

When you've had your fill of Blink's Fry Doe (sic), when you've done karaoke at Lupo's and dribbled away some cash at Skeeball and Pokereno in the Playland Arcade, when your henna tattoo's starting to fade and you don't want to get anything else pierced, it's time to ditch the 24-hour parade of pleasure-seekers on the Hampton Beach Boardwalk and head north to Little Jack's for some fried fish and a beer.

Not that this three-decades-old mainstay isn't hopping. The new owner, Mike Welcome, bought the place after its founder and namesake (and much-loved local character) Reggie Jacques died a few years ago, and he vowed to keep things largely unchanged. That "Immediate Seating Available" sign out front is no joke: Jack's is a 400-seat train station of a restaurant. The ordering window out front is where everything happens, and it can get chaotic; if you ask for lobster or steamers, pick these up inside.

The menu is just as endless, a smorgasbord of old-school favorites designed to fulfill any baked, broiled, fried, and sandwiched surf or turf craving you could possibly have. Check the "Fresh Daily Catch" board by the main door for a list of what just came in, the best bets on the menu at any given time. Try the New England Fisherman's Chowder, a creamy concoction brimming with fresh fish, usually haddock and sole. Or test your endurance with the Catch-22 Platter, which Jack's claims is the largest mixed seafood plate on the East Coast. It comes with belly clams, surf clams (dragged from the ocean floor, not dug from flats), haddock, sole (exceptionally good), baby shrimp, fantail not-so-baby shrimp, and sea scallops. It's all-fried, all-the-time, inexplicably served with garlic bread, a hair shy of $40, and could comfortably feed three or four people, or six on a diet. On the menu of sides, skip the blah rice pilaf and go for the onion rings, medium-thick hoops with a snappy, sweet interior. Jack's also has a homey herb-roasted chicken, and is known up and down the coast for its astounding slow-cooked prime rib–the perfect antidote to too many seafood meals in a row.

Once your order's been called, try to grab a seat in the charming weathered-wood upstairs dining area or at one of the picnic tables outside, near a line of beautiful, beat-up rowboats that have been relegated to the parking lot.

Markey's Lobster Pool

Route 286, Seabrook Beach 603-474-2851 • Open year-round (Fri. to Sun. only from Oct. to April)
BEST BITES: Steamers, fried lobster, lobster roll, onion rings

Lobster lovers, don't panic when you see the line–and you'll see it, snaking out from the glass doors under the blue awnings, sometimes curling all the way around the building to the marsh. These patient people want the Pool's legendary fried eats, big red-checkered cardboard boats of dry-battered clams, scallops, haddock, and oysters.

If you've come to Markey's Lobster Pool ("Maaahkey's" for short) with lobster on the brain, this line has nothing to do with you. Excuse yourself through it and proceed directly to a counter underneath the Lobster Pound sign, where a man–if you're lucky, one wearing the lobster-claw antlers–will help you choose your rascal, add steamers and corn or not, and ask you to wait until your number's called. Try the steamers; Markey's does a flawless job of processing all the sand out, resulting in clean, sweet, gritless bites, and their quarts are closer to a quart and a half. Without the other window's pressure to order and get out of the way, you can hang out here and peer into the tanks of live lobsters–Markey's even has a few crates abutting the tanks to give its tiniest viewers a boost.

You'll still have to brave the line if you like your lobster fried (a Markey's specialty, tasting a bit like the largest shrimp you've ever eaten) or rolled (bulging with meat given the lightest coating of mayonnaise), or if, like most folks, you're after an order of clams and rings. Confer with fellow eaters beforehand: Markey's portions are colossal, and this stuff doesn't reheat well or taste good cold, so agree to split your order or prepare to be faced with left-overs. Not that they'd go to waste. Out back where tables overlook the tidal marsh are gulls by the hundreds, circling like taxis at an airport, all waiting for you to surrender the rest of your meal. Throw a french fry skyward and the birds will battle it out in mid-air; drop it into the murky water below and see if the fish get there first.

Newick's

431 Dover Point Road, Dover 603-742-3205 • www.newicks.com • Open year-round
BEST BITES: Bay scallop pie, crab roll, original clam chowder, Fisherman's Platter

I have only hearsay to back this up, but word on the seacoast is that one of the oldest men in America, a 112-year-old Mainer, was a regular at the South Portland outpost of this New Hampshire landmark before he moved to New York in his twilight years. There, he promptly died, likely because he couldn't get his hands on Newick's Fisherman's Platter, a deep-fried symphony of everything that's locally caught, and big enough for three people of average appetite, or me and my dog if we skipped breakfast. (There's a smaller version available, too.)

The platter is a favorite here, at the original Newick's, a broad gray building up the river from Portsmouth in Dover.

Owner Jack Newick started out simply doing what the Newick family did: They lobstered, selling their catch to local shops and eateries. Towards the end of World War II, whatever didn't sell was brought home, cooked up in their own kitchen, and sold as takeout from a cobbled-together stand by the side of the road here on Dover Point. This moonlighting business became so popular that Jack decided to pursue it full-time, building a restaurant with a fish market on the side.

Though it was rebuilt after a fire in the '80s, the vast dining room has an old sleepaway camp mess-hall feel to it, with checker-clothed trestle tables by the dozens (the place seats 500). And yet, on a summery Friday night, you may still have a short wait for a table–bide your time poking around the gift shop up front, or looking over the photos of milestone Newick family catches like a 700-pound tuna, reeled in after a three-and-a-half-hour fight. Or peruse the fish market and lobster tanks: Everything here is on the menu in some form or other.

I love how Newick's has two kinds of clam chowder, both of them New England–style, both insanely clam-heavy: Order the "original" for a lighter cream base, and ask for it thick if you want it that way. They've won awards throughout the region, and they're completely addictive, as is the lighter, brothy fish chowder.

I've also caught myself daydreaming about the bay scallop pie. It's straightforward stuff, just fresh, pearly scallops drenched in sweet butter and topped with Newick's take on the ever-popular Ritz crumb mixture. They pop it into the oven until everything bubbles and the crumbs get all toasty (a different version swaps lobster for scallops). Lighter appetites might try the excellent Maine crab roll, fresh-picked shreds with a whisper of mayo on a butter-basted bun.

Snag a window table for an eyeful of water views, including the stacks of colorful crates on a little wharf ended by a listing fish shack, and sometimes a bobbing lobster boat belonging to Newick's son. You can also cradle your cardboard tray, head out onto the sloping banks, and cop a squat in the grass if you're not wearing a skirt.

Petey's Summertime Seafood

1323 Ocean Boulevard (Route 1A), Rye 603-433-1937 • www.peteys.net • Open mid-March to mid-November • BEST BITES: Seafood chowder, fried scallops, lobster pie

New Hampshire has a paltry 18 miles of shoreline, and it takes advantage of every last yard. The state's oceanfront is more or less one long beachy boardwalk, so it makes sense that some of the seacoast's favorite seafood joints seem more suited to Myrtle Beach than New England.

In that spring-break spirit, things can get seriously rowdy at Petey's, a double-decker restaurant in Rye that looks like it was cobbled together in a day and propped two car lanes from the beach (and a curious old shipwreck). There's a takeout shop off to the side designed specifically for hungry beachgoers to grab a quick shrimp basket or soft-serve cone before heading back to their towels, and a small ground-floor bar and dining room packed with wooden booths and the usual passel of maritime props. But it's upstairs that Petey's truly comes alive. Follow the creaky stairs strung with decommissioned lobster buoys (some bearing their boat's name) up to the huge indoor-outdoor bar, a terrific perch from which to enjoy the sunset, a fruity drink, and some deeply satisfying junk food.

crib sheet: Lobster Buoys

Small bobbing shapes on the ocean's surface that are attached to lobster traps below, enabling lobstermen to locate theirs. The colors and patterns on a buoy correspond to the same on a lobstermen's boat, which helps prevent trap poaching. Also used in eateries to create insta-shack ambience.

Those wishing there was a T.G.I. Friday's this close to the water will beeline for the jalapeño poppers, potato skins, and spicy waffle fries, but the real jackpot at Petey's is the fried seafood menu. Everything that used to swim, burrow in sand, or crawl the ocean floor can be had solo, in a basket with severely crispy french fries, and in virtually every configuration imaginable for your artery-clogging pleasure. (Though locals agree that the sea scallops win, with the belly clams—which come exclusively from the muddy flats of Essex, Massachusetts—running a close second.)

There's also plenty of lobster on this menu. Have it in a lobster salad roll served on a hamburger bun. Try the Baked Stuffed Lobster Pie & Butter, a crumb-roofed casserole with the decency to call out its key and most copious ingredient right there in the name. Plain old—and very good—boiled lobster can be had as small as 1 pound (for the small-waisted and the coy) and as big as 10 pounds (the mind reels).

Whatever you get, pair it with a bowl of Petey's famous seafood chowder. Its consistency nicely marks the transition between the legendarily thick Massachusetts chowders to the south and Maine's penchant for milky stews to the north. Bobbing in this buttery, intensely seafoody liquid are scallops, clams, haddock, lobster, and whatever else the kitchen threw in that day. It can get a little warm up here to be eating soup; thankfully, there are a few movie set–sized fans strategically placed in the tented room to keep things civilized.

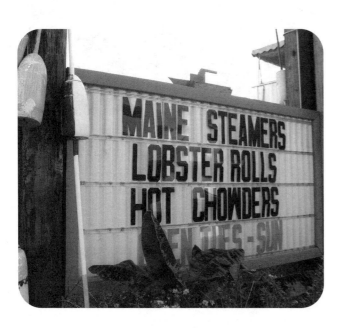

Ten Fried Bites
worth a detour

The Italians have a saying: *Fritta è buona anche una ciabatta*—even a slipper would taste good if you fried it. Probably true, but some fried bites are better than others, and few things complement a crunchy shell of batter like a burst of seafood (or onion) flavor within. These 10 dishes are worth every last calorie.

1. *Haddock,* Westfair Fish and Chips, Westport, CT

2. *Belly clams,* Clam Box, Ipswich, MA

3. *Smelts,* BG's Boathouse, Portsmouth, NH

4. *Oysters,* Arnold's, Eastham, MA

5. *Clamcakes,* Aunt Carrie's, Narragansett, RI

6. *Scallops,* Bagaduce Lunch, Brookville, ME

7. *Calamari,* Flo's Clam Shack, Middletown, RI

8. *Flounder,* The Bite, Menemsha, MA

9. *Shrimp,* Sir Cricket's Fish 'n Chips, Orleans, MA

10. *Onion rings,* Spinney's, Phippsburg, ME

Nancy Drew and the Case of the *Blue Lobster*

The odds of a lobster being born blue—as opposed to the standard greenish brown—are about one in three to four million. Add the fact that the unusually bright color makes them even more vulnerable to prey, and the odds of pulling a blue bug out of the water (even with 46 million pounds of lobster being caught off the Maine coast every year) are slim indeed.

Why so blue? According to Boston's New England Aquarium, the color can usually be attributed to a genetic mutation whereby the shell's standard three-pigment blue/red/yellow balance simply isn't. Yellow lobsters are even rarer: Roughly one in 30 million. There are calico lobsters and lobsters of two different colors—and then there are white lobsters, ones born with no pigment whatsoever. These albino critters are the only exception to a rule whereby cooking changes the color of a lobster's shell, dissolving the bond between its red pigment and protein containing other pigments. In other words, whether it starts out brown, yellow, blue, or pink with purple polka dots, a lobster on a dinner plate will always be the same color: red.

And while some high-end restaurateurs in places like New York City boast a blue lobster dish simply for the sought-after factor (most blues caught in the Northeast wind up at aquariums, living out their days as minor educational celebrities), the egomania of eating this sweet freak of nature is driven home at Shaw's Wharf, in New Harbor, Maine. There, a blue lobster is preserved in a cage (next to his less-fortunate,

ready-for-the-steamer brown brethren) atop which is a sign that reads: "This is a blue lobster. No, we are not going to cook him. But if we did, he'd taste exactly the same."

Additional Listings

Derry

Clam Haven

Route 28 • 603-434-4679

www.clamhaven.com

The Haven's a little farther from the coast than most, but the fried favorites (and the ice cream flurries) at this cute takeout are worth the detour.

Hampton

McGuirk's Seaview Restaurant

95 Ocean Boulevard (Route 1A)

603-926-7000

McGuirk's may be Irish-flavored, but its lobster baguette is always a Hampton Seafood Fest favorite.

The Old Salt

490 Lafayette Road • 603-926-0330

www.oldsaltnh.com

The restaurant at Lamie's Inn looks stuffy at first, but the menu is packed with reasonable, delish seafood stalwarts like fried baskets, raw bar goodies, and a clambake for two.

Sea Ketch Restaurant and Lounge

127 Ocean Boulevard (Route 1A)

603-926-0324

Rowdy spot with a pubby menu heavy on the seafood, right on the Hampton Beach Boardwalk.

Widow Fletcher's Tavern

401 Lafayette Road • 603-926-8800

www.widowfletcherstavern.com

Stop at this clapboard cottage for award-winning chowder and homey fish dishes, and be sure to ask for the story of the Widow herself.

Portsmouth

The Blue Claw
58 Ceres Street • 603-427-CLAW
www.theblueclaw.com

The Claw updates tradition, but not off-puttingly so: The shrimp and roasted corn chowder is worth a detour. Try a bowl, maybe paired with some plump Prince Edward Island mussels or beer-battered fish and chips, and gaze out at the Portsmouth tugboats.

Geno's Chowder & Sandwich Shop
177 Mechanic Street • 603-427-2070

Geno Marconi's daughter Francesca carries on her pop's tradition at this nearly 50-year-old eatery on the back channel of the Piscataqua River. Dock and dine on plump lobster rolls and seemingly effortless bowls of chowder.

Old Ferry Landing
10 Ceres Street • 603-431-5510

Seafood and almost nothing but, fried, broiled, and grilled, by the water for nearly 30 years.

Sanders Olde Mill Fish Market
367 Marcy Street • 603-436- 4568

The Sanders family, who also run the lobster pound around the corner on the wharf, have a small takeout menu of seafood dishes, including a blissfully rich lobster stew that's colored with tomalley and roe.

The Stock Pot
53 Bow Street • 603-431-1851

Portsmouth is chowder city–eat your way around the Pot's chowder menu and back again. The lobster roll is as pleasing as the harbor views.

Rye

The Ice House

112 Wentworth Road • 603-431-3086

The hanging of the Ice House's wooden sign with its painted ice cream cone is, for many, the official start of summer. The mosquitoes can be fierce if you nosh under the trees, but the rewards are rich and wholesome: expertly fried seafood (the fish sandwich is a poem), lush frappes, and an ice cream menu to fluster the most extreme dairy die-hards.

Ray's Lobster Pound

1677 Ocean Boulevard (Route 1A)
603-436-2280

Clam fritters are king at this beachy double-decker saloon. Follow the trail of faded nautical castoffs to the fish market out back for fresh offerings packed to carry.

Rye Harbor Lobster

1870 Ocean Boulevard (Route 1A)
603-964-7845

This tiny pound in a row of shacks on Rye Harbor will cook a few of its products for you on the spot.

Rye Harborside

Route 1A • 603-964-6314

The takeout hut near Rye Harbor State Park caters to tour-boat traffic in the harbor with a menu of dirt-cheap short-order favorites (like a gooey grilled cheese) and a satisfying bowl of clam chowder.

Saunders at Rye Harbor

Route 1A • 603-964-6466
www.saundersatryeharbor.com

Lobsterman Ben Saunders opened this place in the 1920s, and they still make old-fashioned stew to his specifications at this casually elegant spot. Awards have been heaped on the seafood chowder, and the turf menu showcases some ambitious steaks. Poet Ogden Nash was a regular.

Seabrook

Captain Don's Lobster Pound

50 River Street • 603-474-3086

A down and dirty bait-and-tackle shop with a limited takeout menu of unfussed-with seafood.

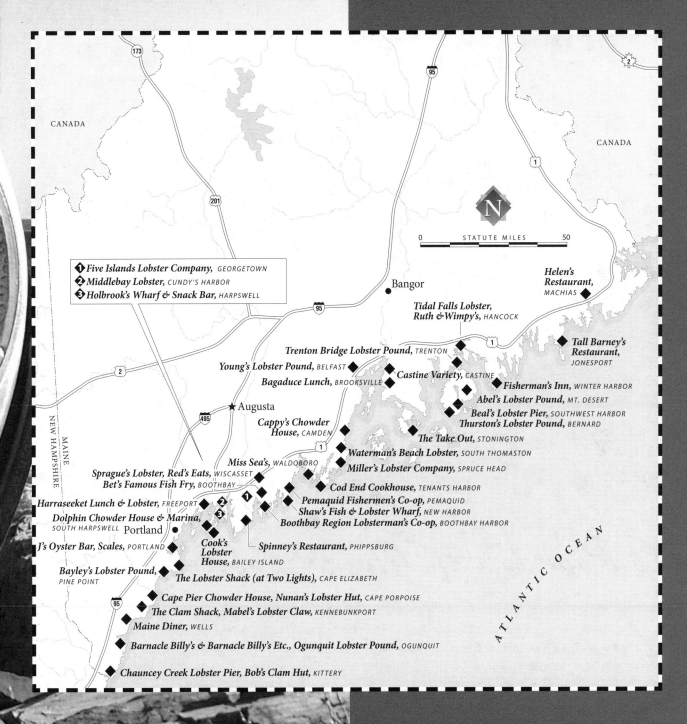

CANADA

CANADA

N

0   STATUTE MILES   50

❶ **Five Islands Lobster Company,** GEORGETOWN
❷ **Middlebay Lobster,** CUNDY'S HARBOR
❸ **Holbrook's Wharf & Snack Bar,** HARPSWELL

Bangor

Helen's Restaurant, MACHIAS

Tidal Falls Lobster, Ruth & Wimpy's, HANCOCK

Tall Barney's Restaurant, JONESPORT

Trenton Bridge Lobster Pound, TRENTON

Young's Lobster Pound, BELFAST
Bagaduce Lunch, BROOKSVILLE
Castine Variety, CASTINE

Fisherman's Inn, WINTER HARBOR

Abel's Lobster Pound, MT. DESERT
Beal's Lobster Pier, SOUTHWEST HARBOR
Thurston's Lobster Pound, BERNARD

Cappy's Chowder House, CAMDEN

The Take Out, STONINGTON

Waterman's Beach Lobster, SOUTH THOMASTON

Miss Sea's, WALDOBORO
Miller's Lobster Company, SPRUCE HEAD

★ Augusta

Sprague's Lobster, Red's Eats, WISCASSET
Bet's Famous Fish Fry, BOOTHBAY

Cod End Cookhouse, TENANTS HARBOR

Harraseeket Lunch & Lobster, FREEPORT
Pemaquid Fishermen's Co-op, PEMAQUID
Shaw's Fish & Lobster Wharf, NEW HARBOR
Boothbay Region Lobsterman's Co-op, BOOTHBAY HARBOR

Dolphin Chowder House & Marina, SOUTH HARPSWELL
Portland

J's Oyster Bar, Scales, PORTLAND

Cook's Lobster House, BAILEY ISLAND

Spinney's Restaurant, PHIPPSBURG

Bayley's Lobster Pound, PINE POINT

The Lobster Shack (at Two Lights), CAPE ELIZABETH

Cape Pier Chowder House, Nunan's Lobster Hut, CAPE PORPOISE

The Clam Shack, Mabel's Lobster Claw, KENNEBUNKPORT

Maine Diner, WELLS

Barnacle Billy's & Barnacle Billy's Etc., Ogunquit Lobster Pound, OGUNQUIT

Chauncey Creek Lobster Pier, Bob's Clam Hut, KITTERY

NEW HAMPSHIRE

MAINE

ATLANTIC OCEAN

A Roundup of Maine Lobster Pounds

hese days, the term "lobster pound" is used very loosely, sometimes to designate nothing more than a seafood restaurant. As a general rule, a lobster pound is a place where–even if there's lots more to choose from on the menu–you can pick a live rascal out of a seawater-filled holding tank, get it cooked on the spot, and chow down nearby, usually at a picnic table, "in the rough." Here are some of my favorites.

Abel's Lobster Pound

Somes Sound Road (Route 198), Mount Desert
207-276-5827

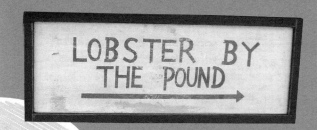

This huge log cabin shrouded in pines at the edge of Somes Sound (curiously, the only natural fjord in North America) is Acadia distilled. Inside and out, the restaurant feels like a resort from another era–until one of the wait-staff tells you that Billy Joel once played the upright piano in the dining room, or that the steamers are Martha Stewart's favorite item on the menu. Trundle down the hill to the pound for a peek at the place where lobster makes a quick stop en route to your plate, and have a chat with a salt-and-pepper-haired gent named Ted, who's been working here since he was six. Folks flock from all over Mount Desert Island for Abel's two nightly sittings, so reservations are a must.

> "Lobster meat, picked still warm from the shell, dipped in melted butter, is one of life's rare, purely transcendental tastes."
> —JOHN THORNE, *SERIOUS PIG*

lingo:
Lobster Pound

From the word *impoundment*, the first type of lobster storage created by seafood dealers in the mid-19th century so they could keep highly perishable lobsters—which people had begun clamoring for along the coast and beyond—alive until they were shipped to market (foolproof portable cold storage was still a few years away). The first "pounds" were gated-off mouths of coves or inlets. When more vacationers began flocking to Maine, a few dealers set up wood-fired pots nearby, thinking folks might get a kick out of picking a lobster, having it cooked, and eating it on the spot. The practice became such a part of the Down East allure that once technology had evolved enough to pump seawater inland to a man-made basin, "pounds" began popping up everywhere—some nowhere near the coast—promising the same pick-your-bug-eat-in-the-rough experience. (Used interchangeably with "lobster pool.")

Bayley's Lobster Pound

Jones Creek Drive, Pine Point
207-883-4571
www.bayleys.com

This place started in 1915 with Ella Bayley selling the leftovers of her husband Stephen's daily catch to neighbors through her kitchen window. Today, the tidy little building in Pine Point is on its third and fourth generation of Bayleys (you can peer at family photos near the takeout counter) and also does a brisk wholesale business. Combined, the outfit sells upwards of 3,000 pounds of the critters on an average summer day. A freezer compartment to the right as you enter stores wonderful, made-here items like stuffed clams, crab and artichoke dip, and portions of lobster stew just begging to be taken home and warmed up after a day at the beach. This may or may not be where the lobster roll was invented (see sidebar). And how can you not love a business whose toll-free number is 1-800-WE-BOIL-M?

shack lore: Invention of the Lobster Roll

Bill Bayley claims it was his grandparents, Stephen and Ella Bayley, who created the seductive sandwich in the lobster pound that bears their name. Not so fast, says Doug Oulton, who runs Borden's Restaurant 470 miles to the northeast in tiny Sackville, New Brunswick. He insists it was his father, Borden Oulton, who came up with the heady combo of lobster meat and mayo tucked into a hot dog bun. "We still make 'em the same way," says a waitress at Borden's. "And they're still popular." Exact dates aren't available, so why don't we call it a tie? Besides, given the roll's popularity, there's more than enough gratitude to go around.

Beal's Lobster Pier

182 Clark Point Road, Southwest Harbor
207-244-7178 • www.bealslobster.com

On Mount Desert Island, the Beal family is synonymous with lobster: They've been hauling it off this pier in Southwest Harbor next to the Coast Guard station for generations. Choose yours from shimmering tanks in the narrow, low-ceilinged pound. Ask for steamers, or not. Everything's dumped into a net, which is tossed into a steamer, and when it's all cooked, watch a sleeves-up kitchen worker crack your lobster with a handed-down knife for easier access. Fried seafood baskets can be ordered one shack over at the Captain's Galley (try the haddock or cod), which is also where you'll find beer and wine, a lobster-pound anomaly. Grab a spot overlooking the harbor, which is especially dramatic at low tide.

Boothbay Region Lobstermen's Co-op

Atlantic Avenue, Boothbay Harbor
207-633-4900
www.mainelobstercoop.net

A meal in the rough is as hard to come by in posh Boothbay as a patch of harbor without a yacht, but the Co-op delivers. Following Atlantic Avenue around the water's curve will lead you to this big, rickety affair known for its no-frills seashore dinners. Order your corn, lobster, and steamers at the wooden stall outside, or head to a takeout window for the fried stuff, creamy chowders, and landlubber fare (the Philly steak is a good non-seafood option), and make note of a third ordering area for later, where the ice cream happens. Sip a Maine microbrew from the drafty lower-deck bar while you wait for your meal, watching the steam billow up from the open-air lobster pots into the late afternoon sun. When your number's called, repair with your tray to a topside table overlooking the harbor, and prepare to crack, dunk, and slurp your way to satiety as envious gulls gaze on.

Five Islands Lobster Company

1447 Five Islands Road, Georgetown
207-371-2990
www.fiveislandslobster.com

Who'd imagine some of the best seafood in Maine would be prepared by a couple from the 'burbs of Detroit? This is food made with love; the pretty harbor and working waterfront are almost gilding the lily. Pick out your lobster in one shingled building, order a crabcake-and-haddock sandwich in another, step up to a third hut for your ice cream, and throughout it all watch fishermen hauling a gigantic tuna into cold storage on the same wharf. Bring a cooler, see the sun set, then come back the next day and do it again. (See more on Five Islands Lobster on page 197.)

shack staple:
The Moist Towelette

Lobster, shell-on shrimp, raw oysters—eating any of these is a contact sport. While some shacks put sinks right near your table so you can hose the lobster goo off your forearms, most stock up on disposable moist towelettes. Millions of shellfish lovers have been saved from a fishy-fingered fate by this humble little square, also known by its most famous trademark, the Wet Nap, invented in 1958 by Nice-Pak founder Arthur Julius. At Shaw's Fish & Lobster Wharf in New Harbor, they go through upwards of a thousand moist towelettes a day in peak season. The figure doesn't surprise J. B. Popplewell, curator of the Moist Towelette Museum (www.moisttowelettemuseum.com), one bit. "It's a dirty world filled with dirty people, dirty animals, and dirty things," he says. "Moist towelettes have historical and cultural significance, but they'll also keep you clean."

Holbrook's Wharf & Snack Bar
984 Cundy's Harbor Road, Harpswell
207-729-0848

Salty, as a word, was invented to describe places like Holbrook's. The kitchen recently changed hands, but new head Jeremy Saxton has stuck with the classics–from perfect lobsters to burgers to shortcakes–on this creaky wharf overlooking Cundy's Harbor. Don't miss the Holbrook General Store next door, where the brass mailboxes offer a peek into its past as the town's post office.

Miller's Lobster Company

38 Fuller Road, on the harbor, Spruce Head
207-594-740 • www.millerslobster.com

Come by car or boat to this cheery red shack with white trim, strung with faded buoys, for a wharfside bite in the pastoral fishing village of Spruce Head. Miller's is very much a family affair: Mark Miller and his brother began accompanying their dad, a lobsterman, out on his rounds as soon as they "had sense enough to not fall out of the boat." The elder Miller set up tanks on his wharf and decided to sell his catch from there; a few years later, picnic tables followed. Today, Mark and his wife Gail run operations, serving lobster and clam dinners, chilled lobster and crabmeat rolls, and the occasional special (steamed mussels or shrimp). And pie, homemade and heavenly. Check out the pies du jour on a little blackboard next to the takeout window, and unless you arrive early, don't be surprised to see the strawberry glaze or butterscotch cream crossed out.

crib sheet: New England Crab

Depending on where you are along the coast, they're called Jonah crabs, peekytoe crabs (a moniker derived from "picked-toe" or pointed-toe crabs), or simply Maine crabs—but whatever you call them, aficionados will tell you there's nothing sweeter. Smaller than their Southern cousins, you won't find these crabs served Maryland-style, with a spread of newspaper and a mallet; everything's pre-picked. Today's tightly regulated home crab-picking industry evolved from fishermen's wives making a little spare cash cooking and shelling the crabs that found their way into their husbands' traps. The tender ivory meat shows up most often in that classic Maine sandwich, the crab roll, but also in creamy crab spreads (try the one at Thurston's Lobster Pound in Bernard) and the occasional pungent bisque.

Ogunquit Lobster Pound

504 Main Street, Ogunquit • 207-646-2516

It's not oceanside, but the rustic atmosphere of this old log cabin nestled in a grove of pines is vintage Maine, feeling closer to Bar Harbor than the two-hour drive from Boston would suggest. Hazel Hancock started the Ogunquit Lobster Pound in 1946; today, her grandkids run the place using Hazel's recipes and sticking to her purist philosophy when it comes to lobster dishes: mostly meat, little filler. Order at the outdoor window, settle into an Adirondack chair, and inhale the scent of the evergreens towering above you; and for dessert—one of the Hancocks' scrumptious deep-dish pies, perhaps—duck inside, where a fireplace warms the dark, cozy room on chilly nights.

Pemaquid Fishermen's Co-op

32 Co-op Road, on the harbor, Pemaquid
207-677-2801
www.pemaquidlobsterco-op.com

The oldest continuously operating fishing cooperative in the United States also runs a peach of a restaurant. The squat, indoor-outdoor wood barn houses a kitchen in the back and a few picnic tables out front, parked under a smattering of nets and other nauticalia. The view of John's Bay is breathtaking, and best when you catch a glimpse of the co-op's fishermen coming in with their haul. Along with fresh, salty-sweet lobsters and steamers and a great crabmeat roll, the restaurant offers an expanded menu of fried seafood (try the light, tender haddock), making it a hit with kids who still think a clam neck or lobster claw is gross. (There's also a swing set for the wee ones.) Don't miss the oyster stew, whose briny bivalves are harvested from the water at the bottom of the hill. The best part? The fishermen eat here too, rubber boots and all.

Shaw's Fish & Lobster Wharf

129 State Road (Route 32), New Harbor
207-677-2200 • www.shawsfishandlobster.com

Once they've called your number and you've ducked out with your tray onto the topside deck at Shaw's, gaze out at the harbor and play a rousing game of Count the Lobster Buoys (there are hundreds). Or watch lobstermen at work on the wharf below, hoisting their catch out of boats on pulleys and stashing it in colorful crates strung by the dozen, snaking out into the sound. There's a bar downstairs but no Fry-o-lator; go for the lobster pie or stew. (See more on Shaw's on page 221.)

Thurston's Lobster Pound

Steamboat Wharf Road, Bernard
207-244-7600

For many, Thurston's is the essence of Maine: a drafty double-decker barn that juts out over a working harbor, serving freshly caught lobster in the rough. Thurston's began as a lobster wholesaling business in 1946, only adding a kitchen in the 1990s, but the restaurant's reputation came all at once. These days, it's known for serving a short but flawless menu that shuts up even the snobbiest seafoodies. Try the trio of intoxicating chowders, the signature Louis spread lush with sweet Maine crabmeat, and one of the legendary boiled lobsters pulled out of the water below. (See more on Thurston's on page 226.)

Trenton Bridge Lobster Pound

Route 3, Trenton • 207-667-2977
www.trentonbridgelobster.com

Since 1956, the Pettegrow family has vowed you'll find "no linen table cloths or fancy glasses" at their rustic eatery right before the bridge to Mount Desert Island. On a stretch of Route 3 that boasts Maine's highest concentration of lobster pounds per mile, Trenton Bridge seems to have that extra something: The lobsters seem pluckier when you snatch them from the tank, the coleslaw tangier, the blueberry pie oozier with inky fruit. And then there's the steam, billowing from the wood-fired saltwater cookers, calling your name as you drive by. The menu's short and sweet; along with lobsters and steamed clams, try the lobster and crab cocktail (like seafood rolls minus the roll, letting the lightly dressed meat speak for itself). When the summer crowds have cleared out and the leaves are turning, get acquainted with the Pettegrows' silky lobster stew.

Young's Lobster Pound

Mitchell Avenue, Belfast
207-338-1160

This big red barn of a building is home, on an average day, to about 30,000 lobsters in brilliant green holding tanks irrigated with seawater pumped in directly from Penobscot Bay. The pound, which has been in the Young family for more than 80 years, offers a bare-bones menu and no-frills dining experience: Once your lobster's been picked out and weighed, choose your sides (corn, potato chips, coleslaw), add some steamers or chowder, and when it's all ready, grab a seat on the upper or lower deck for unstoppable views of sailboats bobbing in the bay. If it's raining, claim one of the red-topped picnic tables inside. And no matter how full you feel now, consider picking up a swordfish steak or some tomalley (sold by the pound) at the seafood market on your way out. You *will* need to eat again.

Bagaduce Lunch

19 Bridge Road (Route 176), Brooksville • 207-326-4729 • Open May to mid-September

The only thing better than the pies at this cockeyed hut on the edge of Bagaduce Falls is the fact that they've been baked fresh since the 1960s by a woman named Vangie Peasley.

I'd heard about Vangie and her pies, but it all seemed too Norman Rockwell to be true. So I asked. "Yep, that's right, my mother bakes the pies," says Judy Astbury who, with her husband Mike, is the third generation of the same family (their kids are the fourth) to own and run this sweet little red-and-white fry hut on bucolic Blue Hill Peninsula, with its rolling farms and winding roads that lead out to perfect little pockets of sea with names like Salt Camp Cove. "They just wouldn't be the same if she didn't bake them."

To sample Vangie's pies–graham cracker cream, blueberry, and strawberry-rhubarb–you'll want to pace yourself with the rest of the menu. Many of Bagaduce Lunch's offerings are fried, and heart-stoppingly (though hopefully not literally) so: Flaky haddock, almost smoky-tasting belly clams, tender scallops, and local shrimp come piled into baskets or stuffed into soft rolls. Also fried is some excellent, juicy chicken. Kids clamor for hot dogs as their parents crowd the takeout window, and hamburgers are served here too, but my favorite thing on a bun at Bagaduce is the crabmeat roll. When cookbook author Brooke Dojny asked Judy Astbury for the recipe, she answered, "Maybe it will be disappointing. I don't put much in it because what I like to taste is the pure, sweet crabmeat." Amen, Judy. Delicate, fresh-picked Maine crab is turned with a dab of Kraft mayonnaise to bring out the meat's natural ocean flavor. Salt and pepper round out the

list of ingredients; add this mixture to the soft, buttery toast of the bun and frankly, it's hard to eat just one. Crab rolls are mostly a Maine thing, but even within the state, good ones are hard to find. This specimen is worth a special trip to Brooksville.

Getting the crabmeat roll without a side of Mike Astbury's legendary double-dipped onion rings would be a mistake. He cuts colossal onions fresh, giving the rings two thorough coats before plopping them into the sizzling fat, but somehow the batter is so light that the extra layer doesn't seem heavy; it just adds extra crisp.

Get your greens in the form of Mike's frothy-light coleslaw, one of the only items on the menu–along with the fries–that could qualify as a vegetable.

When your order's called, load up on wet naps from the bucket at the counter, walk your food down the sloping rocks, and woo your taste buds while you take in the postcard-perfect vista of the reversing Bagaduce Falls. Even on a busy summer Saturday, this spot manages to feel secluded: It's just you and about 750 gulls eyeing your rings.

Don't forget to go back for pie. Get it with a scoop of Gifford ice cream for an only-in-Maine treat.

Barnacle Billy's & Barnacle Billy's Etc.

Perkins Cove, Ogunquit • 207-646-5575 • www.barnbilly.com • Open May through October

BEST BITES: Lobster stew, clam chowder, steamers, Key lime pie

Seventy-eight-year-old Billy Tower's career in food started as your classic 1940s tale: Boy meets Girl. Girl, who works as a telephone operator, is always busy when Boy calls, so Girl No. 2, who's also an operator, takes a message. Pretty soon, Boy's spending more time talking to Girl No. 2, and Girl No. 1 drops out of the picture altogether.

Good thing, too, because Girl No. 2–who became Billy's wife–brought a windfall of plain, delicious Yankee seafood recipes. These came in handy later, when Billy began eyeing an empty storefront on Ogunquit's Perkins Cove. It was 1962, and tourism had only just begun to boom in Ogunquit, a rugged, laid-back alternative to bustling nearby Kennebunkport that had drawn artists like Marsden Hartley and Edward Hopper to its shores. Billy knew Perkins Cove well: He'd been named the town's first harbormaster at just 14 years old, and in the 11 years he spent working as a fisherman, he and his boat called the cove home. "My friends said, 'Why don't you open a lobster pound?'" says Billy. "I went to three banks, scrounged money from my whole family, and bought the place for $50,000. I'd never cooked a hamburger in my life." Entrusting the cooking part to his wife Bunny, he worked on fixing up the place, building decks overlooking the cove, and opened Barnacle Billy's within a few months. Nearly 50 years later, though the area's bohemian days are long gone, a few vestiges remain: Gulls still squawk overhead, stately yachts need to wait for a wooden drawbridge to be hand-cranked to pass into the cove, and Billy and Bunny–along with their kids–are serving the same recipes in the same quaint, cozy restaurant to everyone from local fishermen to George and Barbara Bush.

"They probably come in a dozen or so times a year," Billy says of the former first family. (Sure enough, Barbara

Bush's memoir includes a sunny-day snapshot of her and her husband on the deck at Billy's, complete with a squinting Mikhail Gorbachev in an Angels jacket.) They're among the regular patrons who come to Billy's by boat–the restaurant has docking facilities out back. It's hard to imagine a lovelier end to an afternoon spent out on the water than a dockside meal here or at the sister restaurant next door, Barnacle Billy's Etc., which the Towers opened 20 or so years ago, where an expanded menu includes fried items in addition to the original's steamed and grilled fare.

And what fare it is. "Everybody says our lobsters are better," says Billy, "but we use the same lobster as everyone else." If the largest on the menu, a 2-pounder, just isn't enough, ask about bigger ones they might have on hand. Steamers are another signature item: Dug up in nearby Scarborough, they're pricy but absolutely worth it, sweet, plump, and delectable with their cruet of drawn butter. The chowder is New England through and through, a cream-based, pearly pink mixture thick with clam chunks and little shards of potato, and it has its rabid followers– on one of my visits, a man from Portland (the one in

Oregon) was ordering a few quarts and flying them home to his freezer. You'll want to order one of the rolls for dipping. Yes, it costs extra, but all of the restaurant's bread is homemade.

The only item Billy makes by hand himself is the stupefyingly rich, velvety lobster stew. "Most people just dump lobster meat in a pot with some milk and butter," he says. "But it's not that easy. First, you have to take care in picking the lobster. Then I sauté it in spices and butter—we use butter from Oakhurst Dairy—add milk, strain, measure it out, and make sure there's the right measure of base to lobster in each serving. It's complicated, but you can taste the difference."

In summer, grab a spot on the wraparound deck, order up a simple, delicious lobster or native crab roll, chase it with a glass of rum punch (the recipe's a well-kept secret), and watch as sailboats come and go in the tiny cove. Corn is available only for a short time at the end of the summer—like the rest of the produce, it's delivered fresh seven days a week from Chase Farm in nearby Wells, a family-run operation that's changed hands only once since its beginnings in 1774. Another must-try is the Key lime pie, baked using Nellie and Joe's Key limes from Florida. At the first hint of chill in the air, Billy gets the restaurant's big stone fireplaces crackling. The restaurant closes the Sunday after Columbus Day, leaving you a few perfect autumn weeks in which to follow up a day of leaf-peeping with a bowl of chowder or lobster stew by the fire.

shack people:
"Barnacle" Billy Tower

- *On matchmaking:* "We've had quite a few marriages come out of this place. When you have 140 teenagers working for you every summer, things happen."

- *On shedders vs. hard shell lobsters:* "I can talk out of both sides of my mouth. Hard shells have more meat, but they can be chewy. Shedders are sweeter, but there's less meat—you're mostly paying for water."

- *On presidential palates:* "Barbara Bush says our lobster stew is perfect. Whether you're a Republican or a Democrat, it's still a good bowl of stew."

- *On starting a business:* "Cash flow becomes an issue, at least until you get the hang of it. Don't open a restaurant and buy a Cadillac on the same day."

- *On age:* "People ask me when I'm going to retire. I'm 78 years old. I *am* retired. I love what I do, and I want to keep doing it. That's as good as it gets."

Bet's Famous Fish Fry

Route 27, off the town square, Boothbay • No phone • Open Memorial Day to Labor Day
BEST BITE: Fried fish

Boothbay Harbor has many fans. With its narrow, winding streets and pretty views of the boat-dotted water, it's been a vacation destination since after the Civil War, when hotels and resorts sprang up, adding tourist dollars to the town's fishing and shipbuilding riches. Today, the same holds true, though the ships built tend to be more of the luxury and ferry craft variety, and the general vibe more maritime-themed Disneyland. So

it's not surprising that many Mainers—unless they're in the vacation business—won't touch Boothbay Harbor with a ten-foot harpoon. Still, it's a lovely spot for a few days of strolling, shopping, and eating, but when you're craving something a little more real, hop in your car, drive up to Boothbay proper, and stop at the trailer with the giant mermaid painted on the side.

Meet Bet Finocchiaro: fisherwoman, fry cook, TV host, and all-around local celebrity. Bet's been serving up fried fish and Down East sass out of a trailer on this patch of Boothbay Common for a solid decade. (Not this trailer, specifically; this one's recent, and with its sea-themed murals is a good deal more fanciful than its plain white predecessor—but one thing's stayed the same, and that's the "Free Beer Tomorrow" sign on the side.) She comes from four generations of fishermen, and got her own start at age 12, when her father decided she should find out where money came from rather than just get an allowance. Nowadays she goes out in her own boat, the *Elizabeth*, and what she doesn't sell to fish dealers, she serves out of this takeout window. Not in the mood for haddock? "Then have some fries," she says. And that's pretty much it for the menu at Bet's.

But that's plenty for her fans, who come from all over the world and take home news, photos, and sweet sensory memories of what some say is the best fried fish sandwich anywhere. Filled with thick slabs of cod or haddock, battered and cooked to a dark brown crunch, and served on a kaiser roll with tangy homemade tartar or dill sauce (the fish is also available off the bun with a side of hand-cut fries), it's a dish best measured in inches. The full sandwich stands 6 to 7 inches high. "It's about a pound, pound and a quarter," says Bet. "I don't measure." Unless you haul anvils for sport, the half sandwich order should do you just fine.

And while it's cooking, you get a free floorshow: Bet's booming manner and salty asides–delivered in an accent thicker than her sandwiches–are so legendary that when she was tapped to host her own talk show, producers at the local ABC affiliate suggested that she tone it down a bit. (She didn't.) So clap your hands over Junior's ears and settle in until dinner's served.

shack people: Bet Finocchiaro, owner, Bet's Famous Fish Fry

- *On fame:* "The dry cleaner right there named their store after me. They called it the Centah of Attention. Isn't that sweet?"
- *On her work:* "I don't care about the fish or the damn money. I didn't start this place to make money. It brings people together, my serving food. And good food builds community. I'm a people person— I tell 'em a few stories, send 'em on their way. I have so much fun."
- *On tradition:* "I bread each piece of fresh haddock by hand. It's my grandmother's recipe."
- *On routine:* "All my sauces are homemade, every day. By Thursday I'm so tired of it I call it Kiss My Ass Sauce."

Bob's Clam Hut

315 Route 1, Kittery 207-439-4233 • www.bobsclamhut.com • Open year-round
BEST BITES: Belly clams, lobster roll, New England clam chowder

While some views you get with a meal in Maine have remained almost completely unchanged for decades–a shack on a little cove, lobstermen hoisting their catch–the same can't be said about Bob's Clam Hut in Kittery. As Bob Kraft, who started the squat, shingled blue shack in 1956, has said, "When we were kids, we would swim in the river here, then lie in the road where the pavement warmed us up. Now, if you stub your toe crossing the road, you're a dead man."

This stretch of Route 1 is now called the Golden Mile, home to outlet stores galore, and the first stop in Maine for vacationing bargain hunters. And that's okay for Bob's, because if there's one thing that'll give you an appetite, it's digging through piles of remaindered Ralph Lauren polo shirts at 80 percent off retail.

Bob's has grown up a lot too, adding a 25-table indoor dining room, a patio and picnic tables, and generally sizing its operation to the increased demand (though at the height of summer, the place is still so packed with diners that retreating to your car and chowing down off the dashboard is not uncommon). Yet it still proudly calls itself a "Corny Little Clam Hut by the Side of the Road," and while it may look a lot spiffier today, fans say it really hasn't changed at all. Chalk that up to its high standards for freshness (seafood is delivered daily, without exception–as the staff puts it, "We're too small to store more than that anyway"), its largely unchanged methods (every-

thing is cooked to order, the restaurant makes its own tartar sauce based on Bob Kraft's recipe), or the fact that you still have to work for your meal (pay at one window, pick up your order from another, head this way for condiments, head that way to the soda machine). And the place knows its roots: A 1960s photo of Bob in the kitchen hangs on the wall, not far from the very first guest check, where some lucky soul paid just $1.70 for his clams.

With few exceptions, this place fries; it fries everything. You can smell it from half a mile up Route 1, if the wind's right, and you start drooling before you can even make out the blue and white sign. Sea scallops, bay scallops (cheers for serving both and pointing out the difference), oysters, cod, haddock, shrimp, calamari, and clams. Bob's motto is "Eat Clams!" and yes, you can buy a T-shirt that says so. Or pose for a snapshot next to the mural of Gilligan and the Skipper, both eating Bob's clams. The place serves "specials," clams that are handpicked to ensure a consistency of size: not too big and oozy, but not so small that you can't taste the brine. The bellies (there are also strips) are done up, like all the fried items, in a trademark cornmeal-and-egg coating that renders them somehow both lighter and crunchier than almost any clam I've tasted. The pale fries are an afterthought; make better use of those calories by getting your seafood as a side order (in small, medium, or large containers). The clamcakes, firmer and smaller than most and chunky with bits of bivalve, are good too. Whatever you get, you'll need tartar sauce for dipping. Bob's secret recipe is so tangy, creamy, and utterly addictive that the restaurant's begun selling it in bulk so you can take it home. Which is good, because I'm not above spreading it on toast.

If you can get past the clam-infatuation, head straight for the lobster roll. It's available in two sizes (regular or jumbo), and in two variations (warm, tossed with butter, or chilled, tossed with mayonnaise). Either way, the meaty nuggets are tender, moist, and fresh, and come stuffed into an expertly griddle-toasted bun that's loaded into a little three-sided cardboard boat, and I can't seem to pick a favorite. If you're dining with others, you might want to con one of them into ordering the cold, while you get the warm, or vice versa. Both demand to be tasted and are complemented especially well by an order of thin, crisp onion rings.

Finally, the clam chowder is worth a mention, particularly since Bob's is open year-round, and a cup of this thick mixture can greatly improve one's outlook on a winter day in Maine. It's New England–style and gets its oomph from fresh thyme and Worcestershire sauce, and a 2-to-1 ratio of heavy cream to minced clams. We approve.

There's lots on the menu for the seafood-averse (chicken, burgers, hot dogs) and an endless list of Ben & Jerry's flavors for those with any room left in their bellies.

"We can't wait for the end of summer when the tourists go home, so we can have Bob's Clam Hut all to ourselves for the winter."
—RHONDA, BORN AND RAISED IN KITTERY

lingo: Shore Dinner

A menu term referring to a whole lobster steamed or boiled along with its sides, usually corn on the cob and/or potatoes. When the meal includes steamers or mussels, "shore dinner" is sometimes used interchangeably with "clambake." Usually, everything is tossed into a rope-net bag, with an order number tagged on the handle, and dropped in a cooker.

Cape Pier Chowder House

End of Pier Road, Cape Porpoise • 207-967-4268 • www.capeporpoiselobster.com
Open April to November • BEST BITES: Lobster roll, any and all chowders

Allen Daggett knows lobster. When he turned 18 in 1969, he set out in the family business, joining his dad and brothers, all lobstermen. Between his Cape Porpoise restaurant, his processing plant in nearby Kennebunkport, another eatery in Orange, Virginia (where he and his wife Wanda head for the winter), and a Web site where you can order lobster from pretty much anywhere in the world, Allen Daggett sells a fair bit of lobster. How much lobster? "Oh, a little over a million pounds a year, these days," he says. "I can't take credit for it, though. It's all because of the lobster. Maine lobster is the only way to go."

Panic seized the tiny town when Cape Pier Chowder shut down so that the rotted-out 125-year-old former salt house could be rebuilt, sending locals and visitors alike into serious shack withdrawal–especially from the lobster rolls. "They're our most popular item by far," says Allen. "We almost caramelize the hot dog bun, and we dress the lobster meat lightly in mayonnaise–Hellmann's, nothing else. We've tried all the other kinds, and Hellmann's is the only stuff that doesn't break down." You'll find a few other excellent sandwiches on the Cape Pier menu–try the fried haddock. Or go whole hog and get a lobster dinner–starring rascals up to 3 pounds, sometimes more–with a side of satisfyingly sloppy coleslaw and an ear of fresh corn when it's in season.

Anyone who doesn't come to Cape Pier for the lobster comes for the chowder. "We're chowder people," says Allen, "and we don't sell potato soup." Point taken. The Daggetts' kitchen turns out clam, seafood, and haddock chowders, with nary a cubed russet or other filler kicking around the bottom of the bowl. The chowder recipes all come from Allen's mother, and they're "pretty simple," revolving around hearty stock, half-and-half, and fish and seafood that's fresh off the boat. The first slurp proves his point. A bowl of any of these may seem like madness on a sweltering August day, but a cone of Blake's Old-Fashioned ice cream in, say, black raspberry should cool you off.

Cappy's Chowder House

1 Main Street, Camden • 207-236-2254 • www.cappyschowder.com • Open year-round
BEST BITES: Clam chowder, fried clam roll, Cappy burger, smoked salmon eggs benedict

Camden is stately and beautiful, with its windjammer-packed harbor, its perfect white steeples, and its upscale inns–but it can be a tough place to find a casual bite. So God bless Cappy's, housed for a quarter of a century in both stories of a charming old structure just a short stroll uphill from the wharves. On your way up, you'll come across Cappy's Bakery and Company Store tucked behind the restaurant. This is the place to pick up lobster-motif fridge magnets and some of Cappy's trademark treats, like its famous New England clam chowder, house dressing, and jams (try the raspberry rhubarb), canned or bottled so you can have a little taste of Maine when you get home to Nebraska.

But while you're here, sample the goods at the restaurant, preferably downstairs in the low-lit, always-lively pub of a dining room (if you're not the sing-along type, head upstairs to the mellower Crow's Nest). Grab a rickety table or a seat at the long, wooded bar. Order up a shore special and you'll get a lobster with all the fixins, including a generous helping of the creamy chowder in a dappled, well-worn enamel mug–this stuff is so good, *Gourmet* magazine requested the recipe. And while it gets less attention, you should stry the smoky, kielbasa-laced seafood stew. It's is a meal unto itself, or works nicely sided by a roll bursting with fried belly clams if you have a growing boy's appetite. Cappy's turns out a whole array of its own sauces, like the spicy mustard–see if they'll throw some for you onto a luscious char-grilled Cappy Burger, a standout in the turf category. Brunch is a big deal here on the weekends, and the thing to get is Cappy's eggs benedict with smoked salmon. For a fusty sailor's bar with lobster traps on the ceiling, this place makes a mean hollandaise. Try some of the homemade gingerbread for dessert. It's especially good on a crisp fall day.

Those with dependents will love Cappy's, which has a menu, balloons, and crayons for your kids, and a warm smile, an ear scratch, and even a water bowl for your pooch.

183

NEW ENGLAND'S FAVORITE SEAFOOD SHACKS

Castine Variety

Main and Water Streets, Castine • 207-326-8625 • Open year-round
BEST BITES: Lobster roll, crab roll

Each year the Lobster Promotion Council asks Mainers to elect the state's best lobster roll; the Variety–since about 1920, the hub of all activity in the genteel town of Castine–has won more than once. The roll is huge and heavenly (as is the crab version), with more meat than any bun could handle; a fork is required. The truth is, a dirt sandwich would taste good if it was served at the scruffy lunch counter in this throwback five-and-dime, where the specials are inked onto paper plates clothespinned to a jag of wire dangling between two hooks. This little store scoops more Maine-made Gifford's ice cream than any other dining establishment in the state; maybe the sign above the counter ("Without ice cream, life would be darkness and chaos") has something to do with it. Wash it all down with a bottle of Moxie, flip a wave to proprietor Big Ernie–who'll probably be on the phone with someone who's called to ask about the tides–and walk back out into the 21st century.

shack staple: Moxie

Why not wash down that Maine lobster roll with an icy gulp of Pine Tree State history? Before Coke, before Pepsi, there was Moxie, the country's first mass-marketed soft drink. Originally sold medicinally as "nerve food" by creator Dr. Augustin Thompson of Union, Maine, who prescribed it for "loss of manhood, paralysis, and softening of the brain," it was bottled as a soft drink in 1884. With its catchy name, addictive cough-syrupy taste (gentian root and wintergreen drove the flavor), chipper orange-and-blue logo, and kicky slogan and jingle ("Make Mine a Moxie!"), it became the nation's most popular beverage in the early 20th century. Today you don't find it much outside the state of Maine, but its following remains strong and devoted—more than 30,000 turn out each July for the annual Moxie Festival in tiny Lisbon Falls.

Chauncey Creek Lobster Pier

16 Chauncey Creek Road, Kittery • 207-439-1030 www.chaunceycreek.com • Open Mother's Day to Columbus Day • BEST BITES: Lobster, Chauncey Crock Beans, mussels in garlic and wine

First impressions being what they are, Kittery, the first town across the border from New Hampshire, certainly makes a good one for the state of Maine. It may be home to just 9,000 people and a slew of outlet malls, but it's spoiled with two places where you can eat the kind of seafood you rhapsodize about years later. Bob's Clam Hut is one (see p. 180), Chauncey Creek Lobster Pier is the other, and it can be said without dispute that the latter wins in terms of set-

ting. Set far away from the steamy, sooty traffic of Route 1, Chauncey Creek is a sprawling red building with white trim tucked amidst the colonial cottages of Kittery Point. Shrouded in lush spruce on either side, the restaurant juts out into the eponymous tidal creek with views down into Pepperell Cove—even the parking lot could be called bucolic.

This place started out serving lobster and nothing but. The great-uncles of current owner Ronald Spinney used to fish lobster off the pier at Kittery Point as early as the 1920s, and in the early '50s one of them splurged on some picnic tables, deciding he'd try to make a few dollars by boiling some of his catch and serving it, plain or on a roll. He encouraged patrons to bring whatever they wanted to supplement the lobster-only menu—from corned beef to beer—and this tradition continues today. Chauncey Creek is blissfully BYO everything that they don't have on hand. Show up with a birthday cake, and the staff will light the candles. Chill your own Chardonnay, and they'll happily dig a corkscrew out of a banged-up wooden drawer. Add this to the fact that lobsters here are consistently priced a dollar or so lower per pound than at many other restaurants, and it's hard to imagine a better bargain—even with all those outlet stores just a steamer's throw away.

The menu has expanded since the early days, and the number of picnic tables has grown to 42, but lobster remains the reason vacationers time their drives in and out of Maine to pass through Kittery around lunchtime. Choose your own from the tank. Anything in a shell is wonderful here, from sweet local steamers and raw bar fare like cherrystones and Malpeque oysters to meltingly tender mussels swimming in a garlicky white wine broth. There's also a pair of good seafood salad rolls, lobster and crab, that come on a bun studded with sesame seeds, the fresh-picked meat tossed with Miracle Whip, seasoned with celery salt, and allowed a hit of paprika for color. The Chauncey Crock Beans are a twist on the Boston baked classic, drawing their musky intensity from salt pork and a few secret ingredients. Shrimp lovers can choose between a steaming pile of the peel-and-eat variety or fried popcorn shrimp, one of a few fried offerings at the restaurant. Mini-pizzas and a couple of chicken dishes will keep the turf crowd happy. Finally, a perfect, towering slice of homemade blueberry pie leaves no doubt that you've arrived in Maine.

Unless it's chilly, you'll want to skip the half-dozen indoor seats and grab a Technicolor picnic table on the long wooden deck, either out in the open (there's a roofed bit for rainy days) or tucked under a screened-in awning that's perfect for dinners at dusk, when it gets buggy with black flies and mosquitoes. At the end of your feed, march up to the main building for a wipe-down and a taste of Maine humor: a paper toweling dispenser nailed to the wall, crowned with a plaque that reads "Finger Bowl."

lingo: Claw Shot

The salty liquid left at the bottom of a lobster claw shell after you've extracted the meat; tossed back in the manner of a tequila shot.

pie for breakfast

"To a foreigner, the saying goes, a Yankee is an American. To an American, a Yankee is a Northerner. To a Northerner, a Yankee is someone from New England. To a New Englander, a Yankee is from Maine. And in Maine, a Yankee is someone who eats pie for breakfast."

—Nathaniel Reade

A muffin is just cake masquerading as breakfast for the guilt-afflicted. Why not do what Yankees do, and call a spade a spade? Here are five great places where you can unapologetically start your day with dessert.

1. *Moody's Diner* (Route 1, Waldoboro, ME; 207-832-7785)
They bake five dozen pies a day at this 70-something 24-hour diner. The walnut is famous, and for good reason.

2. *Modern Diner* (364 East Avenue, Pawtucket, RI; 401-726-8390)
Any pie will do in this 1930s train car, the first diner added to the National Register of Historic Places.

3. *Agawam Diner* (Route 1 at Route 133, Rowley, MA; 978-948-7780)
The pies here are stunning. Try the coconut cream, then the apricot cream, in that order.

4. *Olga's Cup and Saucer* (261 West Main Road, Little Compton, RI; 401-635-8650)
Delightful fresh-fruit mini-pies, just big enough to split.

5. *Maine Diner* (Route 1, Wells, ME; 207-646-4441)
There is a succulent lobster pie, but at 7 AM, the excellent blueberry's probably more reasonable.

The Clam Shack

Route 1 (at the bridge), Kennebunkport • 207-967-2560 • Open Mother's Day to Columbus Day
BEST BITES: Fried clams, lobster roll, fried haddock sandwich

Kennebunkport has its share of gourmet restaurants, the better to cater to a clientele looking to park their yacht and grab a quick panino before heading out to fish bass with expensive lures. It's not for nothing that generations of Bushes have vacationed here, making the Secret Service as common a sight as seagulls. But even the leisure class needs to let down its hair every so often.

When they do, they often head across the bridge to a little white shack with gray trim, where the parking is impossible, the lines are long, utensils aren't provided, and the seafood is like summer on a plate.

Clams are masterful here: Crumb-battered and fried to a brittle crunch that keeps the bellies juicy, they're one of the menu's biggest draws. The lightning-fast staff serves these up in waxy, cardboard boxes with a racing stripe and pinked edges, the kind that have been used at clam shacks forever. (Big fried scallops are just as good.) A framed letter from Barbara Bush hangs nearby, singing the praises of these clams. Get here on a weekend and you'll have plenty of standing-in-line time to read the whole thing.

Then there's the lobster roll. It's round, on a toasted hamburger bun piled high with meat that's still warm because the lobster's cooked fresh—steamed over seawater pumped in from the tidal river below—cracked, and hand-shredded for you on the spot. (Owner Steve Kingston does everything by hand: Oxidation brought on by knives or spoons would taint the flavor.) Choose your poison, butter or mayo, or ask for both and see if you raise an eyebrow. Bostonians drive miles north for this lobster roll; locals brave tourist-choked roads for it–perhaps the ultimate compliment. A note to those eating in pairs: Get your own. Sharing this dish is difficult.

These lobster rolls are so unstoppably good, the Clam Shack's begun selling them in an at-home kit, complete with everything from buns to bugs. They'll overnight the kit to you, and it's also available from the sweet gift shop next door. Don't just pop your head in there, go all the way to the back–the shop turns into a terrific fish market where cheery men in aprons filet the morning's catch. If you're not driving far and your destination has a kitchen, this is one of the best places around to pick up some fish for dinner.

There's not much in the way of dining surfaces at the Clam Shack, and that's part of the fun. Car hoods and roofs are popular options. Or improvise and perch your cardboard tray on a foot of bridge railing, the better to inspire looks of naked longing from those stuck behind the wheel as traffic inches across the bridge. Just remember that the seagulls are hip to this trick, and they're not above dive-bombing you so you'll fluster and send your succulent meal into the water below, at which point they totally win.

Ten Lobster Rolls You Won't Want to Miss

Lobster roll: The official sandwich of paradise. Everybody has a favorite, and no two are alike. These 10 places make a memorable version of the summery treat.

1. *Abbott's Lobster in the Rough,* Noank, CT
Hot, unadorned meat on a hamburger bun with butter on the side for dipping.

2. *Moby Dick's,* Wellfleet, MA
Picked, packed into a roll, and plated—it doesn't get much fresher than this.

3. *Quito's,* Bristol, RI
Fat shreds of lobster get a little zing from fresh dill in the mayonnaise.

4. *Helen's,* Machias, ME
It's served as lobster on toast here—a roll would simply disintegrate under all the meat and butter.

5. *Castine Variety,* Castine, ME
A statewide favorite, served with potato chips from the back of a 1920s variety store.

6. *Cove Fish Market,* Mystic, CT
A magical mound of mayo-and-lettuce-laced lobster salad on a butter-griddled bun.

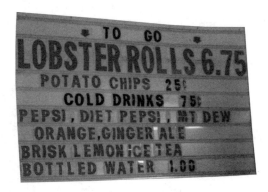

7. *Kelly's Roast Beef,* Revere, MA
Celery, mayo, and a full quarter pound of lobster meat. Bliss.

8. *The Clam Shack,* Kennebunkport, ME
Purists may recoil at the sight of a hamburger bun. More for the rest of us.

9. *Red's Eats,* Wiscasset, ME
Possibly the most famous lobster roll on earth—and for good reason.

10. *Miss Sea's,* Waldoboro, ME
Less than a fiver gets you a mini-version of the regular roll: luscious nubs of meat tossed with Missy's special dressing on a warm bun.

Cod End Cookhouse

Commercial Street, Tenants Harbor • 207-372-6782 • www.codend.com • Open Memorial Day through September • BEST BITES: Mediterranean seafood stew, fish chowder, onion rings

There's something about Cod End that captures Maine for me. After a pretty, spruce-scented drive down St. George Peninsula from Rockland, you arrive in bucolic Tenants Harbor, where pale cottages and crusty shacks on stilts stipple the water's edge, and old skiffs live out their days in small, grassy gardens, their hulls sprouting Queen Anne's Lace. Cod End Cookhouse is right at home here: All gray shingles and cranberry trim, the building looks like a tavern from the front but juts out far over the water in the rear, tapering into a wharf with a few picnic tables and, further, a spot where you can tie up your vessel and come in for lunch. A sign painted on driftwood and hammered to the side of the building with rescued nails is a paragon of Yankee understatement: "Good Seafood."

Duck in through the front door—next to an old engine propeller nestled among clutches of forget-me-nots—and the fish market greets you first. (Owner Anne Miller started Cod End as a market 30 years ago and tacked on the restaurant part later.) Everything on ice here is spanking fresh, with colors popping just the way they should, each orange salmon slab and pale pink scallop a testament to the high standards maintained within these walls. Anything you don't see here, you can ask about (tongues, cheeks, and livers? no problem); and everything on the premises can be prepared to your specifications on the spot.

Pass the lobster tanks and turn left, through the creaky screen door, and you're at the Cookhouse part of the operation, a small annex with a takeout window and menus corralled by a piece of thin rope strung between two thumbtacks. So much is good here, you'll want to return over and over again so you can taste everything. People love the Mediterranean seafood stew, a sopa do mar-cum-bouillabaisse in a garlicky, herby tomato broth, overloaded with fresh fish and shellfish from clams and mussels to cod and pollock, depending on the day. On misty Maine afternoons, when tufty tips of pine trees poke out of the fog across the harbor, dip into Cod End's fish chowder, a richly flavored, medium-creamy concoction packed with tender hunks of white fish, slicked with butter, and freckled with thyme.

Fried everything is light and crunchy (try those scallops, they're exquisite); and Anne's own fish cakes—made with russet potatoes and hake, and seasoned with Old Bay, fresh dill, and a dash of Tabasco—elevate the thrifty staple to new heights. Vegetarians, take note: the kitchen can even make a cheese and tomato sandwich sing. They use biting cheddar and griddle the whole affair on oatmeal-and-molasses anadama bread from Tenants Harbor's own Schoolhouse Bakery. Pies here are worth a return trip, with impossibly flaky homemade lard crusts and oozy fruit centers (not surprisingly, the blueberry is popular), but you'll want to try the excellent blueberry cake, too. Wash it all down with a plastic-cup pint of local brew and linger as you watch fishing boats chug out to sea.

As you leave, be sure to peek at the impressive collection of navigation charts or pick up some local jam for tomorrow's breakfast.

try it once: # The McLobster

In Taipei, you can get your McRice Burger with chicken or beef. In Quebec, McPoutine is a quick, warm bite on a cold day. McCubans haven't hit Ybor City yet, but Miami's got them—and we all remember John Travolta's fondness for the French Royale with cheese in *Pulp Fiction.* So it makes sense that in New England, McDonald's verve for regional variations would lead straight to you-know-what. That's right: the McLobster.

This fast-food lobster roll only shows up on Golden Arch menus in summer, and even then not all Mickey Ds on the coast offer the questionable treat—look for the signs (a recent set read "Real Lobster. Less Than 4 Clams"). What to expect: frozen-shipped real Maine claw and knuckle meat (no tail), mayo, and lettuce, piled into an untoasted, squishy, four-inch long bun, and served colder than a McFlurry. (For best results, bring your roll to room temperature.)

And the taste? In the words of Ron Ellinger, a lifelong Mainer, "Good in a pinch."

Cook's Lobster House

Route 24, Bailey Island • 207-833-2818 • www.cookslobster.com • Open mid-February through December • BEST BITES: Steamed mussels, fried scallops, fish chowder, lobster stew, clam-and-mussel mix

Anyone with a TV, even if they haven't set foot in New England, is probably familiar with Cook's: They do take MasterCard, they don't take American Express, and they're seemingly located at the end of the world.

Cook's was the destination Visa chose a few years ago for a commercial where a suit gets a craving, hops in his car, ditches the city, and shoots north, driving until he runs out of road and reaches a spot as far from his daily life as it gets, only to be told he can't use Amex to pay for his meal. It's telling that the commercial crew did nothing but light the restaurant for the cameras. There was no need to quaint the place up, because the shingled bungalow with water on three sides is already the movie set of any director's dreams. Besides, while the cameras were rolling, meals were being served to regulars on the other side of the building. Business as usual.

It's been that way since 1955, when Cook's–the only tenant on this craggy finger of land that points out into Casco Bay–began serving up unfussy food to locals and the visitors willing to make it out as far as Bailey Island, pushing forth along two-lane Route 24, where the weather-worn cottages grow fewer and farther between, replaced by deep-water inlets and tidal bays with names like Mackerel Cove.

But Cook's is no shack in the strict sense. The dramatic, desolate setting doesn't prepare you for the full-fledged restaurant beyond the porthole in the front door. A vast dining room warmed with wood and brass has enough windows to take in the 240-degree ocean view, offering every diner the opportunity–fog conditions permitting–to spy the lobster boat that hauled in his dinner from Merriconeag Sound. On the walls, everything tells a story, from the framed antique maps to faded photographs of generations of fishermen. In good weather, head out and grab a seat on Moby's Deck, pairing your Casco Bay ale with something salty from the raw bar.

The kitchen here does everything from scratch–chalk it up to challenging geography and the exacting standards of the Parent family, who own the restaurant. They pull their own lobster traps, cut and trim their meat, make all the extras like coleslaw dressing, and bake the desserts.

For a sampling of everything Cook's does best, steamed, fried, and ladled from a kettle, order one of the Down East Shore Dinners. The centerpiece is either a plain boiled or baked and stuffed lobster (Ritz crackers are the secret ingredient), which you can side with clams

(steamed with butter and broth or fried to a golden crunch), plump steamed mussels harvested right off the rocks nearby, and one of Cook's legendary chowders. Try the velvety fish kind made with haddock, the creamy clam, or the simple, decadent lobster stew. Steaks are broiled over a charcoal fire for a smoky, intense flavor. Try the Maine blueberry cake or the buttery apple crisp for dessert.

Walk wee ones down to search for shells on the little shore beyond the restaurant (just be careful of poison ivy). On your way out of Bailey's Island, peer at the Cribstone Bridge before you cross it: This engineering marvel is the only bridge of its kind on earth, a structure made up of granite slabs held together by nothing but weight. Nifty.

If you're near the Harpswells on July Fourth, Cook's famously hosts its very own fireworks show, right over the water.

collector's item:
Bachelor Lobstermen of Maine Calendars

They're rough. They're rugged. They smell like bait. Firemen, put your hoses away: In Maine, people are hanging a whole other kind of hunk on their walls 12 months a year.

It was just a matter of time until lobstermen were recognized as calendar pin-up material, though it took an entrepreneurial couple from Rockland (the self-proclaimed Lobster Capital of the World) to recognize it. Will Cook and Joanne Gray sold their first *Bachelor Lobstermen of Maine* calendar in 2001, featuring fishermen from up and down the coast posing on their boats and wharves, along with personal tidbits about each hunk and useful trivia like lobster trap regulations. It sold out almost immediately, and some national media attention left Graycook Productions scrambling to print more. Others followed, and soon the *Lobstering Women of Maine* calendar threw their female counterparts into the spotlight. Want one? Head to www.mainemade.com and order early.

Dolphin Chowder House & Marina

515 Basin Point Road, South Harpswell • 207-833-6000l • www.dolphinchowderhouse.com
Open May through October • BEST BITES: Seafood chowder, lobster stew, Grape-Nut custard

There was a brief, heady time during which you could call up the Dolphin Chowder House from anywhere in the country, declare that you were craving their fish chowder, and they'd pack up a quart or six for you and ship it overnight. Fed Ex rates being what they are, this was a pricey proposition, but then this is no ordinary fish chowder.

The Dolphin calls their chowder "the best in the universe," and if you haven't had it before, here's what will happen when you do: On the first slurp, you realize they're actually being modest. On the second, you see the face of God. On the third, you wonder how you've lived this long without it, realize you could never, ever replicate it, and start plotting how soon you can come back to this little poke of land for more. It's not too thick, not too thin; rich with cream, bulging with flaky, sweet fish, and singing with the flavors of the sea. It comes in a cup or a bowl. Don't order a cup.

The Dolphin Chowder House served the first helping of this stuff for a few nickels on the first day they opened, in 1966; to this day, only about three people have been privy to the recipe. "That's Malcolm," said the woman who rang me up on my last visit, pointing to the faded photo of founder Malcolm Saxton from the '60s, hung next to the first guest check. "He knew the recipe, but he's dead." Lore has it that in the 1980s, *Gourmet* magazine heard about the chowder, sent someone out here to Harpswell Neck to taste it, and quickly dispatched a letter, requesting the recipe for publication. For a while, the letter was hanging on the wall by the restrooms. But the Saxtons refused. "They wanted to keep it in the family," the woman tells me.

As sad as I am that the Dolphin no longer ships to your doorstep, it never was quite the same. The chowder was ambrosial as ever, but it was missing a few key

accompaniments. The salt air mingled with diesel fumes wafting off the working marina. The boats bobbing in glassy Potts Harbor, and the stark silhouette of Halfway Rock Lighthouse in the distance. The unpretentious atmosphere of the restaurant itself, its sideboard loaded before 11 AM with a day's worth of oyster crackers, stacked in a tidy pyramid of baskets. Even after a recent round of renovations, the little wooden dining room gives off an air of life half a century ago, of blue-plate specials and bingo nights. Most crucially, eating the chowder anywhere but here meant missing out on the other thing the Dolphin is known for.

"All our entrées come with a fresh-baked blueberry muffin," said the server on one of my first visits. "Some people eat 'em right away while they're still warm, some people even dip 'em in the chowder—personally, I think that's kind of weird—and some people get 'em wrapped up for breakfast the next morning." Whenever you eat them, the caramelized crust and inky bursts of berry beneath send the muffins over the top.

As delectable as the fish chowder dish is, the Dolphin's lobster stew runs a close second. A salty-sweet pink concoction that packs almost equal parts cream and butter, it's brimming with huge chunks of tender lobster meat. Get your vegetables in the form of fresh chopped parsley sprinkled on top for color.

Beyond these, there's a full menu of simple, fresh seafood standards, some of which I've sampled and loved—including a satisfying Maine crab roll and a wholesome tasting, incredibly sweet hard-shell lobster—but these days, it requires determination and willpower that I don't possess to order anything but that chowder. Sometimes I follow it up with pie, the flavors of which change daily. They also make a gooey-good Grape-Nut custard.

One note: The fish chowder is the only item you can't order in a regular serving to go, but the fridge behind the register is always full of cold-packed quarts you can reheat at home. Ask them to throw in a few muffins on the side.

photo op:
Lobster Boat Races

You probably know when football and baseball seasons start, but what about lobster-boat race season? Life for Maine's more competitive lobstermen gets more interesting each June, with the first officially sanctioned heat in Boothbay Harbor, and the season wraps up seven races later in late August in Searsport (fog permitting). Entries are classed by boat length and engine horsepower, and the grand prize barely covers the cost of fuel to fill up one these guzzlers—but bragging rights in this century-old sport are the real catch of the day.

Fisherman's Inn

7 Newman Street (at the flagpole), Winter Harbor • 207-963-5585 • Open mid-May to mid-October

BEST BITES: Smoked sampler, lobster bisque, finnan haddie, clam chowder

This little restaurant goes back to 1947 and looks it, though these days its menu is homey in some spots, and sophisticated in others, mirroring Winter Harbor's twin century-old histories as a hardscrabble fishing village on the one hand, and on the other, a getaway discovered early on by the wealthy, who promptly built elegant summer mansions and called them cottages.

Portobello mushrooms run rampant, there's a whole slew of vegetarian options, and I saw the words "spicy Thai" on the menu, but the Inn's motto still fits: "Real food, done well." This is the place to order finnan haddie, a slab of fresh haddock in a bubbling creamy sauce, or a buttery, satisfying lobster potpie. Fried foods are less common here, but the Maine clams done in a cornmeal crunch should be enough to satisfy your fry jones. You may want to beeline for the clam chowder, one of the Inn's specialties; it's creamy and chunky with sweet clam slivers, and the awards it's won are all over the restaurant. I like the lobster bisque, too, rich with cream, niblets of rosy meat, and enough sherry to warm up a nippy day.

You'll also find more than a few recipes here based on smoked things from the sea, and for good reason: Owner Carl Johnson also runs the nearby Grindstone Neck of Maine, a smokehouse known well beyond Winter Harbor for its small-batch-smoked local seafood free of preservatives and artificial anything. Try the crispy smoked salmon cakes—sort of the lovechild of smoked salmon and a crabcake—or a garlicky pizza appetizer topped with cold-smoked sockeye salmon. Or go simple and get the Grindstone Neck smoked sampler, where salmon shares the plate with shrimp, scallops, and mussels, all intensely flavored, peppery, and not for the seafood-shy. Or just stop by the smokehouse afterwards to inhale the aromas of sea and smoke, and stock up on snacks for later.

Five Islands Lobster Company

1447 Five Islands Road, Georgetown • 207-371-2990 • www.fiveislandslobster.com
Open Mother's Day to the end of Sept. • BEST BITES: Lobster, steamers, fried clams, the Jenny special

We've all had a moment like this: You're on vacation in an achingly pretty place (in this case, Georgetown, Maine), and you're eating something good made even better by the surroundings (blue water flecked with fishing boats and a cluster of pine-tufted islands). Maybe you're well into a pint of local Allagash Ale and wishing you didn't have to go back to wherever it is that you call home. You start wondering–out loud–if you could just quit your job, pack everything into a U-Haul, and open a lobster shack on a dock in Maine.

Chances are, you'll return to your old life with a camera full of snapshots and some warm memories, and that will be that. But for Jenny Butler and her husband Chris, a couple of thirtysomething food hound Maineiacs who'd been trekking Down East year after year from their Detroit suburb, the idea didn't fade away. These days you'll find them spending almost every hour of the summer on this dock–which many have called the prettiest in Maine–running Five Islands Lobster, serving visitors and lobstermen alike, and not quite believing their luck. "I mean, just look at this place," laughs Jenny of the postcard she calls home. "It's just so cool. We only bought it a few years ago, so people have been coming here long before me. We wanted to be a part of all this and do a good job."

Here's how it works: If you want a lobster (and you do; the waters off this dock are some of the deepest and coldest in Maine, which locals claim makes for the sweetest-tasting lobster), head into the red Lobster Company building and pick one out. The staff in here will take a break from cracking a big barrel of lobsters for the day's rolls to cook your bug, with some corn and steamer clams on the side. While that's happening, you have a few minutes to pop over to the Love Nest Grill next door (so-named because of the upstairs apartment, where lobstermen used to hide away with their sweeties in between fishing sorties). This gray shack with the spruce trim was built in 1868 and looks it; inside, crowd around a big old blackboard and order up something from the grill or the fryer. Try the hand-dipped rings, which Jenny calls "sort of blooming-onionish," or the unusual salmon fish and

chips, or the crumb-battered fried clams, dug near Portland. There's fresh grilled tuna, when they can get it. Leon Kelly, one of the 32 lobstermen who work off this dock, recommends the Jenny Special, a double-decker sandwich with a fresh haddock fillet and a lusty crabcake, (these are entirely breadcrumb-free, resulting in a sort of pancake of the sea). Try it with all three sauces, which Chris's dad makes himself: a tangy mustard-dill dip, a creamy cilantro mayonnaise, and a tartar sauce with dill and capers that you'll be talking about the next day. Luckily, you can buy a bottle of the stuff to go.

As you wait for your number to be called, score a pic-nic table on the wharf, crack open your cooler or your brown bag, and breathe in: seaweed and cooker steam, fry oil and–if you're lucky–a whiff of gasoline from a fishing boat motoring out to sea or coming into the harbor, its sternman piling bright green and orange crates full of just-caught lobsters onto the wharf a few feet from yours. There's a third building where you can get a lick of Coffee Toffee Thunder or Minty Mint Cookie from Annabelle's, New Hampshire's best-loved ice cream artisans. And while you watch the teen pack your cone, know that in the back of that same building, there's a bait cooler where fishermen are packing a 300-pound tuna on ice.

shack people:

Jenny Butler, Five Islands Lobster owner, and Leon Kelly, lobsterman

Jenny: "I love it all. I even love dipping the onion rings—the mix is just like silk on your fingers. All the smells, the view, the people—just being on a working wharf. When I see the fishermen come in and open the bait cooler to put their catch on ice, it's exciting."

Leon: "It's the best place in the world. Out here on the water, everything works together; it's how it should be. Even on a bad day, it's pretty good."

Jenny: "Leon fishes off this dock. We serve a lot of his lobsters, and he's one of our best customers."

Leon: "I like the Jenny Special, myself. Crabcake and haddock on a bun. You could say I've eaten a few of those."

Jenny: "Leon's dad was a lobsterman."

Leon: "Yep, started with my father right here, when I was six, in 1957 . . . Tried having an office job once, but I couldn't do it. I never knew if it was raining or shining out. I was so miserable, my wife threatened to divorce me if I didn't quit."

Jenny: "And now Leon's daughter is his stern-woman."

Leon: "The best seafood in the world comes from Maine, and the best seafood in Maine is fished right off this dock. I'll go get you one of the shedders we just brought in. You'll see."

Harraseeket Lunch & Lobster

Town Landing, Freeport • 207-865-3535 • Open end of April through Columbus Day
BEST BITES: Onion middles, the Lobster Delight, whoopie pie, strawberry shortcake

People tend to know the town of Freeport as an outlet mall disguised to look like a quaint 1890s New England hamlet. Local laws won't have it any other way: Even the Gap here is tucked away in a white clapboard structure right out of *Little Women*, with brass fixtures and a Yankee-fied sign out front. It's a shopper's paradise, but the pursuit of $20 cashmere can make you lose perspective.

A dock on the other side of town, well removed from the bustle of bargain hunters and the waft of remaindered bayberry candles, is where you go to get that perspective back. At Harraseeket Lunch, an almost 40-year-old landmark perched on the Town Landing overlooking the Harraseeket River, your priorities shift: You're on vacation, the sun is shining, and cashmere takes a back seat to lobster, devoured as you watch boats go about their business in Freeport Harbor.

Before the smell of fried food and steaming seawater hits you, your stomach might grumble at the sight of the place alone. Patriotic colors are popular in New England, but this place takes it to a whole other level: Harraseeket looks like a July Fourth parade paused mid-march, set down its tubas, and started selling seafood off the side of the floats.

If you want lobster, steamers, boiled red potatoes, and corn, follow the signs instructing you to circle the building and order from a window on the water. (You can also purchase seafood, and take it home to cook, at the window under the "Live" sign.) Those wanting their food fried or sandwiched line up on the roadside, where you also go for drinks. It's a good idea to have someone hover near the tables if you're dining outside; on busy days, they fill up fast. (There's plenty of additional seating indoors, but unless it's really cold or pouring, it'd be a shame to head in here and miss all the activity outside.)

Harraseeket does a bargain of a clambake, the Lobster Delight: At this writing, $16.95 netted you a snapping-fresh 1-pound lobster, steamers, and just-shucked corn piled onto a tray and served up with butter and broth. And it's always excellent, though in truth, I'd order something called the Lobster Delight even if it wasn't. I think I'd order pretty much anything called the Lobster Delight, anywhere, for any price. (The lobster roll is a beauty here too: slight mayo on the meat, shreds of lettuce at the bottom, and a perfect, butter-basted bun.)

Be advised: The kitchen's not afraid to serve clams sized for giants. Huge bellies burst and ooze when you bite into them, releasing the salty snap of the sea and sending you straight to quahog heaven. (Be sure to ask for crumb-fried, not batter.) The second-best fried item on this menu is a brilliant byproduct of Yankee thrift. Many a restaurant tosses the center of each onion it cuts for rings, to keep the frying time on this side dish more or less uniform. At Harraseeket, these centers become a whole other menu item, like the hole to a doughnut: onion middles, batter-fried and full of crunch. If you like rings but feel the tart oniony insides are too often overpowered by heaped-on batter, these nuggets are for you. I'll take the middles over the rings any day, even if they do require a breath-mint chaser.

Get one of two desserts to go: Harraseeket makes a delectable whoopie pie, the classic chocolatey Maine treat; they also pile fresh strawberry chunks onto a baking powder biscuit, topping it all off with whipped cream for a classic, scrumptious shortcake.

local specialty:
Anadama Bread

Bread made with molasses and cornmeal, said to have originated in Rockport, Massachusetts, in the early 20th century. A fisherman was so tired of the dinner his wife Anna made every night (cold corn meal and molasses) that he got fed up and decided to bake bread with it, muttering "Anna, damn her" as he cooked. Today, it pops up on menus all along the coast (try some at Cod End Cookhouse in Tenants Harbor, ME).

shack classic: Whoopie Pie

Whether you spell it whoopie or whoopy (and whether it was invented in Maine or in Pennsylvania Dutch County, as is sometimes alleged), you haven't really had a meal Down East until you've capped it with one of these decadent treats. Spongy, bittersweet cocoa discs sandwich a gooey layer of marshmallow cream filling, the whole thing creating a salty-sugary duet to make your Hostess Cupcakes and Ding Dongs pale in comparison.

Helen's Restaurant

28 East Main Street, Machias • 207-255-8423 • Open year-round
BEST BITES: Seafood stew, lobster on toast, broiled haddock burger, blueberry cream pie

*M*aine's nickname, Vacationland, applies more in some parts of the state than others. Heading north of Mount Desert Island, there are more trees than people. After a while Route 1's traffic thins, the bracing scent of pine wins out over salt air, restaurant signage dulls (no googly-eyed lobsters in sailor hats here), and–as a waitress in Portland put it when I revealed the plan to eat my way to the Canadian border–you enter the land of "the locals, the die-hards, and the crazies." (For the record, I encountered no crazies, unless you count putting 14 blueberry desserts on a menu as a pathology, which some might.)

In part due to the lighter tourist traffic, and also to the fact that many from these parts consider eating out an indulgence, the far Down East is not known for its restaurants. But if you do make it this far, a stone's throw from Nova Scotia, your rewards will be sweet indeed. Also, you'll get to test my theory that the farther north you go, the more godly the chowder. It gets very cold up here, it's foggy more often than not, and it's populated by a lot of fishermen who'd rather not pay a king's ransom for a hearty, hot meal. (You see a lot of liver and onions on menus way Down East.) If ever a climate demanded a good bowl of soup, this is it. Helen's Restaurant in Machias is a prime example, a wonderful old diner whose only concession to cute is the knife, fork, and spoon that make up the *H* in Helen.

All the seafood is caught locally, meaning it's pulled out of the coldest Atlantic waters off the U.S. with almost no travel time from wharf to plate, and you can taste the

difference. Chowders are called stews at Helen's, and they're milky mixtures started with painstakingly rendered stock. On the average day, you're hard-pressed to choose between the crab, the scallop, the lobster, and the shrimp. "You're in luck, dear," said the woman behind the counter. "We have seafood stew today. Only make it once a week, on Sunday." A single slurp of the buttery broth–chunky with scallops, blushing shrimp, bits of clam, and more than one fat lobster pincer–is exquisite, but also genuinely painful once you realize, if you're from far away, just how much driving will be required to experience this bliss again.

Another bit of genius from this kitchen is the lobster on toast (not to be confused with the lobster roll, Helen's decent, chilled version of the standard). The menu calls it Lazy Lobster, but it has an entirely different appeal from dishes going by this name elsewhere, which tend to be simply meat warmed with butter. (Not that there's anything wrong with that.) Think of it instead as a hot lobster roll so buttery it couldn't hold, soaking through the grilled bread with its sheer moist lobster-ness and simply falling apart on the plate. I'll take two.

Helen's also has a vast menu of non-seafoody down-home dishes, many with definite local flair. Try the ham steak, something right out of 1950s-era *Better Homes and Gardens,* or the "crock and a half," a bubbling, cheesy bowl of French onion soup served with half a ham- or turkey-club sandwich.

Dessert at Helen's is a big deal. Big glass cases full of backlit pies greet you when you enter. It comes down to choosing between two kinds of blueberry pie, cream or plain, both made with tiny berries from the pickers down the road. There's no manufactured goo holding these little suckers back; half are cooked, half are fresh, and they burst forth from between the crusts, squishing all over the

place, making this a dish best eaten slowly, precisely, and while wearing black. (The strawberry cream pie is a local favorite and just as good.)

Park yourself at one of the stools or booths in the front seating area, head back into the dining room done up with Shaker details like buckets and lanterns hung from the beams, or on a warmer day, snag the lone red picnic table in the grass by the boat ramp, near a tiny lighthouse. Helen's also has a gift nook where you can stock up on everything emblazoned with lobsters, blueberries, or the map of Maine.

J's Oyster Bar

5 Portland Pier (off Commercial Street), Portland • 207-772-4828 • Open year-round
BEST BITES: Raw scallops, oyster stew, oysters Mornay, Izzy's cheesecake

In Portland's Old Port, there's a big, stately ship where you can feast on a huge lobster dinner served by attentive waitstaff who'll cater to your every whim. The wine list is extensive and the water views unbeatable. It's called DiMillo's Floating Restaurant, and right next to it is a tarbox of a pub where the beer is cold, the food is good, the game is on, and the accents are local. The place is crowded with fishermen and off-duty cops. On a wet autumn night, as the fog rolls in, you'll see bright yellow slickers slung over the backs of bar stools, dripping rain onto the floor. Welcome to J's Oyster Bar, the sweetest little dive in Portland.

On a stretch of waterfront whose dining options can sometimes be touristy in the extreme, J's is a breath of salt air. A big U-shaped wooden bar dominates the room, and while you can no longer light up in restaurants in Maine, J's proud past as a smoky hole in the wall still lingers in the air. Low tables dot the room's periphery, but sit at the bar or you'll miss all the action: the food coming out of the kitchen, the conversations going on around you, the barmaid's brassy repartee. (That said, in warm weather try to score one of the few wharfside tables that J's sets out. Portland has a working waterfront, so this is one of the rare opportunities to grab a bite with your toes in the ocean.)

The menu is pub grub with a nautical bent and mostly old-fashioned flair, and in truth, J's Oyster Bar isn't always about the food. Some say the place shouldn't even be allowed to have "oyster" in its name, because they find its raw bar middling at best, or sniff at the fact that it tops oysters with cheese. If you know and accept that going in, an evening at J's Oyster may be one of the best you'll spend in Maine.

Oysters are served up a few different ways. Try them "raw and nude" (ask what kind they have that day—they're always local, but there's some variety), Rockefeller (baked with spinach, bacon, and cheese), or Mornay (topped with a Swiss cheese–based mixture and broiled); or get the oyster sampler, which serves up a taste of each, plus a stuffed variety. There's also a milky oyster stew on the chowder menu, good for a cold day. Come February, when oysters are at their tastiest and most abundant, J's offers them—plain, on the half shell–free during happy hour.

Give J's raw scallop cocktail appetizer a try. You don't see raw scallops on a lot of menus; the texture can be off-putting to some, but the tenderness and sweetness of the pearly pink flesh must be tasted to be believed. Mussels come steamed in white wine, and steamers, available in bucket sizes (the large is big enough to split), go especially well with the J's experience. The flavor is wonderful but the steamers can be mammoth, so if you gross out easily at fat clams, ask how big they are on the day you go. (Maine doesn't have the size restrictions on their clams that Massachusetts does, given its less sandy coast and the fact that clams are harder to come by.) You'll be tempted to toss the shells on the floor like so many peanut hulls.

Order up a local beer to go with your steamers; J's has an impressive selection from Maine microbrewers, including Shipyard Brewery, who sponsors J's Oyster Shucking Contest each September.

The lobster roll dominates an extensive sandwich menu (from a non-seafood standpoint, try the Reuben). *Gourmet* sang the roll's praises a few years ago, and I'm willing to bet that alone accounts for some of J's minimal tourist traffic. Chunks of unadulterated lobster meat crowd a soft, chewy bun (the kitchen seems to have a light hand with the toasting, so if you like your roll well-done, order it that way). The seasoning of the seafood rolls is a self-serve affair: Both the lobster and crab sandwiches (the latter is a Maine thing, and it's equally unadorned and satisfying) are served up with a little foil packet of mayo on the side.

Other popular mains include a homey dish of scallops with buttery crumb sauce, a winningly simple seafood casserole (featuring "a combination of today's fresh catch"), and of course a lobster dinner, served up clambake-style with a mess of steamers, corn on the cob (in season), and a little mound of deliciously peppery coleslaw. When I've stopped by, there's been exactly one item on the dessert menu: Izzy's cheesecake, from the swell Portland bakery of the same name.

tracking your lobster,
From Trap to Plate

Before you reach for the metal cracker, take a look at your lobster's claws. If the rubber band bears the question "Who Caught Me?" along with a four- or five-digit number, get ready to meet your lobster's maker. Well, its catcher, at least.

At Lobstertales.org, that number and a few clicks will bring you face to virtual face with the lobsterman who pulled your critter out of the water, and you can learn a little about him and the Maine community where he plies his trade. The idea was born out of a simple notion at the Maine Island Institute—namely, tagging lobsters to track their migration in the ocean. But quickly, an additional idea was born: Why not also create a link between Maine's fishing communities and people who enjoy their most famous export?

And based on the site's interactive map, they're fairly far-flung: Lobster lovers from as far away as Albania, Saudi Arabia, and the pacific islands of Vanuatu and Palau (names *Survivor* fans will recognize) have accessed the site since its inception in 2002, matching up their dinner to its origins on the site.

So next time you eat a bug, be sure to check the band. Because every lobster tells a story.

The Lobster Shack (at Two Lights)

225 Two Lights Road, Cape Elizabeth • 207-799-1677 • www.lobstershack-twolights.com
Open end of March through October • BEST BITES: Lobster, lobster roll, clam chowder, whoopy pie

"Unbeatable view" gets a lot of use in guidebooks (even this one), but here, it really applies. Locals call it the Two Lights Lobster Shack due to its enviable view of lighthouses on either side (including Portland Head Light, famously painted by Edward Hopper), and it's about as close to crashing surf as you can get while still technically being at a restaurant. Feeling sea spray on your face while you suck pearly meat from a lobster leg is just one more reason why you can't argue with the Maine state motto, "The Way Life Should Be." There's nothing to prevent you from just running into the surf–no railing, nothing. (Parents of curious toddlers, take note.)

Line up to order at the main counter, where a half-hour wait on a summer Saturday is not unusual. In such a dramatic setting, the food could be middling and it would-n't matter; happily, it's good, sometimes very good. (It also tends to be slightly pricier than the norm, but again, have I mentioned the view?) The lobster roll, pure meat with just a glisten of mayo, often tops local polls as the region's best, even beating out legendary roll purveyor Red's Eats in nearby Wiscasset. The lobsters are lovely, each served with pick, bib, fork, and a waxy cup of melted butter, a paper ramekin of coarse coleslaw crowned with a round of pickle, and a baked biscuit. The rest of the menu is straight-up shack fare, highlighted by butter-creamy clam chowder; dense, chewy clamcakes; fried clam bellies and shrimp on the juicy side; and straightforward, milky lobster stew. The Shack gets points for pairing nearly everything with a cardboard boat heaped with earthy crinkle-cut fries.

A dozen or so glossy red picnic tables cover a sandy patch of land separating the stocky restaurant from the water. They're spaced just far enough apart that you can really tear into your lobster without sending splatters of goo onto other diners. There's nothing to stop the wind here, and when it picks up, so will your lobster bib–right into your face. Remember, this close to the sea, it's a seagull's world, and you're just passing through. It can be hard to hear your number called over their screams and the hubbub of hungry diners–not to mention the blast of the nearby fog horn–so stay alert.

Get dessert to go. I recommend the Lobster Shack's version of the Maine classic whoopie pie (spelled "whoopy" here), fudgy cake crescents with a frosty cream center–and walk off your meal with a stroll to check out the lighthouses. I learned from a fellow diner that one of them is now a private residence. Jealous, much?

Ten Sweet Pit Stops

Need a little sugar rush to carry you 'til your next lobster roll? Treat your sweet tooth to . . .

1. *Penny candy at Gray's,* America's oldest General Store, tucked away since 1788 in a bucolic hamlet (4 Main Street, Adamsville, RI; 401-635-4566)

2. *Murdick's fudge,* made from the same recipe used at their original shop on Mackinac Island, Michigan, since 1887. (21 North Water Street, Edgartown, MA, one of three locations on Martha's Vineyard; 888-553-8343)

3. *Strawberry shortcake,* cossetted with cream, at Jim's Bagel & Bake Shoppe. (24 Washington Street, Gloucester, MA; 978-283-3383)

4. *Long stretches of sizzling-hot dough* at boardwalk landmark Blink's Fry Doe. Get them dusted with sugar (classic) or clouded with whipped cream, just two of the 21 sweet and savory toppings available. (115 Ocean Boulevard/Route 1A, Hampton Beach, NH; 603-926-4887)

5. *Spicy fresh-baked gingerbread* at Cappy's Bakery and Company Store. (1 Main Street, Camden, ME; 207-236-2254)

6. *An orange freeze at Captain Frosty's,* its most popular dairy menu order by far. Like the world's best Creamsicle, in a cup. (219 Route 6A, Dennis, MA; 508-385-8548)

7. *Soft, melty (read: dental work-friendly) saltwater taffy* at Perkins Cove Candies. (103 Oarweek Road, Ogunquit, ME; 207-646-7243)

8. *Frozen pumpkin pie custard* (flavors change daily) at Classic Custard, before hitting the outlet shops nearby. (150 Route 1, Freeport, ME; 207-865-4417)

9. *A honey-dipped or old-fashioned cake doughnut* at Kane's, where they've been hand-making them the same way for 50 years. (120 Lincoln Avenue, Saugus, MA; 781-233-8499

10. *Cinnamony Granny Smith apple crisp* at Chopmist Charlie's. The killer ingredient? A generous shot of brandy. (40 Narragansett Avenue, Jamestown, RI; 401-423-1020)

Mabel's Lobster Claw

124 Ocean Avenue, Kennebunkport • 207-967-2562 • Open April to October
BEST BITES: Lobster stew, baked stuffed lobster, fried clams, clam chowder, blueberry pie

Mabel's Lobster Claw, a Kennebunkport institution, is known for two things: serving some of the freshest lobster in the Kennebunks, and serving it to the 41st president of the United States, who comes by fairly often in summer with Bar in tow. A photograph of the former first family with Mabel's staff is the centerpiece of the sweet wood-paneled dining room, which feels more suited to tea and popovers than to seafood. Reportedly, Bush Sr.–whose "cottage" is just up the road–orders Mabel's famous lobster special.

The dish can be overwhelming for those who like their rascal unfussed-with: a sizeable lobster bulging with scallop, onion, bacon, and bread stuffing, toasted and dripping with butter. It's sort of like five dishes in one, and I'd be hard-pressed to finish it in one sitting, but it is very, very good. Mabel's menu is teeming with this kind of dish–complicated, luxe takes on surf and turf that you'd expect to be served at a wedding. Those who haven't led the free world may opt for some of the simpler, shack-style fare. Mabel's lobster roll is a classic, packed with claw and tail meat, and even sweeter when shedders come on the market. The lobster stew (pricey, but colossally portioned) takes a while because the kitchen believes it's a dish best made to order, and the lush hunks of meat drunk on cream and slicked with butter are worth the wait. The whole affair tastes even better with a few good cranks of black pepper.

Fried clams here are fairly stupendous, but they disappear from the menu in late summer when blueberry season hits, reportedly because local clammers can make more money picking and selling the tiny wild fruit. The fact that Mabel's would rather stop serving one of its most popular dishes than stoop so low as to serve nonnative clams says something about this kitchen's uncompromising standards. The same goes for the clam chowder–it may or may not be the chowder of the day. If it is, get it; it's a straightforward, tummy-warming concoction, heavy with clam morsels and cream, laced with fat chunks of potato, and sprinkled with fresh chives. Oyster crackers would almost be overkill.

Desserts are a big deal at Mabel's, and you'll have trouble choosing between the "famous" peanut butter ice cream pie, the homemade fudge cake (it comes with ice cream, napped with extra fudge sauce), and the heavenly blueberry pie.

Maine Diner

Route 1, Wells • 207-646-4441 www.mainediner.com • Open year-round
BEST BITES: Seafood chowder, lobster pie, she-crab soup, cod cakes, Indian pudding

"These two women came in for lunch once," says Myles Henry, who owns the Maine Diner with his brother Dick. "They'd gone on a three-month chowder excursion from the mid-Atlantic all the way up to the Maritimes, and they'd tasted more than a thousand bowls of chowder. They said only one other place, up in Nova Scotia, had chowder that even came close to ours." He pauses. "That was pretty cool."

Myles Henry thinks food in general is pretty cool, and he plays around with recipes and ingredients with the jazzed verve of a big-city chef–but without any of the pretension. "Food is just fun," he says. "Diner food, five-star food, doesn't matter. And I think it should always reflect its place. I'm not knocking chain restaurants, but I think it's a shame to take a bite of food and not know whether you're in Boston or Omaha, Nebraska."

Like everything else on the menu at this cheery coffee-shop edging Kennebunkport on Route 1, there's no big culinary secret to the seafood chowder in question. "We just do it right," says Myles, who tinkered with the recipe for months until he was satisfied. "Cook each ingredient separately, but in the same liquid, straining in between batches and reducing the broth. It's not hard; it's just a lot of work, and most places don't take the time." The finished product is an intoxicating bowl of chowder: a divinely rich cream-based broth with bobbing bits of scallop, tiny shrimp, flaky haddock, and a lobster claw or four.

Chowders are bestsellers at the Diner. This seafood variety is wildly popular (they go through about 20 big kettles of the stuff a day) as is the New England clam. A

few years ago Myles added she-crab soup to the menu, using locally caught crab. "No one else up here has it," he says of the almost bisquelike mixture spiked with Old Bay and sherry. It's definitely more mid-Atlantic than Maine coast, which may be why patrons–many of them locals– were skeptical at first. But Myles did what he always does with a new recipe: He handed out free samples. "It was just a question of getting them hooked," he says. Now he'd be hard-pressed to take it off the menu.

There's a quality lobster roll here, chunky, unadorned, served warm with a deep ramekin of melted butter on the side and a pickle. But it's all just a preamble to the Diner's signature item: lobster pie, an elegantly simple recipe handed down from Myles and Dick's grandmother. Fresh hand-torn gnarls of luscious meat are crammed into a low chafing dish, drizzled with butter, and topped with a crumb mixture that gets its smoky tones from a few generous gobs of tomalley. The whole affair is browned until it bubbles and served up with a dense cloud of hand-mashed potatoes. It's a dish to restore faith to the unbelieving, the stuff of cravings that won't go away. Only in polite company should you resist the urge to run a fingertip along the dish's bottom. Raise a glass to Myles's grandmother when you're done.

For the lost soul who doesn't like lobster, there are other fishy standouts on the menu. Cod cakes offer a satisfying twist on the home-kitchen favorite born of Yankee thrift: Salt cod is smushed into those mashed spuds, shaped into nuggets, and deep-fried to a perfect crunch. These are sided by a crock of toothy, saucy, bacon-studded brown beans. Or try the crispy fried or crumble-baked haddock. There's also a fried clam platter, the Henry brothers' own tribute to their favorite boyhood shack: "El's Fried Clams, on Route 1 in York," says Myles. "El would dig his own clams every morning and close up shop when he'd fried the last one. The place is gone now, but that's still our barometer for the perfect clam."
Myles is so reverential of good fried clams that

he only uses bivalves from the northern reaches of Maine and southern Canada–"If we can't get 'em, we take 'em off the menu."

For dessert, more lobster pie. No? Then swirl your spoon through the Maineiest of sweet treats, a bowl of gooey Indian pudding.

crib sheet:
Tomalley and Roe

Sounds like a vaudeville act, but it's actually indispensable lobster jargon. Tomalley is the lobster's liver, recognizable by its gooshy consistency and gray-greenish-mustardy hue. The roe—unfertilized lobster eggs—is sometimes called the coral because the dark stuff turns bright orange when cooked.

Chefs call these the best part of the lobster; many use them as the base for lobster broth, while true die-hards simply spread the stuff on toast. No less an authority than Julia Child frowned upon any recipe that would discard either.

Order the lobster pie at the Maine Diner in Wells for a delectable introduction to tomalley, which is tossed with butter and fresh-picked meat in their lobster pie.

Middlebay Lobster

45 Ellen Way, Cundy's Harbor • 207-798-5868 • Open Memorial Day to Labor Day
BEST BITES: Lobster stew, fried haddock sandwich, steamers

On the front of its Xeroxed yellow menu and on the mini-marquee outside, Middlebay Lobster calls itself Maine's best-kept secret, and I almost want to keep it that way.

Just a couple of years young, Middlebay Lobster is a comfy roadhouse with all the concrete-floored allure of a bait shop, tucked in a grove of pines. And in the little kitchen in the back, Elizabeth Hurd, who owns the place with her lobsterman husband Jeff, concocts the best lobster stew that's ever passed my lips. Quite simply, this stuff is trumpets-sounding, angels-singing, sun-breaking-through-clouds good. It manages to distill the flavor of a full lobster dinner into each spoonful, which is what many lobster stews aspire to but not so many pull off. I complimented the cook, saying the stuff tasted like it was just lobster, butter, and cream, hoping I might eke some information out of her. "You don't say," she responded. Translation: You'll pry the recipe out of my cold, dead hands. I can live with that. Just as long as they keep it on the menu.

There's also a fantastic fried haddock sandwich, with a medium-thick fillet easily twice the size of its bun and curling out into crisp points on either side. A broth-and-butter-sided bucket piled high with husky Maine steamers makes a contenting meal unto itself and was a bargain at $5.95 in '05. A pair of decadent, chilled seafood rolls, made with fresh-picked Maine crabmeat and lobster, come in three sizes each, the rosy meat shimmering with a spring coat of mayonnaise. Middlebay's crab bisque looks and smells promising–I managed to pry my eyes from my plate to notice bowls of it flying by–and I desperately want to try it, but I don't see that happening anytime soon, because of the damn lobster stew.

lingo: Down East

To the uninitiated, logical mind, "Down East" (or "Downeast") Maine might suggest Portland or Kittery—points that are down, as in to the south. Not so. The term has its origins in age-old sailor-speak: Those hauling cargo in Maine's waters noted that prevailing winds were southwestern, blowing their vessels downwind and to the east. Today, even though Down East is used outside the state as a blanket term for Maine, it technically refers to the swath of coast starting around Ellsworth and stretching north. Misuse of the term is proof positive that someone is "from away"—another bit of colloquial fun, used to designate someone who's not from Maine.

Miss Sea's

Route 1, Waldoboro • 207-542-0179 • Open May through December
BEST BITES: Miniature lobster and crab rolls, lobster on a stick, bacon cheese dog

Miss Sea has no official address, but as you're zooming through the little village of Waldoboro on Route 1, you'd be hard pressed to miss the takeout's signage: lobster flags, stenciled plywood, and a sandwich board advertising . . . lobster on a stick? Miss Sea herself, a.k.a. Missy, admits it's a bit of a gimmick to drum up business. "It's just a lobster tail on a stick, you know, with butter," she says.

One thing that's not advertised as loudly is my favorite thing on the menu: the mini-lobster roll. For just a few dollars ($3.50 in summer '05), you get a generous help-ing of meat swirled in light dressing and lumped into a hot dog roll about 4 inches long, griddled on the spot by Missy herself. There's also a mini-crabmeat roll, prepared the same way using fresh Maine crab she buys from a place a little farther down Route 1–it's just as delicious, and even cheaper. These mini-rolls don't require much commitment; they barely require an appetite. They're like the Krispy Kremes of the seafood world: too cheap and tasty to not pick one up every time you drive by.

Along with regular-sized lobster and crab rolls and hot dogs piled with crumbled bacon and cheese, Missy does steamers, full lobster dinners, and the odd meatball sub here (a big blue tarp juts out to either side of her trail-er, roofing a few picnic tables well suited to this messier fare). You can also pick up live lobsters and clams to go.

Missy adds hearty seafood chowders and stews to her menu in leaf-peeping season, and starting in November, sells Christmas trees and wreaths in this spot.

lingo:
Bug
Fisherman slang for lobster.

Nunan's Lobster Hut

9 Mills Road (Route 9), Kennebunkport • 207-967-4362 • Open year-round

BEST BITES: Lobster, lobster stew, steamers, clam chowder, homemade blueberry pie

rown-bag your own booze to this workhorse of a shack near the mouth of the inlet in Cape Porpoise, just a few minutes north of Kennebunkport on Route 9. You'll feel like you've stumbled into the attic of an old sailor: The shingled walls and sloping rafters are hung with tangles of buoys, ship prints, and other grubby curios (like a sign that reads "Two happiest days in the life of a boatsman: the day he buys it, the day he sells it"). Nunan's Lobster Hut is what newer restaurants try to emulate with their studied retro-whimsy, but it's an atmosphere that can't be faked with a few garage sales and a staple gun. This kind of crustiness takes years to acquire. Fifty-three, to be precise.

Bertha Nunan's been serving the simplest menu to locals and vacationers to the Kennebunks since she opened the place in 1953. Now semi-retired, she comes by on and off but lets her sons run the business. Still, it's Bertha's exacting standards of quality–only the best, freshest lobster, cooked to her specifications (see sidebar)–that have made the place home to generations of lobster lovers. The restaurant's motto is simple enough: "We catch 'em, we cook 'em, we crack 'em, you eat 'em!" And that's exactly what happens, to the tune of about 700 pounds of lobster on the average summer evening.

There's no view here, unless you count the parking lot and the marsh out back. From the outside, with its cheery red and yellow trim and inimitable sign, the black-clapboarded restaurant looks almost dollhouse-sized, but it's four rooms long within; still, by 5:15 PM, right after the restaurant opens (it's a dinner-only place), every last picnic table inside is full and hungry crowds wait their turn out front (or as Bertha calls it, "in the pasture").

And the menu? Choose your lobster (from $1\frac{1}{8}$ pounds, solo or twinned, up to $1\frac{1}{2}$ pounds–if size matters, you can discreetly inquire about bigger bugs), served up with a roll, potato chips, and a pickle. Then maybe pick something to whet your appetite while you wait for your lobster to cook. Try the thick, peppery New England–style clam chowder or get those clams au naturel in an order of steamers. The latter, like the lobster, are dumped onto a well-worn stainless steel tray and plopped onto your table; you get a ramekin of broth for rinsing and another of drawn butter on the side. The lob-

ster stew is an insanely rich, buttery, briny broth buoying hearty chunks of lobster meat. Get the small order of stew or skip an entrée entirely and have the large. Wash it all down with whatever you BYO-ed or ask for a root beer, Nunan's own. And whatever you do, don't skip dessert: Bertha bakes the restaurant's blueberry pie, served up plain or à la mode. (There's apple, too, but you're in Maine–are you really going to do that?)

Nunan's recognizes that lobster is messy business if you do it right: Grab the plastic bib provided if you're wearing something you're attached to. When you're done, just march over to the big stainless steel sinks lining the wall and wash up.

There's always someone loudly exclaiming they can't believe Nunan's charges extra for coleslaw–usually a dad whose kids are staring down at their feet, totally mortified. Call it a petty move, or chalk it up to the restaurant's quirks. Besides, it's tasty coleslaw worth the $1.50, not the standard soggy afterthought.

And that's it. There's no fish at Nunan's, unless you count the tuna salad, one of a small selection of sandwiches (peanut butter, open-faced grilled cheese, tuna salad, a basic burger). That, along with the juicy Delmonico rib eye dinner, constitutes the Hut's only acknowledgment of a world without lobster.

cooking lobster: The Bertha Method

"I'm always surprised at what people will do to a lobster," says Bertha Nunan, shaking her head. "Some pre-cook it and throw it back into boiling water for a minute just before serving." She opened her Cape Porpoise restaurant in 1953 and has been cooking lobsters the same way ever since. Here's how she does it:

1. Pour 2 inches of water in the bottom of a big pot—whether you're cooking one or a dozen lobsters.

2. Swirl in "a few good plops" of table salt.

3. When the water's boiling, add the lobster(s), cover the pot, and cook for 20 minutes. "Not a minute more, not a minute less," says Bertha.

4. Cooking your lobster in batches? Bertha says her secret is washing the pot in between. "Practically nobody else does this," she says, "but it's what makes our lobster taste better than anybody else's. Lobsters can get all dirty and greasy from eating bait," she says, pointing to the sediment left in a pot after cooking. "So start with fresh water every time."

Red's Eats

Route 1 on the west side of the bridge, Wiscasset • 207-882-6128 • Open April through September
BEST BITES: Lobster roll, fried shrimp, crabcakes, the Yumbo

Devotees pledge that Red's Eats–a crimson-colored tool shed that started dishing out dime-lunch fare in 1938–serves the best lobster roll in Maine, and therefore on the planet: the ne plus ultra of lobster on a bun. Perhaps more crucially, these same people are willing to drive across the country and stand 100-strong in line for up to two hours to get their hands on one; this, in turn, brings cars to a near-standstill in both directions on Route 1 as it stretches across the Wiscasset Bridge, infamously creating the worst snarls in the state. And a lobster roll that stops traffic is the kind of thing that makes CNN send a camera crew. As a result, this may be the most photographed takeout window in America.

All of which fuels the fire of naysayers, many of them locals, who claim that the reputation of Red's roll is based entirely on its hard-to-get-ness, on the thrill of the chase.

They say the sandwich is all show, famous for being famous, and too expensive–the Paris Hilton of seafood. Debate aside, two things are indisputable: Whether or not it's the best tasting lobster roll on earth, it's without a doubt the most impressive and tastiest-*looking,* and Red's has drawn people from all over the world to Wiscasset– the self-dubbed "prettiest little village in Maine"–to taste it.

There's also no denying a certain magic in the air on a summer Saturday when, between 9:30 and 10 AM, a small crowd starts to gather in front of the shuttered trailer. (Red's officially opens at 11, but sometimes, the reality's closer to 12:15.) The first in line are usually the most haggard-looking, weary from their trip and cranky from hunger. Soon, the line starts to grow at a rate of about one person a minute. As 11 AM nears, the crowd gets antsy; by 11:10, if Red's still isn't taking orders, civilization's veneer wears thin and things start to acquire definite mob potential (as much as a group made up of Mormon newlyweds and retirees in golf shirts can).

Finally, the Maine equivalent of the velvet rope is lifted–the takeout window's red shutters swing open–and word makes its way down the line, which often stretches along the sloping sidewalk and well onto the bridge. In observance of Red's tradition, the cashier asks the first person in line where they're from, and this tidbit gets announced over the PA system to great whooping and applause from the hungry crowd, which at this point is primed to applaud pretty much anything.

And then, the first roll is served, and the lucky patron cradles it in tinfoil and marches it victoriously down the

line to one of the plastic picnic tables set up behind the trailer. Red's claims to pack more than a whole lobster's worth of meat into each roll, and you'll certainly have trouble picking it up and eating it like a sandwich. The top-loading bun is perfectly toasted and brushed with butter; the meat is moist from the lobster's natural juices alone. (You'll be asked if you'd prefer butter or mayo on the side for dipping.) Rusty-colored claws protrude from each end of the bun; huge, hand-torn chunks of meat bulge from the center; and the sandwich is crowned with an entire, glistening lobster tail, split in two.

Amazingly, there's an entire menu here of items that aren't lobster rolls, mostly of the fried variety: Some like the fried mushrooms or zucchini, others go for the clam or crabcakes–both straightforward and tasty–or crispy fried Gulf shrimp. There's also a really good toasted ham and cheese sandwich on a sesame bun called the Yumbo, a steal at $2.95 in '05, and Round Top ice cream served out of a side window, towards the bridge.

the big questions: Shedders vs. Hard-Shell Lobsters

Unlike much of the sea's bounty, which is at the peak of its quality and taste in colder months, the lobster world delivers what some believe to be its tastiest treat in summer. That's when soft-shell lobsters—also known as shedders or new-shells—start showing up in traps. These critters have molted, discarding their hard shell as a crab would, and are in the soft-shell phase of growing a new carapace.

Shedders have their naysayers, claiming that the texture and flavor of the meat isn't quite up to snuff during this period, pointing to the fact that a shedder can yield 30 to 50 percent less meat than a hard-shell, and saying you're mostly paying for water.

Feh, I say. First, shedders are cheaper, by as much as $3 per pound, primarily because they don't ship well, and because they do carry more water weight than hard-shells. And then there's the flavor. Georgetown, Maine, lobsterman Leon Kelly is a new-shell die-hard: "They taste much sweeter! At least I think so. And the meat's more tender. I'll take a shedder any day," he says, plopping a live one down in front of me. Almost springy to the touch, the shell is so thin that, once cooked, it's possible to eat a shedder without the aid of metal crackers—just peel and eat. Like the tangerine of the sea.

So next time you're ordering a lobster in the summer months, ask if they have shedders. Try one, and see if you agree with Leon.

Ruth & Wimpy's Restaurant

792 Route 1, Hancock • 207-422-3723 • Open early April to December
BEST BITES: Shore dinner, steamed mussels

*I*t was inevitable, really, in a state known for lobster and a country known for superlatives, that sooner or later somebody somewhere would lay claim to the largest lobster. That somewhere is Ruth & Wimpy's Restaurant, near the mouth of Mount Desert Island, a cozy restaurant that you can't miss precisely because of Wilbur, the 20-foot fiberglass crustacean who makes his home out front, next to the lobster cookers puffing steam up to the sky.

I think maybe when Ruth and Wimpy decided to erect a colossal lobster statue in their parking lot, they didn't know just what a sensation he'd stir. Nowadays, only nightfall and torrential rain quell the steady stream of visitors eager to be photographed with Wilbur. He's one part of the affectionately touristy appeal at Ruth & Wimpy's; there's also a roped-off 1950s Pontiac done up in candy-cane colors on display near the front door, and the restaurant's walls and ceiling are almost fully grown over with nautical gimcrackery. Unless you get here very early, you'll probably have a wait, albeit a short and pleasant one. Ale aficionados will happily pass the time reading the labels on hundreds of beer bottles lining the shelves, and the rest can bask in the cheery mayhem of servers dispatching twin lobsters straight from the cooker, steaming bowls of mussels, clams, and chowder, and trays piled high with fried seafood. Large groups should try to score the party room tucked away on the right; if the weather's cooperating, go for the roofed cluster of picnic tables outside, where you can watch the action at the lobster pots and keep Wilbur company–as if he needs it.

Ruth & Wimpy's Giant Lobster

Full Name: Wilbur, the Giant Lobster
Stats: 20 feet in length; fiberglass shell
Claim to Fame: Biggest lobster in Maine, perhaps in U.S.
Factoid to Drop at Parties: Kirstie Alley once signed over a blank check to take him home, but the owners ripped it up

Ten Chowders, Stews
and One Mind-Blowing Bisque

Few dishes anywhere have roots that run as deep as chowder in New England—or are as hotly debated. These 10 concoctions are some of the headiest to ever hit a bowl.

1. *Seafood stew*, Helen's, Machias, ME
A religious experience, which may explain why Helen's makes this dish only on Sundays. Hunks of shellfish and haddock pack a light cream chowder broth—just a handful of oyster crackers away from the perfect autumn-day meal.

2. *Lobster bisque*, Chopmist Charlie's, Jamestown, RI
People buy this velvety concoction to use as a recipe base—heavy with cream, spiked with sherry, very lobstery.

3. *Seafood chowder*, Maine Diner, Wells, ME
Rich, intense flavor buoys tender clams, Maine shrimp, and pillows of sweet lobster meat to the buttery surface.

4. *Clam chowder*, Captain Parker's Pub, West Yarmouth, MA
Over and over again, Gerry "The Captain" Manning's creamy clam chowder wins local and not-so-local chowder-offs.

5. *Scallop chowder*, Thurston's Lobster Pound, Bernard, ME
This local institution makes a different chowder every day, but my favorite is the scallop: Generous chunks of the sweet shellfish lace a milky, light gray broth, buttery and flecked with thyme.

6. *Haddock chowder*, The Take Out, Stonington, ME
Even on sweltering days, people go for a Styrofoam cup of this stuff. Flaky hunks of haddock are swirled around in a tasty cream base that gets its oomph from an unusual suspect: tarragon.

7. *Creamy clam chowder*, Newick's, Dover, NH
Newick's has a lot of chowders on its menu, but it's this—the extra-thick clam—that brings you back.

8. *Fish chowder*, The Dolphin Marina, Harpswell, ME
The restaurant calls this stuff "the best fish chowder in the universe." They're not kidding.

9. *Lobster stew*, Middlebay Lobster, Cundy's Harbor, ME
The flavor of a full lobster dinner, in a bowl. Crammed with sweet, pink meat, it's one of those things that's wildly complicated in the kitchen but tastes simple and perfect on the spoon.

10. *Mussel chowder*, Sesuit Harbor Cafe, Sesuit, MA
It's not a regular menu item, but it should be. Creamy thick, briny-flavored, and buttery, and studded with slivers of dark orange mussel.

Scales

25 Preble Street, at the Public Market, Portland • 207-228-2010 • Open year-round
BEST BITES: Fried haddock with hand-cut fries, fisherman's stew, raw bar

Portland is an eating town, and if you have any kind of crush on food, its Public Market will make you fall harder. The vast, cathedral-ceilinged structure houses stalls selling goods from far away and close by, and an hour spent winding through this place is a pleasing and filling one: Here, sample a sliver of Irish gubbeen, a washed-rind cheese; there, slice yourself a hunk of still-warm bread baked with honey and spread it with creamy farmhouse butter; a little farther, at a produce stand, taste the reason why Maine is synonymous with blueberries.

One corner of the market had trouble finding its feet. A few different fish purveyors moved in, but nothing seemed to click until Sam Hayward and Dana Street showed up. (They're the wonder-duo behind Portland's Fore Street restaurant, home to spit-basted rabbit and pan-roasted mussels hopped up on almonds; if you haven't been, get your car keys now.) Like Fore Street, Scales is all about local goods, but it's primarily a fish market: Piles of plump gray shrimp abut shiny-shelled cherrystones and littlenecks on ice; kicky live lobsters are irrigated in a low tiled bath; and special requests are embraced as challenges (need a whole monkfish liver? They know a guy). It's also a raw bar (picks and lemon wedges make eyes at you from the oyster station) and a bit of a restaurant too, where everything is cooked to order. Cornmeal-crusted clams, oysters, and scallops are fried and served in paper cones, which, aside from absorbing the nonexistent grease, just look nifty. They're served with fries, as is the puffy battered haddock. These fries are hand-cut, French bistro–style, caramel colored and earthy flavored, and served with spicy homemade ketchup (but a jolt of malt vinegar makes them sing). Try the codfish cakes with smoky baked beans, the crab-and-shallot salad, a crock of luscious fisherman's stew, or the lobster roll. On the shy side of $20, this roll may be pricey, but it's a cut above: Your lobster is cooked to order, picked on the spot, and stuffed into a crisp, pillowy bun barely able to contain the buttery juices that'll make their way down your arms if you brave it without knife and fork. Scales gets white tie, too, with elegant dishes like sautéed skate wing, and they'll prepare pretty much anything they have in the market for a small fee.

A few tables dot the sidewalk in warm weather, and there's also a handful of seats inside–or you could perch on a stool at the fish counter itself, ideal for soaking up the bustling sights and sounds of the market.

crib sheet: Maine Shrimp

Winter in Maine is called a lot of things ("unholy freezing nightmare," for instance), but my favorite has to be "shrimp season." Maine shrimp (a.k.a. Northern pink shrimp) are fished only in midwinter, when they migrate south from the polar circle to the northeast Atlantic to hatch their larvae. These tiny suckers—head-on, they're less than 5 inches long— are fantastically sweet and flavorful. If you get them fresh, the less done to them the better; many restaurants will simply steam and serve them for your peel-and-eat convenience. Luckily, they freeze well, so they pop up on menus in the summer—try them fried at the Lobster Shack in Cape Elizabeth, ME.

Shaw's Fish & Lobster Wharf

129 State Road (Route 32), New Harbor • 207-677-2200 • www.shawsfishandlobster.com
BEST BITES: Lobster potpie, lobster stew, lobster roll

The salty fishing village of New Harbor is like something out of a movie–specifically, *Message in a Bottle*, where it stood in for a fictional South Carolina town.

You'd be forgiven for missing the schmaltzy Kevin Costner vehicle; not so if you make your way to this part of Maine without coming to Shaw's. Unimpeded harbor view, check. Lobstermen hauling traps onto wooden scales mere feet away, check. Picnic tables on a weathered topside deck, check. Shaw's has it all, without an ounce of pretension, and it serves some of the freshest, simplest shack food on the mid-coast.

There's no fried food here, so as to not mess with a good thing: a menu built on chowders, stews, and seafood rolls. Shaw's lobsters, fished from these waters and delivered hours ago, are done up a handful of delicious ways, though it's hard to resist the simple allure of a shore dinner featuring a whole lobster, or two or three–yes, three. A fisherman at Shaw's bar first tipped me off to the triple lobster special, a favorite betting meal around these parts– as in, "I'll bet you a triple at Shaw's you can't get her phone number." (He also told me that up until recently, you went at your lobster the old-fashioned way, with a wooden mallet. But lobsters aren't crabs and this was a messy affair, so metal crackers have taken their place.) Go for the potpie, freshly chunked lobster napped with a buttery sherry cream and bubbling under a toasted cracker crust. If Ritz crumbs and booze strike you as overkill, downgrade to the lobster stew, whose ingredients can be counted on the fingers of one hand. The secret to this transporting mixture is twofold: It gets some depth from a smack of dry mustard, and it's always allowed to sit overnight for maximum lobster-ness. If even that's complicating things too much, have Shaw's lobster roll. The meat shimmers with mayonnaise and a drop or two of lemon juice, nestled against a single leaf of crisp lettuce in a perfectly buttered bun. They reportedly serve up to 10,000 of these in a summer. Finally, there's the Lazy Man's Lobster: meat, butter, and paprika. It's one of the kitchen's most popular dishes.

Have the roll for lunch and then come back in the late afternoon, parking yourself at the bar downstairs– where half the stools face out over the harbor, with its deep green waters, bobbing fishing boats, and pine-shrouded, white-shingled houses across the way–and order a pint of something local on tap.

Spinney's Restaurant

987 Popham Road, Phippsburg • 207-389-1122 • Open May to November
BEST BITES: Onion rings, haddock chowder, blueberry pie

*M*y French father is a man of predictably Gallic tastes: He has a glass of red wine every morning with breakfast, makes his own meaty terrines from scratch when the mood strikes, and is perplexed by peanut butter and marshmallow fluff. He's also a man who's driven more than 300 miles to Spinney's, a rickety restaurant perched at the edge of Phippsburg's Popham Beach, for a plate of sizzling, salty onion rings washed down with a frosty mug of Shipyard Ale.

These are important onion rings. On our initial visit, when my dad asked what the server recommended, they were the first item out of her mouth. The kitchen starts with thin bangles of sweet colossal onion that are hand dipped in a dry crumb crust and fried until perfectly crunchy, inside and out. There's nothing revolutionary to the process and yet–unlike the rings from so many other kitchens–these emerge greaseless, while the pearly flesh within is just shy of cooked and popping with mellow, oniony flavor. One bite suggests that they might be lacing the fry oil with some sort of human catnip. The same goes for all the fried items on the menu, each as satisfying and expertly done as the last, and made from fresh seafood that arrives daily. Spinney's also makes some blissful chowders, including the haddock, which is creamy, medium-thick, and bobbing with nuggets of fish and toothy potato cubes.

There's no rush to finish your meal here, so linger awhile as you gaze out at one of the only sandy beaches in this otherwise rocky stretch of Maine. Belly room permitting, get yourself a slice of homemade pie oozing with warm blueberry filling to go with that last sip of Shipyard.

Or take a cue from my dad and get a second order of onion rings "for the table," even though everyone else is full.

walk off the meal: Fort Popham Stroll

Get your onion rings with a side of history. From Spinney's, it's a short walk to the tip of Hunnewell Point and the hand-cut granite walls of Fort Popham, built (and never finished) during the Civil War. On this same peninsula, the first English colony was established in 1607—13 years before the pilgrims landed on Plymouth Rock. They shipped back to England from this same spot on the *Virginia*, the first documented vessel built on American soil.

Sprague's Lobster

Route 1, west of the bridge, Wiscasset • 207-882-1236 • Open mid-June to the weekend after Columbus Day • BEST BITES: Lobster roll, crab roll, shore dinner

You'd be forgiven for missing this takeout on the edge of the Creamery Pier—the grandstanding at Red's Eats across the street (see p. 215) is enough to distract anybody. But many locals say Sprague's is the better of the two, with its straight-up menu of steamed, boiled, and fried classics, including terrific hand-cut fries and the shore dinner, a whole lobster, corn on the cob, a roll, and—a hard-boiled egg? "That's our specialty," says Frank Sprague, who owns the place with his wife Linda. "We took it off the menu in the '80s, when there was all that talk about eggs and cholesterol, but folks kept asking, 'Where'd the egg go?'" He claims cooking the egg with the lobster gives it the slight tang of the sea. Served with less fanfare, Sprague's lobster roll is slightly cheaper than the one across the street, and absolutely excellent (its little brother, the fresh crabmeat roll, is worth your time and travels well). And the best part? Hardly ever a line.

shack staple: Top-Loading Bun

To many, a lobster roll that's not served in a top-loading bun (also known as a split-top, or, in New England, a frankfurter roll) isn't a lobster roll at all.

Real top-loaders look a bit like two vertically squashed slices of white bread, providing maximum surface for grilling, toasting, or griddling your bun before loading it up with hot or cold lobster, or crabmeat, or fried seafood. Shacks along the coast tend to favor buns by J.J. Nissen, Freihofer, and Pepperidge Farm. Unlike a regular side-loading hot dog bun, these tight sheaths don't fall apart when filled—unless the filling involves inordinate amounts of buttered lobster, which is a good problem to have.

These unusual rolls are hard to find elsewhere— another reason why it's nearly impossible to replicate a real lobster roll outside of New England.

Tall Barney's Restaurant

Main Street (Route 187), Jonesport • 207-497-2403 • Open year-round
BEST BITES: Fried clams, seafood platter, blueberry pound cake, breakfast

Jonesport is a peninsula-tip town where the streets get narrower, cottages peeling with paint jut off the land at precarious-looking angles, and water views are broken up by tiny islands with names like Pig and Little Sheep. Jonesport doesn't have a movie theater or a store, but it does have commercial fishermen, basketball games at the local high school, and fog. It also has Tall Barney's, a stubby diner in the middle of town where fishermen start their days at 4 AM with breakfast and an hour or so of jawing about yesterday's catch, the game scores, and whether the fog's going to lift.

Perhaps because entertainment can be scarce in these parts, the usual one-that-got-away tall tales are elevated to an art form at Tall Barney's—so much so that its daily gathering of salty raconteurs has been affectionately called the Liar's Table, which has gained notoriety well beyond the peninsula. One of their favorite topics is Barney Beale, a Jonesporter from the 1800s and the restaurant's namesake. Barney was more than 7 feet tall, liked his drink, and—if you believe the stories—was so strong, he once stumbled out of a bar in a brawling mood vowing to hit the first person he encountered. All he saw was a horse, which he wound up knocking dead with a single punch between the eyes.

The fishermen of Jonesport almost lost their beloved meeting place a few years ago, when Tall Barney's went on the market and no one bit. Just as the owner was threatening to close the place down, NPR did a story on the Liar's Table; a few hundred miles south, New Jersey insurance salesman John Lipinski happened to tune in. He didn't know a thing about running a restaurant, but he knew he was looking for a change. A few phone calls and moving vans later, he and his wife Linda were setting their alarm clock a whole lot earlier as Tall Barney's new proprietors.

A few novelties have snuck in since the Lipinskis took the helm—Barney Beale might have looked askance at, say, veggie burgers served within these old walls—but mostly, the menu's staples remain unchanged: fried seafood, hearty chowders, and meat, all served up in portions that might also kill a horse. Try the haddock burger or the sweet fried clams and scallops, or nibble a little of everything on the Seafood Platter. It's so gargantuan that if you manage to finish it, dessert's on the house. (At this writing, only one customer had taken John up on the offer.)

Desserts are best enjoyed on a stomach that's at least partially empty: Linda bakes all pies, cakes, and crisps herself, and many star ample amounts of the wild blueberries for which this part of Maine is known.

lingo: Clambake

A method of cooking clams, mussels, lobsters, corn, and potatoes by rigging a fire in a pit, letting it burn down to the coals, piling it with rocks, and layering the food with wet seaweed on top. Everything steam-cooks, thanks to the kelp's moisture, acquiring a particularly oceany flavor. Said to have originated with New England's Native Americans. Also used on some menus to mean a lobster cooked along with its trimmings (steamers, corn, potatoes).

The Take Out

134 North Main Street, Stonington • 207-367-2211 • Open Memorial Day to Labor Day
BEST BITES: Crab roll, haddock chowder, fried shrimp

I didn't measure, but the Take Out may be the tiniest eating establishment in this book. If a real seafood shack should look like it could be towed away, the Take Out wouldn't even require a truck. A foursome of firemen could do the job after a couple of pints of Geary's.

The gray trailer with the lobster-and-spruce sign, set back on the west side of the road that winds down the Blue Hill peninsula, is a perfect place to stop and gather energy on your drive to Deer Isle or the Isle au Haut Ferry.

The quality standards at this pit stop are in inverse proportion to its size. Somehow, there's room for a fryer in this hut, and it turns out scrumptious piles of golden shrimp, scallops, and haddock in baskets or rolls; turn to the second page of the two-Xerox, one-staple menu for "just fried clams." The haddock in the sandwich is available broiled, too; you can skip these and get your fill of fish from the haddock chowder, whose humble presentation–ladled into a Styrofoam coffee cup–belies the magical concoction within. The broth is thin but you can still taste the butter in the cream, and the chubby hunks of fish barely fit past the mouth of the cup. The whole thing is liberally seasoned with fresh tarragon, which gives it a subtle, unusual licorice kick. I'm hooked.

The other standout on this menu is the crab roll. You're in crab roll country down here, but the Take Out's version really is spectacular: You don't quite know where the sweetness of the crab ends and that of the creamy dressing begins. And if you fork out the filling as you go, as some do, you're left with a few deliciously gooey bites of buttered toast that taste winningly like crab. It's a trick I learned from a customer who had one half-eaten crab roll in her hand and a second waiting on the table. I tried her method, and she's right. I challenge even the most die-hard carb hater not to eat this bun. There's also a long list of meaty subs available and finger-food of the buffalo wing variety.

Just a few picnic tables painted with maritime scenes separate the Take Out from the road, and during the week, it seems as if every worker in Stonington pulls in on their lunch break to pick up an order of something salty and good. But beware of peeling out: A stern sign taped to the kitchen door informs the clientele that "Squealing of Tires Is Not Going to Be Tolerated: You Will Personally Be Asked Not To Come Back." And that would be a real shame.

Thurston's Lobster Pound

Steamboat Wharf Road, Bernard • 207-244-7600 • Open Memorial Day through Columbus Day
BEST BITES: Scallop chowder, shore dinner, Joey's crabcakes, crab Louis spread

*I*t's nice to sit on one of the decks at Thurston's on a blue-skied midday, watching the bustle of fishing boats in action and the glint of sunlight off the water of Bass Harbor, cracking your way through a plump, succulent lobster on a yellow tray. But my first visit to Thurston's, on a dull, chilly day just before dusk, got me hooked on more than the food. As far as I'm concerned, this ramshackle wharf was made to be experienced at twilight, in a thick sweater, surrounded by pea-soup fog. It was impossible to see more than a few feet beyond the screened-in deck to the outside–you could barely make out the outlines of the lobster boats, but you

could hear them, some close and others farther away, water slapping against their hulls, their ropes creaking on the moorings. Low tide and moist air made the harbor especially fragrant, and the musty smell of seaweed made everything taste better. It was chowder and ale weather, so that's what we had–that, of course, and lobster.

Looking at the place, with its rusted fixtures and weathered shingles, you'd never guess the restaurant's only been around since the early 1990s. That's because there's been a lobster wholesaling outfit in this location since Fred Thurston founded it in 1946. Wander beyond the lower decks or past the little porch puffing with steam from the broad propane-fueled cooker, and you'll see that this part of the business is still very much thriving today. Hundreds of green and yellow wire traps, crusty with dried seaweed and barnacles, sit stacked seven and eight high on the next dock, littered with faded buoys and coils of heavy rope. Thurston's great-grandson, Mike Radcliffe, runs it all today, buying the legendary lobsters served at Thurston's off the 70-odd boats that call Bass Harbor home.

Once you choose your lobster from the basin by the register, where a kitchen hand weighs and sorts them by size, preparation is straightforward: Your bug and whatever else (steamers, mussels, corn) get stuffed into a net with handles and a numbered wooden chip and dropped into boiling seawater out back while you decide on any extras. The lobsters are untouchable here, especially the new-shells: They're sweet and musky from the seawater, especially towards the end of the day, when the water's flavor has intensified from everything it's touched. Luscious

milky broth infused with herbs and cracked black pepper.

The mussel chowder zings with white wine, cream, garlic, and shallot, while the scallop gets its kick from pungent oregano leaves. All three chowders are served up with generous, tender chunks of the key ingredient, and all three get their richness from a kitchen trick: They're aged for a full day before being served.

If you still manage to be hungry after all this, stain your teeth with a slice of oozy-good homemade blueberry cake.

Maine crab stars in three dishes: There's a yummy, inexpensive roll on the sandwich menu (which includes some kid-friendly dishes like hamburgers, hot dogs, and PB&J); Joey's crabcakes, savory broiled pucks light on filler, with smoky chipotle sauce on the side; and the crab Louis spread. There's not much to Thurston's version of this West Coast classic—mostly the crabmeat's moistened with mayonnaise and cream, before a dash of chili sauce and cayenne bring the heat. Spread it on crackers as you sip one of the local brews; I love the Casco Bay Riptide Red and the Bar Harbor Real Ale, both on tap here.

Finally, you'll need to hit Thurston's three days in a row to sample the chowders of the day. Everyone has their favorite; mine is the scallop, but the mussel and haddock have a loyal following. Each begins with a buttery,

Lobster by the Numbers

50: Percent of body weight adult male lobsters carry in their claws

1: Distance in miles a lobster travels in a night in search of food

6–8: Number of weeks it takes a lobster to re-grow a lost claw (which is why one is usually bigger than the other)

44: Number of lobsters scarfed down in 12 minutes by Sonya "the Black Widow" Thomas (the world record) at the 2005 World Lobster Eating Championship in Kennebunkport, ME

150: High end of a lobster's life expectancy, in years

44.6: Weight in pounds of the largest lobster ever recorded, caught off Nova Scotia in 1977

8: In feet, the length of lobsters caught by pilgrims in the early 1600s, according to their diaries

3.25: In inches, the distance between the eye socket and the start of the tail for a lobster to be of legal harvesting size

10,000: Average number of eggs a female produces at one time

10: Number out of those 10,000 that make it to harvesting size without being eaten on the ocean floor

20,000+: Pounds of lobster served during the five-day Maine Lobster Festival in Rockland

800: By law, number of traps a Maine lobsterman can set at one time

15: Maximum number of traps attached to a single lobster buoy

7,000: Number of working lobstermen in Maine

46,000,000: Pounds of lobster they haul in a year

Tidal Falls Lobster

Tidal Falls Road (off Eastside Road), Hancock • 207-422-6457 • Open June through Labor Day
BEST BITES: Garlicky mussels, hot crab dip, lobster, blueberry squares

I'm amazed that this restaurant is still something of a secret. But then again, if you drove a ways until you hit a little clearing with a stunning vista–where you could linger over delicious seafood at a picnic table perched over falls inhabited by eagles, ospreys, and a seal or two–maybe you wouldn't tell anybody, either.

For such a small menu, it's surprisingly hard to choose. You can't go wrong with a lobster–as heavy as 4 pounds, which may require an extra serving of drawn butter–and metal crackers available for a $2.00 deposit. But there's so much more to taste at Tidal Falls, where everything is homemade with locally grown or caught ingredients. Maybe kick things off with a ramekin of the hot crab dip, where sweet fresh-picked Maine crab (also available in an excellent roll) is tanged up with a mixture that includes cream cheese, onion, and lemon juice. The mussels are done up in a style more reminiscent of the shores of Brittany than Maine (which makes sense: One of the owners married a French woman). The inky mollusks are harvested from rocks nearby where they grow wild–getting their particularly clean, intense flavor from the tidal falls' constant swirl–and are kept in the lobster tank until you order them. Once steamed (over seawater pumped in from the bay), the mussels are simply

bathed in garlic and butter, which mingle with their briny liquor. Use an empty shell as a spoon to catch every last drop at the bottom of your bowl.

Desserts are just as good–try the blueberry squares, baked several times daily in the Tidal Falls kitchen. For a few weeks each summer, during raspberry season, these are picked nearby and added to the recipe, giving the squares a tart sultriness that almost requires a Cognac chaser, if it were that kind of place. Cart along a bottle of wine to go with your meal here, or try the fresh-squeezed lemonade, spiked with zest and shreds of mint.

Picnic tables (each with a trash bucket dangling off the end for lobster shells and the like) line the bank where grass slopes down to a pebbled inlet, and there's a screened-in area for dining on buggy evenings.

But the most plum seat in the house is one you won't see unless you go snooping around to the back of the building. Here, up a slim flight of weathered, wooden stairs, is the Captain's Deck, a contender for the most romantic place to dine al fresco in all of Maine: It holds a single table and offers the best vantage point from which to enjoy an already hard-to-beat view. This is the only seat in the house that takes reservations, and the $25 fee goes straight to the Frenchman Bay Conservancy, so that those nesting egrets you spy over dinner can be sure to have a home here for a long time.

And if you really want to see the falls in action, get your hands on a local tide chart or call ahead: Within an hour of low tide, water flowing into Frenchman Bay collides with that flowing out of Taunton Bay, and the roiling result is like Discovery Channel dinner theater.

try it once:
Lobster Ice Cream

Tourist gimmick, or an idea whose time has come? The puzzling concoction—vanilla ice cream pocked with chunks of fresh, salty Maine lobster— is the brainchild of Ben and Bill's Chocolate Emporium (66 Main Street, Bar Harbor, Maine; 800-806-3281), but you'll also find a version at the Lobster Barn Café (Route 27, Harpswell, Maine; 207-725-2745), where a sign claims there's "nothing fishy about it!" You be the judge.

Waterman's Beach Lobster

359 Waterman's Beach Road, South Thomaston • 207-596-7819 • Open Thursday through Sunday, Memorial Day to Labor Day • BEST BITES: Lobster, steamers, raspberry pie, rhubarb pie

*A*ny place that serves rhubarb pie gets my vote. As I learned from a foodie friend who's an ardent rhubarb buff, many cooks want to use the stalky treat, but they worry about scaring off your sweet tooth and add some other, wimpier fruit to cut the tartness with something sweet and less challenging—usually strawberry, sometimes peach. A pie made with straight rhubarb, he says, is the true mark of a confident chef and a gauntlet thrown to his customers.

Whether or not you agree, this is a madly delicious slice of pie. It's just one of the dishes worth the lush detour south of Rockland, through towering spruce and rolling farms dotted with the odd lobster-buoy scarecrow, to Waterman's Beach Road and this humble shack perched on the Atlantic's edge. Here, from Thursday through the weekend in summer, two women ready the morning's catch for eager eaters who run their dogs through the surf while they wait for dinner to steam. Its unbeatable location, between a meadow and the sea, might lead lesser cooks to take the easy way out, phoning in their fare using only the best and most frozen fare Mrs. Paul has to

offer. Not so at Waterman's Beach—and don't take it from me: No less an authority than the James Beard Foundation has bestowed its laurels on Waterman's Beach, which won an America's Regional Classics award in 2001. The fact that co-owners and (sisters-in-law) Lorri Cousens and Sandy Manahan are so quick to downplay the honor as "nothing gourmet or anything" makes the place all the more winning (after enough customers asked to see the inscribed award, they eventually gave in and hung it on the little shack's wall). You can't expect a place with Xeroxed menus and yellowing, hand-drawn signs taped to the trash lids reminding people not to throw away the lobster crackers to get their knickers in too much of a twist over this kind of thing.

Waterman's Beach serves nine dishes, six of which involve lobster, some of the freshest you'll ever eat. Get there early, peer out at the ocean between the islands, and you might see men hauling in the traps that held your meal—chances are, it's Lorri's husband or one of her three sons, or perhaps one of Sandy's sons, all lobstermen. This explains why the crustaceans come through the kitchen door just a couple of hours out of the water. Cousens and Manahan steam the lobsters over the saltwater they came from, sealing in the ocean's tang. Order 1-pounders solo or twinned, or a 1¼- or 1½-pound lobster dinner, served with melted butter, potato chips, and a roll. There's also a mound of steamers, almost 2 pounds' worth, sweet and silky and wonderfully messy to eat. Seafood rolls are grilled hamburger buns stuffed with fresh-picked meat and a suggestion of mayo (go for the crab). The lone landlubber option is a hot dog, if a very good one. Sides of potato or macaroni salad, coleslaw, and corn on the cob are yours for a dollar or so.

Seating is strictly in the rough, at a handful of red and blue picnic tables on the deck, which has a roof for rain, or in the field, which doesn't.

> "We don't add anything to it—it's the lobsters that are so fresh."
>
> —LORRI COUSENS,
> *EXPLAINING THE SECRET TO HER LOBSTER ROLL*

As for the pies, Lorri's mother-in-law Ann Cousens (who started the little restaurant in 1986) gets up at 5 AM to bake each and every one, and locals know to show up early, because they go fast. Lorri claims there'd be rioting if her mother-in-law stopped making the pies, and I believe her. There are nearly as many varieties of pie on offer as there are items on the rest of the menu: Depending on the day, you can cap your lobster meal with one of nine kinds, from lemon sponge and raspberry to blueberry, pecan, or pumpkin, to name a few. And, of course, rhubarb. Get it à la mode.

Additional Listings

Bar Harbor

Chowdah's Restaurant

297 Main Street • 207-288-3040

A full-service spot in the middle of town with steaks and a raw bar.

Bath

Morse's Lobster Shack

Bath Road • 207-725-2886

Recently opened outpost—in a 1950s red drive-in—of Morse's in nearby Harpswell. Get the haddock sandwich.

Belfast

Maine Chowder & Steak House

139 Searsport Avenue (Route 1)
207-338-5225
www.mainechowderhouse.com

Views of Penobscot Bay go nicely with scallop stew (ask for some hush puppies on the side).

Weathervane Restaurant

3 Main Street, on the Public Landing
207-338-1774

This seafood chain—sort of like a homier Legal Sea Foods—crops up throughout New England. Belfast's outpost is right at the bay's edge, offering an exceptionally nice view.

Boothbay Harbor

Chowder House

22 Granary Way, by the footbridge
207-633-5761

Take in the nautical theme indoors (the bow of a boat found at Hendrick's Head Lighthouse sits in the dining room) or sit outdoors under the striped yellow awning and quell your chowder jones. Homemade desserts are also worth the trip—the Tollhouse squares are big sellers, as are the pies from local baking maven Cindy Lewis.

The Daily Catch

93 Townsend Avenue • 207-633-0777
www.realmainelobster.com

Try a bowl of Lulu's lobster bisque or the Boothbay seafood pie (shrimp, scallops, and lobster nestled

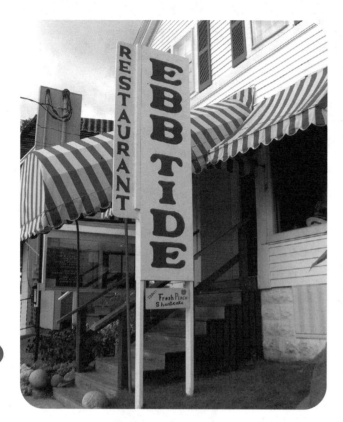

beneath a buttery crab-crumb topping), and finish with the place's baked-to-order roasted Tollhouse sundae.

Dunton's Doghouse

Sea Street • 207-633-2403

This takeout is not much bigger than a doghouse, and there's always a crowd. Mostly á hot-doggery, it does an exceptional fried haddock sandwich.

The Ebb Tide

43 Commercial Street • 207-633-5692

In tourist-loving Boothbay, this old-school eatery's peppermint-striped awning is a welcome sight. Don't leave without sampling the fish chowder; make a special trip for the peach shortcake (they hang a shingle outside on days when they're serving it). Great breakfasts, too.

Kaler's Crab and Lobster House

48 Commercial Street • 207-633-5839
www.kalers.com

The vibe at this big restaurant on the harbor is a tad T.G.I. Lobsters (the signature frozen drink is the "Boothbay Mama"), but the classics are good enough and the gimmicks (a "touch" aquarium out back for the kids, meet-and-greets with "Dan, Dan, the Lobster Man") are hokey-sweet enough to be forgiven.

The Lobster Dock

49 Atlantic Avenue • 207-633-7120
www.thelobsterdock.com

If the Boothbay Co-op just up the road is a madhouse, fall back on this multi-patio, pet-friendly standby with a killer view of the harbor, in a spot that housed a ship-yard in the late 1800s. Owner Mitch Weiss's signatures, like seafood fra diavolo and mussels marinière, are fancier than the casual spot suggests, but the classics–especially a warm lobster roll–are your best bets.

Brunswick

Fat Boy Drive-In
Route 24 • 207-729-9431

Car-hopping your food since 1955 (there are booths, too). Home of one of the cheapest lobster rolls around (half a tenner at this writing); also try their Canadian bacon BLT.

Camden

Bayview Lobster
1 Sharps Wharf • 207-236-2005

Suck down shore dinners and good fried scallops on the dock as you watch the tall ships come and go in the harbor and the steam rise off Bayview's lobster pots.

Cape Porpoise

Wayfarer Restaurant
Route 9 • 207-967-8961

Slide into a red vinyl booth and let head waitress Bert serve you a cup of haddock chowder from paradise.

Castine

The Breeze
Town Dock • 207-326-9200

Pop down to a weathered gray shack on the water for the lyrical menu alone. Order an Off-Necker (fried scallops), a Back Shore Basket (fried belly clams), or the Starvin' Marvin (a little bit of everything).

Dennett's Wharf Restaurant & Oyster Bar

15 Sea Street • 207-326-9045

www.dennettswharf.com

Casual dining in a winning waterfront house built as a sail and rigging loft in the early 1800s. Ask about the dollar bills on the ceiling.

Columbia Falls

JudyAnn's Seafood Restaurant

Route 1 • 207-483-2045

Looking for Perry's Seafood? It's JudyAnn's now–but the lobster rolls are still excellent.

Freeport

Lobster Cooker

39 Main Street • 207-865-4349

Shopping at the L.L. Bean outlet is hard work; grab a bowl of award-winning lobster, corn, and leek chowder at this place down the street.

Georgetown

Lisa's Lobster House & Grill

80 Moore's Turnpike Road • 207-371-2722

The road to Lisa's starts out rustic and turns *Deliverance*-scary, but press on to the end, where you're rewarded with dirt cheap, trap-fresh lobster and rolls in a fish shack overlooking Sheepscot Bay.

Eastport

Eastport Chowder House

167 Water Street • 207-853-4700

Wonderful lobster rolls and views of Passamaquoddy Bay (say that 10 times fast) and Canada.

Ellsworth

Jordan's Snack Bar

200 Route 1 • 207-667-2174

A roadside stand near the Mount Desert Island turnoff. Standard fried eats and rolls, plus a big ice cream menu.

Sea Shack

190 State Street at Route 1A • 207-664-8982

Not a restaurant–not even a takeout–but a great seafood market on wheels, where you can purchase a yummy and very local specialty: pickled wrinkles.

Union River Lobster Pot

8 South Street • 207-667-5077

Try the Clam Slam for a bivalve three-way (chowder, fried, and cake) or get the shore dinner–besides lobster, steamers, and mussels, it comes with chowder (try the Down East fish kind) and homemade biscuits.

Harpswell

Estes Lobster House

1906 Harpswell Neck Road (Route 123)
207-833-6340

The drive from the mainland to this great, lumbering mess hall is lovely, all woods and deep tidal coves.

Lobster Barn Café & Ice Cream Parlor

Route 27 • 207-725-2745

Serviceable shack food and the only place outside of Bar Harbor to find lobster ice cream–if, for some reason, you wanted to.

Morse Lobster

Allen Point Road, off Route 123 • 207-833-2399

The Morse family's been catching lobster for generations, and they'll cook one for you.

Hulls Cove

The Chart Room

Route 3 • 207-288-9740

Lovely old restaurant with adventurous additions (think blackened yellow fin tuna and macadamia nut crusted halibut) right on the cove.

Kennebunkport

Old Salt's Pantry

Dock Square • 207-967-4966
www.oldsaltspantry.com

If you're not in the mood to wait in line or devote time to a sit-down lunch, this postage stamp–sized old-school delicatessen makes a winning lobster roll.

Kittery

Cap'n Simeon's Galley

90 Pepperell Road (Route 103), Kittery Point
207-439-3655

Open since the late '60s. Dine right on the wharf, and don't miss the onion rings or the homemade cherry cheese pie. Or Frisbee's General Store right next door, one of the oldest in the country.

Sea Hags Seafoods

2 Badger Island West • 207-439-2883

Hard not to love a place that gets its name from a pair of cartoon mermaids who look like Vegas cocktail waitresses past their prime. This sweet market right by the bridge to New Hampshire also serves good seafood rolls and solid chowder.

Warren's Lobster House

11 Water Street (Route 1) • 207-439-1630
www.lobsterhouse.com

Sprawling old-fashioned dining room right on the water, with views of the bridge to Badger Island.

York Seafood and Roast Beef

Route 1 on the York/Kittery line • 207-439-3401

They short-order succulent shack-style surf and turf bites. You'll know it by the blue "Fried Clams" sign on the roof.

Lincolnville Beach

Lobster Pound Restaurant

Route 1 • 207-789-5550

A nice spot with warm staff who'll serve you yummy things like steamer chowder and homemade chocolate pudding. Linger over a microbrew or a glass of wine before your ferry to Isleboro.

Little Deer Isle

Eaton's Lobster Pool

Blastows Cove Road, Little Deer Isle
207-348-2383

Shore dinners in a remote spot with wraparound views of Penobscot Bay—and a fireplace.

Machias

Blue Bird Ranch Family Restaurant

Lower Main Street (Route 1) • 207-255-3351

Sweet, plain, old-school diner. Highlights include heavenly seafood stews (get the lobster, not always available) and decadent blueberry desserts by the dozen.

New Harbor

The Sea Gull Shop

3119 Bristol Road, next to Pemaquid lighthouse
207-677-2374

As you watch gulls skim the water right outside the wall of windows or swirl around Pemaquid Light itself, have a cheap cup of silky fish chowder, or splurge on a Fisherman's Platter (a sampling of fried everything that's fished locally), and save room for shortcake.

Northeast Harbor

The Docksider

14 Sea Street • 207-276-3965

At this little white house just up the hill from the harbor, lobster on the patio feels like a backyard clambake. Plan ahead for the blueberry pie.

Old Orchard Beach

Barefoot Boy

45 East Grand Avenue (Route 9)
207-934-0185

Barefoot Boy is plunked right on the strip that's home to the seaside town's sweetly junky '50s motels. Breakfast is big here, but you'll also find a simple seafood menu.

Dewey's

15 Old Orchard Road • 207-934-0025

There's surprisingly little seafood to be had on the boardwalk at Old Orchard Beach (though you'll never run out of pizza or taffy). Head to Dewey's takeout for fried clams.

Ogunquit

The Clam Digger

314 Route 1 • 207-646-8998

Solid shack fare on the cheap side in a spot that tends to be less crowded than others nearby. Love the cartoon sign featuring a clammer in a sou'wester getting squirted in the eye by his prey.

Port Clyde

The Dip Net

On the dock (next to the Monhegan
Boat Terminal) • 207-372-6307
www.dipnetrestaurant.com

Perfect views on a wharf in the fishing village of Port Clyde, and winning food with some sophisticated touches.

Port Clyde General Store

4 Cold Storage Road, next to The Dip Net
restaurant • 207-372-6543

Worth a visit to see the quaint old store itself, but while you're there, you'll want to ask if they've made any haddock chowder that day. "Ours is special," says the woman minding the till. "It has sherry in it. Lots of sherry."

Perkins Cove

Lobster Shack

Right on the Cove • 207-646-2941

This 1910 fishing hut doesn't look like much, and lucky for you that sends most of the cove's heaving weekend crowd elsewhere. Chowder here is sensational.

The Oarweed

Just off Shore Road • 207-646.4022

Lobster barn on the water serves steamers in cardboard, as it should be. Wash down your Roby's Down East'r (lobster roll, cup of chowder, and a coffee) with a mug of rum punch.

Pine Point

The Clambake

Route 9 • 207-883-4871
www.theclambake.com

Just like in Texas, everything's bigger at the Clambake, from the seating (it can pack in 700) to the salad bar (vast) to the portions (hefty, justifying the higher-than-average prices). Family-friendly in the extreme, it overlooks a pretty saltwater marsh near Old Orchard Beach.

Portland

Beal's Ice Cream

344 Cottage Road, South Portland
207-799-4410

Beal's is a household name in Maine for its old-fashioned ice cream, but this parlor, grafted on to a gas station, also serves a succulent lobster roll.

Gilbert's Chowder House

92 Commercial Street • 207-871-5636

Fishermen and dock hands head here for pints of wintry ale and sustenance from gooey-thick chowders (clam, fish, corn, and seafood—order "super seafood" for a bowl with twice the goods). If moving your spoon through one of these seems too athletic, try the hearty lobster club sandwich. Dine inside, under the mounted swordfish, or on the tiny rear patio.

The Lobster Station

501 Cottage Road, South Portland
207-799-4008

At this writing, Lori Hillier's eatery had been open for 38 days. The shiny restaurant next to a Del's Lemonade may be (and look) new, but the kitchen's already hit its stride, offering shack classics; at $6.95, the (big portion of) fish and chips is a yummy steal.

Newick's

740 Broadway, South Portland • 207-799-3090

Only Maine outpost of the New Hampshire seafood landmark.

The Portland Lobster Company

180 Commercial Street
207-775-2112

This small Old Port newcomer already has legions of fans.

Susan's Fish-n-Chips

1135 Forest Avenue • 207-878-3240

While visitors trawl the Old Port for a quaint bite, locals head for the edge of town to this cavernous rec room next to Bill's Brake & Exhaust Shop, where they scarf down mounds of dirt-cheap, expertly fried seafood (and equally fried ice cream). Owner Susan Eklund proudly displays her shack's many awards on the south wall.

Prospect Harbor

West Bay Lobsters in the Rough

Route 186 • 207-963-7021

You'd be forgiven for driving right by it; after all, the sign says "West Bay Floral." But what's on offer here is better than any bouquet: shore dinners served up in an old campsite setting, sided with homemade baked beans and flaky-crusted home-baked pie for dessert.

Rockland

Conte's Fish Market and Restaurant

Next to Rockland Public Landing
No phone

Who needs a phone or a formal menu? This ruddy bait shack hums along happily without either. The day's dishes—heavy on the seafood—are scrawled on a massive roll of butcher paper, a fat loaf of crusty bread waits on every newsprint-lined table, the wine list consists of one or the other (red or white), and candle lanterns hang from the ceiling.

Rockland Café

441 Main Street • 207-596-7556

I'd be remiss in not mentioning a place with an "All You Can Eat Seafood" special.

Round Pond

Muscongus Bay Lobster Co.

On the harbor • 207-529-5528

An unfussy lobster pound with outdoor tables right on the water and a more extensive menu than the shack next door (though not by much), including oysters on the half shell.

Round Pond Lobster Fishermen's Co-op

On the harbor • 207-529-5725

Lobsters, clams, and corn—period—served out of an out-house-sized lean-to surrounded by traps piled higher than the building itself.

Scarborough

Dunstan School Restaurant

Route 1 • 207-883-5261
www.dunstanschool.com

This place eschews stuff-your-face stigma by renaming its $15 seafood special an "All You Care to Eat" Buffet. (It's even cheaper for kids.)

Ken's Place

207 Pine Point Road (Route 9) • 207-883-6611

Ken Skilling started frying in 1927, and pretty soon his restaurant became famous for clams (the chowder's good, too). There's also a raw bar. Pull in at the red-and-white awning.

Seal Harbor

Seaside Takeout

On the pier (by the Seal Harbor Yacht Club)
No phone

A heady find in chichi Seal Harbor, this shack serves cheap and cheerful lobster rolls and unfussed-with steamed seafood dinners that include winkles, crabs, and anything else that came in with the catch.

Searsport

Anglers Restaurant

Route 1 • 207-548-2405

Try the scallop or oyster stew, followed by some Grape-Nut custard.

Sedgwick

Country View Drive-In

4200 Snow's Cove Road (Route 15)
207-359-2214

Stop en route to Deer Isle, grab an order of fried haddock or scallops or a heady (and cheap) crab roll, and dine overlooking blueberry barrens and unimpeded sunsets.

Southport

Robinson's Wharf
Route 27 • 207-633-3830
www.robinsonswharf.com

Sweet place in an even sweeter location overlooking Townsend Gut, on a dock just over the swing bridge separating Boothbay Harbor and Southport. It's all about fresh lobster here.

Stonington

Carter's Seafood
Oceanville Road, just north of Stonington
207-367-0900

Buy lunch at the fish market and snag a picnic table outside.

Fisherman's Friend Restaurant
5 Atlantic Avenue • 207-367-2442

This diner recently moved from its spot on School Street, but the grub—simple seafood classics—remains deliciously unchanged.

The Harbor Cafe
Main Street • 207-367-5099

Exactly the kind of sweet, bright, friendly (and cheap!) little eatery you wish was around the corner from your house. Try the crab stew with a side of onion rings or the Mate's Plate, a sampling of their fried seafood. Hard to find anything over $12 on this menu.

Island Cow Ice Cream Co.
Main Street • No phone

Along with heavenly Smiling Hill Farms ice cream, this yellow hut with the pink trim serves a delectable crab roll.

The Maritime Cafe
27 Main Street • 207-367-2600
www.maritimecafe.com

Upscale, but worth the splurge for flavorful fins and shells served right on the heartbreakingly beautiful harbor.

Trenton

Gateway Lobster Pound
Bar Harbor Road (Route 3)
Next to Hancock County Airport
207-667-2620

Amazing fried scallops, great lobster roll, Elvis nights with dancing, and Precious Moments figurines in the gift shop.

Kathy's Breakfast & Chowder House
Bar Harbor Road (Route 3), in the Sunrise Inn
207-667-8452
www.kathysb-c.com

Kathy Hamor's unfussy eatery boasts lobster 14 ways, like Lobster Alfredo and Lobster Eggs Benedict, but simpler fare is available (and best) at this cute spot.

Lunt's Lobster Pound

Bar Harbor Road (Route 3), across from Hancock County Airport • 207-667-9459

Excellent New England–style clam chowder, topped with butter, parsley, and paprika.

Maine Luau Lobster Pound & B.B.Q. Pit

Bar Harbor Road (Route 3) • 207-667-6320

For those who like grilled seafood and cartoon lobsters in grass skirts.

Trevett

Trevett Country Store

Barter's Island Road, at the swing bridge
207-633-1140

The movie *In the Bedroom* may have put this little town

(and its bridge) on the map, but savvy eaters have long been making the trek down to Trevett. There's a deck over the water, an old-fashioned store, fresh-made lobster rolls, and ice-cold Moxie. Bliss.

Vinalhaven

Harbor Gawker

Main Street • 207-863-9365

Heartwarming, plain little restaurant with a pond view offers straight-up fare, like an excellent, cheap crab roll. Worth the ferry ride to pretty Vinalhaven Island.

Waldoboro

Moody's Diner

Route 1 • 207-832-7785
www.moodysdiner.com

Here since 1927, this 24-hour diner is hip to its own appeal, but lovably so–and besides, you have to come here at least once for the walnut pie.

Wells

Billy's Chowder House

216 Mile Road • 207-646-7558

Huge portions of the classics served in a pretension-free spot overlooking the wildlife reserve.

Lord's Harborside

352 Harbor Road • 207-646-2651

Settle in for a meal overlooking Wells Harbor–the Lord's lobster pie is a religious experience.

Winter Harbor

The Barnacle
159 Main Street • 207-963-7733

Inconspicuous takeout spot with fried seafood only (try the haddock sandwich), plus burgers and pizza.

Wiscasset

Sea Basket
Route 1 • 207-882-6581
www.seabasket.com

Excellent fried seafood served in this homey spot. Look for the shingle advertising lobster stew.

Tasty Maine LOBSTER Stew

Yarmouth

Cindy's
Route 1 at Exit 17 • 207-865-1635

A must, if only for the nonstop tchotchke action (it looks like a garage sale from the road), the banter with owner Bob Pottles, and the fried clams and succulent, amber-battered o-rings.

Day's Crabmeat & Lobster
Route 1 at Exit 17 • 207-846-3436

Day's market has a 70-year rep for fresh seafood. It also has a takeout window and serves a few simple, scrumptious dishes, including a copiously meaty lobster roll.

York

Bos'n's Landing
Route 1 • 207-363-4116

For 30-plus years, this sweet, rambling restaurant overlooking the York River has been serving classics like oyster stew and lobster rolls—the latter is their biggest lunch seller by far.

Fox's Lobster
Nubble Point, York Beach • 207-363-2643
www.foxslobster.com

There's been a lobster pound on this patch of land with views of Nubble Light since 1936, and while it's changed hands (and names), the idea remains the same: good seafood classics, devoured in the rough.

Sun and Surf
1 Ocean Avenue, York Beach • 207-363-2961

Solid clam chowder, fresh haddock, crabmeat on a homemade croissant, and blueberry pie paired with perfect views of Long Sands Beach.

index

C

NEW ENGLAND'S FAVORITE SEAFOOD SHACKS

Index

NEW ENGLAND'S FAVORITE SEAFOOD SHACKS

Index

NEW ENGLAND'S FAVORITE SEAFOOD SHACKS